CW00530498

# PROGRESS AND INEQUALITY IN
# COMPREHENSIVE EDUCATION

# PROGRESS
# AND INEQUALITY
# IN COMPREHENSIVE
# EDUCATION

Edited by
ANTHONY G. GREEN and STEPHEN J. BALL

ROUTLEDGE

First published in 1988 by
Routledge
a division of Routledge, Chapman and Hall
11 New Fetter Lane, London EC4P 4EE

© 1988 A.G. Green and S.J. Ball

Printed in Great Britain by Mackays of Chatham PLC, Chatham, Kent

All rights reserved. No part of this book may be reprinted or
reproduced or utilized in any form or by any electronic, mechanical, or
other means, now known or hereafter invented, including photocopying
and recording, or in any information storage or retrieval system, without
permission in writing from the publishers.

British Library Cataloguing in Publication Data

Progress and inequality in comprehensive
    education.
    1. Great Britain. Comprehensive education,
    1965–1988
    I. Green, Anthony G. II. Ball, Stephen,
    *1950–*
    373.2'5'0941

ISBN 0-415-00551-5

# Contents

# Contents

# Contributors

| | |
|---|---|
| **Peter Aggleton** | Senior Lecturer in Education, Bristol Polytechnic. |
| **Stephen J. Ball** | Lecturer in Sociology of Education, Centre for Educational Studies, King's College, University of London. |
| **Steve Baron** | Lecturer in Sociology, University of Stirling. |
| **Robert G. Burgess** | Senior Lecturer, Chair of Department of Sociology and Director of Centre for Educational Development and Appraisal, University of Warwick. |
| **Roger Dale** | Senior Lecturer in Sociology of Education, South Bank Polytechnic, London. |
| **Miriam David** | Head of Department of Social Sciences, South Bank Polytechnic, London. |
| **William Dubberley** | Community Education Tutor at Darton, Community Education Centre, Barnsley, Yorkshire. |
| **Anthony G. Green** | Lecturer in Sociology of Education, Institute of Education, University of London. |
| **Tuula Gordon** | Research Officer, University of Joensuu, Finland. |
| **David Hamilton** | Lecturer in Education, Department of Education, University of Glasgow. |
| **David Hartley** | Lecturer in Education, University of Dundee. |
| **Bernadette O'Keefe** | Senior Research Fellow, King's College University of London. |
| **Jenny Thewlis** | Teacher-in-charge of Individual Tuition, ILEA, Division 10, Editorial Group of Teaching London Kids. |
| **Barry Troyna** | Lecturer in Social Aspects of Education in the Department of Education, University of Warwick. |

# Introduction and Overview:
## Choice, Progress and Inequality

Anthony G. Green

At the centre of educational <u>progressivism</u> is choice, individuality conceived as emanating from or the property of human beings in moments of socially supported autonomy. The social strategy of progressivism (in education, social welfare, etc) is designed to extend those moments of autonomy on the basis of mutuality and cooperation minimally compromising the interests of others while accumulating general social benefit. It is here that comprehensive educational and the progressive principles can find engagement in a sociality which celebrates positive differences in personal and cultural qualities and self-motivated activities, in a system which, in turn, constitutes mutually productive, ever extending systems of both needs and satisfactions - social individualism, as distinct from the egotism of aggressive self-interest.

The chapters of this book form a collection which, though not reflecting a tight coherence, directly and indirectly addresses the current crises in British comprehensive education.[1] The main themes concentrate on social aspects of comprehensive and progressive ideals and practices and implications for their realisation and articulation against the background of current developments in education. These crises throw into relief differences in alternative conceptions of 'choice' and their importance in education. From the 'left' critique of 'progressivism' it is pointed out how progressivism tends to overemphasise 'choice' at the level of individuals, ignores sociality and the contexts of 'equality of opportunity'. In so doing it displaces attention from obstacles to achieving social enpowerment faced by those placed at cultural and economic structural disadvantages in the competitive game of choice making and turning opportunities into achievements. There are pernicious differentiation of individuals and spurious celebration of many success stories. The objective of social individualism found in a division of labour which is constituted in equality of esteem and symbolic rewards remains an impossible objective. In this point of view, so long as the situation is misperceived or perceived only dimly by those too demoralised to do anything about it, the educational terms 'progressivism', 'child centredness', 'choice' etc. become empty (though powerful) rhetorical devices of complacency formation in radical egotistical individualism. In these terms the crisis of comprehensive education is a moral and political one, a theme woven into the fabric to different effect of each contribution to this volume.

The critique of comprehensivisation from the 'right' profiles choice, diversity and differentiation in a way which underplays the structuring of choices as an issue. Modelled in either cultural elitism or conservative political expediency with its idealisation of the benign possibilities of the rigours of market forces, the term 'choice' becomes a powerful cultural weapon in the hands of those committed to differentiation without equality. This systematic differ-entiation is to be fuelled anew by the numerous, but proportionally small minority who capitalise from below on their opportunities. They choose to join the ranks of the advantaged who continue to choose to reap the benefits allocated to them by their favourable place in the game. Here it might be supposed the best advice as far as making choices is concerned is to 'choose your parents wisely'.

With these general perspectives in mind we move to the main interests of the book, the period since the mid-1960's, noting that it has been marked by a variety of developments and changes in British society and culture. Several particular ideologies, policies and practices in education have competed for respectability and hegemony under the banners of progress and the extension of opportunity. Our interest is in progressivism and comprehensivisation. Rarely are they considered in relation to each other. Partly, this is because progressivism has generally been associated with child-centred primary education while comprehensivisation has tended to be interpreted as a set of problems in secondary education and, in particular, as part of a social democratic philosophy aspiring to extend opportunity to acquire and participate in social goods 'more equally'. Comprehensivisation is often taken to be about social

2

aspects of education and the role of educational provision in changing wider social relations, while progressivism, is usually discussed in terms of teaching and learning practices in schools. Simply put, these issues divide on schools' social context and their practical content in what is generally taken to be interesting about educational developments.

Comprehensivisation, by whatever definition, has hardly been achieved once we proceed beyond the label to the reality. It has been subjected to a series of influential critiques and educational policy initiatives which show several signs of successfully undermining what achievements have been made. Central and local government policy moves seem to be designed to achieve transformation of education in the name of 'modernisation' with, and for, social and economic 'restructuring'. 'Equality of opportunity' and 'treating each child according to his or her needs' are no less evident than previously as tokens in the rhetorical play of educational debates and legitimation practices. They are being reworked through a re-insistence on 'freedom of choice' (especially for parents and in part, for children) and re-invocation of national economic priorities for 'modernisation' (see Hamilton, Dale, Hartley). Developing over ten years, a new educational language appears to be providing an effective vocabulary for the 'new right'. This discourse re-structures the appearances, and at the same time operates to shift the realities, of power in and around educational institutions. This is especially so with respect to pressures to change forms of accountability and responsibility which, amongst other effects, weaken teachers' claims to professional standing with regard to both parents and their employers as well as to 'the community' and local commercial interests. New disciplines of accountability and market mechanisms are articulated with and through these discursive activities and link to new balances of opportunities and constraint for education.

The contributions to this collection variously report upon specific current developments and experiences in the '80's, in some chapters, and in others review trends and changing patterns over the period from the late 1960's. This introduction holds in tension two contrasting views. One, that in some ways what was 'progressive' about progressivism has been reversed and a new 'regressive' era is emerging. And two, that the crisis in secondary education has in fact uncovered the reality of progressivism as a set of practices providing for individualising social disciplines, now

3

constituted in rhetorics of 'modernisation' and economic efficiency, with and for the social harmonisation of increasingly tense and conflictual social situations.

The contexts for the discussions below are the relations between political and economic developments as they influence education (for the most part) and are influenced by it (to some extent) in the production of social and cultural forces in the division of labour in Britain. These include the following: the general crisis of capital accumulation 'for Britain' during the 1970's and the various policies and proposals covering the place of education in the solution to these problems - the spin-offs of attempts to reconcile the 'need' for social harmony with the 'need' for economic prosperity founded upon the contested arena of economic relations. This is partly specified in the 'problem' of the relationship between education and work, and attempts to reposition 'education' in relation to that problem by shifting definitions of education towards practices of training for production; these, in turn, are set within the constraints and disjunctures arising from high levels of (especially youth) unemployment accompanying the restructuring of British capital; the social, political and cultural relevancies of 'education' for different sections in the changing relations of the social structure - in particular, the 'working classes' and 'new middle classes'; the articulation of pressures for social accountability and the tensions this raises for educational professionalism; the expression of ideals and practices associated with equalising social and economic opportunities in a society becoming increasingly aware of race and ethnic divisions as well as social differentiation associated with gender. Comprehensive and progressive educational ideals and practices concerning the contexts and contents of secondary education are thus rendered problematic in a variety of complex ways. These include centralising finance and certain general planning for educational organisation, curriculum and teachers' pay and responsibilities, plus deconstructing local educational authorities' powers and 'breaking up' some of the 'high spending' and politically difficult (generally Labour controlled) authorities such as the Inner London Education Authority. At the same time educational market led privatisation is encouraged, with schools taking responsibility for their own budget planning within set allocations and with the likely expectation that they will raise further funds on their own initiative. Finally, vocationalisation of the curriculum may well be significantly undermining longstanding (if often poorly realised) commitments to liberal education (as for its 'own sake' and for the development of individual young people), and reinvigorating mechanisms of differentiation in the form of disguised tri- or bi-partism in state education. This had, to some extent, been weakened, but never entirely eliminated, over the last twenty years of the comprehensive school experiment.

The development of state secondary education in Britain began as part of the economic and social changes of the late nineteenth century which continued during the twentieth century. These developments were constituted at several points of social tension which they both variously reflected and expressed. These are found for instance, in problems of reconciling social differentiation with social equality in mass education. Broad economic, cultural and political imperatives combined in the formation of a division of labour in economic production realised in complex structures of paid occupations and labour processes. In relation to this, the national system of education would ideally make available, as a right to each citizen, high quality and agreed values (ideal and material), at negligible, immediate cost to participants and their families. Set against this is the aim of treating education as investment in human capital formation as a factor in and opportunity cost for other productive investment. Here the tension within education has two major dimensions. The first is concerned with reconciling the preparation of the young for responsible adulthood in industrial and social productive activity (domestic and non-domestic), with education in and for critical personal and cultural exploration and creativity, plus personal, political responsibility. The second tension concerns the problem of reducing injustices in a system in which social inequality of origin tends to powerfully influence outcomes and achievement in education. The tension here between extending the opportunities for choice through welfarism; minimal distribution of necessary social goods, delivered through local state agencies, and progressivism; satisfying and developing the opportunities for individual expression of 'common' differentiated values of responsible individualism in a complex division of labour, connected with the educational aspirations of comprehensive schooling fought over in the last eighty years of British experience.

David Hamilton's contribution traces aspects of this history in his discussion of curriculum development activists (largely referring to teachers) back to the progressives of the late nineteenth century, and beyond to Comenius' account of the potential but partially unrealised role of the state in regulating teachers' curricular and pedagogic initiatives in the services of regulating the social order. Hamilton identifies some of the problems of the progressive state's attempt to impose a technology of education founded upon illusive professionally devised and applied natural laws of learning. This aspiration for harmonious social development, exploiting the latest developments which science and technology have to offer to educational efficiency, resurfaced in the 1960's and especially in the context of our interest in the 1970's, symbolised by the then Prime Minister, Callaghan's speech at Ruskin. Here, the issue of control was subordinated to an emphasis upon 'standards'. It implied that there had been slippage in educational achievement levels. Playing upon implementation of appropriate schooling in the curriculum, it embodied an assertion that teachers need to re-appraise their own work for being misguidedly progressive. It was wrapped in an underlying commitment to tying education closely to labour market economic imperatives, and so to realising suitably up-to-date standards of educational 'relevance'.

Dale's piece describes this and subsequent moves in educational funding provisions which reflect shifts in the 'structure and ideology of the educational system'. These developments continued to undermine teachers' professional autonomy within the established three way partnership for educational provision of state, local education authorities and the teachers' organization. The context was set for further displacing the meaning of child-centred progressivism and shifting the meaning of equality of opportunity as a social value associated with comprehensivism. Hamilton sees a long continuity in the progressivist and loosely specified ideals about making education relevant to the needs of the children themselves and to their future 'true' positions in the occupational structure, Dale identifies a sharper recent shift and reformation of educational ideologies, powers and practices as teachers became, during late 1970's and through the 1980's, more closely 'regulated'. Key points left open in each paper concern the specifics of this regulation are the nature and types of potential spaces between the regulative rhetorics, progressive or otherwise and realities of state policies which are available for teachers' 'resistive' activity. Both pieces recognise degrees of autonomy for teachers in the disciplinary potentialities of and for them and the children they educate. Such discipline is articulated within human relations educational managerial control procedures, management by cooptation and consent. For Hamilton these possibilities are part of the continuous general constitution of state licenced professionalism in education, and, one might suggest (though not part of his account), part of the constitution of the state sector of educational middle class professional social regulation and social harmonization procedures, whether it be through earlier 'multi-lateral' or contemporary 'comprehensive' forms of secondary school organization. For Dale it is evident that there is a more overt contemporary re-modelling of the tri-partitism, the latter having never been fully eliminated from secondary 'comprehensive' education as it has developed since the 1960's. In each account the ambiguities of position of teachers makes their work potentially both a site of protest and of social harmon-isation.

David Hartley's description of recent specific changes in Scotland offers contrast and connective ironies for progressive comprehensivism when set against Hamilton and Dale's chapters. He presents a description of state imposed child-centredness in 'progressive' pedagogy and curricula. Hartley's is an image of 'centralised progressivism' as part of the 'management of consent' of both difficult to manage low achieving secondary school pupils and their teachers. This is mobilised through the spurious democracy of human relations management in education and through cooperative 'consultative centralism'. Social harmony and the avoidance of structural social criticism are the prizes to be won by the State's administrative procedures in these forms of collaborative control of both teachers and taught. The question is whether this leaves 'spaces' to be exploited by progressivists or constitutes institutional ties to control them.

While Dale identifies in England and Wales centralising developments in the regulation of teachers, intended to create a fluent articulation between education and production (despite the widespread cynicism on this point, by both teachers, parents and pupils), Hartley's acount indicates that in Scotland teachers are being 'forced to be free' to practice child-centred methods in preparation for

7

the attenuation of the connection between educational credentials and employment. The strategy in the context of potentially long term unemployment, is to shift school leavers' balance of critical energy away from the political and economic system to the self. What was once, perhaps, a hidden curriculum of control using progressive methods, has now been quickly formalizing into overt practices in a social and vocational skills curriculum using 'progressive' methods. This curriculum of control, is a good example of the ways in which expressive orders of schooling can be 'instrument-alized' to turn pupil-centred 'progressivism' on its head.

If Hartley's account is correct, what appeared in the late 1960's and during the 1970's as 'progressive' policies and practices, which had the indirect ideological effect of buttressing social harmony by defusing social criticism and the aspirations of pupils (and their parents) as it personalised low educational achievement and failure, is, in the late 1970's and 1980's in Scotland, a purposefully designed strategy aimed to have just such effects. In turn, Hartley describes a collaborative model of teacher professional development which disguises the educational centre-periphery dynamics it aims to realise. As with Dale's account, Hartley's picture is of closely framed teacher work providing limited educational discretion. The pattern is of 'guided volunteering' for the teachers. Along with 'guided discovery' for difficult pupils this 'neatly encapsulates the isomorphism in the forms of control ... for pupils of low academic standing and their teachers'. This construction of 'progressivism' contradicts comprehensivism. It maintains social divisions disguised as individual responsibility. Inequality is rendered obscure and difficult to make problematic.[2]

The theme of social progressivism, constituted by benign state institutional agencies and innovations may be identified in the communitarian wing of educational innovation. Here, principles of comprehensivism and progress mutually informed the policies behind community college education. The educational needs of the whole community from child to pensioner are to have been incorporated into a structure of opportunities intended to cut across inequalities of class, age and more lately, gender and ethnic differences and those of physical and mental disadvantage. By the same token, community schools, being selective by geographical areas rather than the needs of individual children, tend in working class 'problem' areas to encourage social pathology rather than individual pathology models for identifying educational difficulties, and paradoxically, combine this with a self-help perspective on their solutions. Baron's chapter reviews the place of 'community' in the politics of comprehensive education from the 1960's and focusses attention upon a pattern of tensions and contradictions in provisions intended to reduce boundaries between young and old, work and recreation, schools and their contexts. As in the case of the educational aspirations of, say, Courtesthorpe College, it is intended that other boundaries are changed, for instance, between teachers and pupils, between disciplines, between academic and vocational needs - progressivism and comprehensivism articulated here in the practices of one highly visible and (in the case of Courtesthorpe) vulnerable institution.

A problem for social democracy is to balance the interests of capital with popular concerns and to simultaneously reduce the appearance of regionally based vicious cycles of deprivation. In Baron's account, the concept of 'community' was a vehicle for promoting the idea of common culture through education. At the same time it was to strengthen the ever present opportunities for talents to find their 'correct' location in the functionally differentiated social order. The aim was to reduce to impotence the dis-harmonising possibilities of polarising class expressions of politics and culture. Community education could not and cannot bear these burdens. A basic problem is that, for instance, one class catchment areas severely restrict comprehensive cultural mixing and highlight the inherent contradiction of using a geographical area basis for attempting to create justice with efficiency in a systematically divided society.

Baron draws attention to the non-communal way in which comprehensive community colleges were created. Rather than arising from a democratic analysis of organic community needs and the complex patterns and diversity already in place, they were imposed, top-down, by local state agencies. His account reveals how influences condensed around benign professional expertise with power to define the 'needs' of a 'community' - another irony of, and tension within, progressive institutional reform where it 'imposes' that on which it professes to rely, namely, 'community-centredness'. This is part of the central dynamics of social democratic political practice in education. Community comprehensive education is

frequently legitimised with reference to Henry Morris'
concept of village colleges, especially through nostalgic
rural organicism. Baron argues that to do so is to
misunderstand Morris' project and politics. His strategy was
developed in a specific historical context of declining rural
church and landowning power with the aim of resisting the
consequences of the resulting political vacuum particularly
where it was being filled by urban commercial capital
interests. Morris intended to mobilise organic interests
rooted in local cultures and practices rather than introduce
solutions by outside administrative structures.

The internal dynamics of community colleges in
transition, during the late 1970's to early 1980's, are
considered here by Tuula Gordon. Points of complementarity
with Baron's account emerge where Gordon reports on
specific workings of 'Greenfield' College against the broader
context of political and economic restructuring during the
late 1970's and early 1980's. Its central theme, which is
reflected indirectly in Dale and Hamilton's pieces elaborates
the potential for critical educational work in the range of
'oppositional spaces' which progressive comprehensive
community colleges may constitute. She identifies how such
spaces were constituted in problematic and contradictory
ways and how the opportunities for educational practices
critical of patriarchal relations, never very firmly
established in the college, were put under severe strain by
economic and political re-structuring in the wider society.
Comparing liberal, libertarian and socialist educational
ideologies, Gordon elaborates features of the gender
problematic for progressive pedagogies and comprehensive
secondary education. Student-centred libertarian individualism may well be performed by teachers as critical activity
designed to dislodge gender-based inequalities institutionalised upon sex differences. There is the irony of teachers
being drawn into deepening the problems with solutions
offered by these very oppositional spaces. Most
immediately, for instance, young women's freedom to
choose their own curricula may result in the reproduction of
gender differences as the students choose to do conventional
'girls' activity. The oppositional space becomes a cage for
both teacher and taught in that it cannot withstand wider
cultural pressures. Nevertheless threr are opportunities in
Gordon's account for critical work where students choose to
cross and criticise gender lines in their work. What is
difficult however, is to undermine the existence of the

cultural gender line itself within the limited opportunities available in the educational activities of the students and teachers. As in other areas of education, progressive procedures can encourage critical activity but cannot radically transform the cultural 'tones' of gendered social relations in the imaginations and practices of teachers and students without hugely increasing the autonomy of the school and the authority of the teachers vis-a-vis the culture of the 'community' and the students. Paradoxically, this re-emphases the authority, however enlightened of educational professionalism. The political and economic imperatives of the 1980's have, as Gordon describes them, made even the defence of these oppositional spaces difficult to maintain. It is of interest that while Hartley sees the state working to impose a progressivism of control in Scotland, Gordon sees the political and economic imperatives of restructuring the social relations of production as both challenging and undermining the critical spaces of oppositional progressivism available in English community colleges. The tension between potential for control on the one hand, and critique, on the other, in so-called 'progressive' educational practices is neatly illustrated by this contrast. At the same time these issues are illuminative of some of the difficulties of pinning down degrees of relative autonomy of educational processes from 'wider' social processes, in particular, of specifying the determinate role of the state and cultural forces with respect to education.

The comprehensive secondary school is, of course, a place for adults to earn a living and pursue a career as well as for students (and those adults) to pursue education. The principles of balanced social mixing and equality of opportunity of comprehensive schooling are confronted by social patterns and their cultural expressions which often work against these principles where, for instance, patriarchy and occupational professionalism articulate. This process is often exacerbated in the context of shrinking career opportunities concomitant on falling school roles. This raises interesting issues about equality in comprehensive school management in the 1980's. Robert Burgess' report here complements in close detail Baron's more general study of community education as well as Gordon's accounts of partriarchy working and being partially resisted in a community college. His focus is upon the gender issues which arise in teacher career development and job appointments in schools. The chapter gives an indication of the structures of social relations in a school which, in Burgess' case, has a strongly implicated religious culture (Roman Catholicism) providing rationales and rhetorics for patriarchal practices in appointment of teachers. It is an open question as to the extent to which the positive aspirations of comprehensivism and progressivism can flourish in the institutionalised contexts of these kinds of infrastructures of inequality of power, influences and outcomes.

The gendered division of labour in British society has become more clearly visible in recent years and along with it some of the range of inequalities and structures of power articulating contexts and contents of education which evolve around the home-school nexus of relations. The 1960's/early 1970's marked a high point since 1945 of social democractic social policy on the home-school connection as educational and wider local and national state programmes were enacted to 'compensate' for inadequate domestic conditions of largely working class families. These social progressive moves which aimed to extend opportunities and reduce class differences in educational achievement were gender neutral in principle, though not in practice. They tended to ignore certain patterns of gender differentiation and gendered inequalities of opportunities in the home and in the work/paid production context. The problem, which implicitly and explicitly held the attention of these policies focused upon childrearing and 'first education' aspects of the home-school 'partnership' and was defined as an issue of mothering, as distinct say, from the more gender neutral 'parenting'.[3]

The reality of a gendered approach to social policy on the family and parenting endorsed assumptions about the nuclear family model for child-rearing and placed the main responsibility upon the mother for preparation and sustained support of children's primary and secondary schooling while at home. In reviewing these issues from the 1960's through the 1980's, Miriam David draws particular attention to a significant shift in the attitudes of state policy. Namely, while in no way shifting the burden of responsibility from mothering (especially with reference to the pathology of working class children's underachievement), there has been a re-alignment in the construction of the home/school relationship. The rhetoric of children's 'needs' and the 'needs' of economic realities is coupled with a liberal concept of 'choice'. The implication is that the family or parents are to become the beneficiaries of greater opportunities to 'choose' - between local state schools; and between the maintained and the private sectors; and between local authority maintained schools and a new special arrangement (City Technology Colleges and Opted Out Schools) for those unable either to pay for, or acquire economically assisted places into the private sector. Here the liberal progressive rhetoric of individual 'needs' and 'choice' is used to describe market driven mechanisms of educational development in which the home and the family are the prime site of choice making for private social responsibility, and whose influence, along with that of the demands of industry and commerce, are intended to improve educational standards by sharpening competition between schools. Connecting directly with Dale's account of funding changes in education, at this point, David indicates how this does little to transform gender relations in the domestic context or in society at large. Nor does this have any real chance of shifting the social class balances of opportunities. That is to say, it is the middle class parents who are generally more likely to increase both their involvement in the educational partnership and to have the resources - cultural and economic - to use any increased opportunities for 'choice'. While the early 1970's saw the then Conservative government using an ideology of 'choice' to delay comprehensive re-organization, the 1980's sees this rhetoric of 'choice' being mobilized to further undermine comprehensive education.

The key social and political issues are, that in the context of tighter financial controls in state education re-introducing parental choice to the inner city secondary schools, in the form proposed, can only divert resources away from the local state system and privilege those already privileged parents who are able to 'choose' the more selective, 'better' schools. At the same time, the social progressive ideal of using education to enhance the chances of the structurally less well-placed has been edged to the periphery of the political agenda. Now, even amongst some Labour controlled education authorities (such as the Inner London Education Authority), as David points out, aspirations are returning to the aim of having these children achieve only up to minimal standards of general 'attainment'. There are probably few more graphic indications than this of the current demoralisation in the social democratic educational tradition. It leaves little possibility for instance, of reducing inequalities of educational opportunity where class and gender are articulated in the home-school relationship since female-headed single parent families are amongst the poorest of these households.

Progressivist comprehensive education requires in major part that schools operate as communities in which there is a high measure of consensus on curricular and pedagogic issues. This means that whole school policies are required and, since the 1970's, have been strenuously advocated in areas such as language and communications (Bullock, 1975) and mathematics (Cockcroft, 1982). Barry Troyna's chapter concentrates upon whole school initiatives in multi-culturalism and anti-racism as features of what might be seen as the moral curriculum of schools. This chapter attempts to tread a very careful path through a complex minefield of issues encountered when the concept of 'institutional racism' is made problematic as a conceptual tool for understanding racism in schools. Central to his approach (along with others such as Jenny Williams) is the view that while there are many features which perpetuate racial inequalities in schools; teachers' attitudes; hidden and overt curricular practices; differential status and authority of minority culture teachers, and pernicious role modelling in the perceptions of majority and minority students. Proposed solutions, which reduce to the question of changing teachers' minds or attitudes, for instance, through 'racial awareness training', are sociologically naive and education-ally unavailable in progressive terms. To Troyna, the social and educational project of initiating multi-culturalism and anti-racism requires liberation from exclusive reliance upon 'racially relevant variables'. His chapter raises the question of the need to locate the success or failure of any particular progressive anti-racist policy initiative within what can be seen as the non- or a-racist institutional structures of some schools. The description he provides illustrates the case of a failure to establish clear and specific anti-racist whole school policy in an academically oriented 'high achieving' community college, in which there was clearly racial tension. Staff loyalty to subjects and a powerful sense of subject professionalism presented a basis for their resistance to comprehensive social principles. This was enacted through professional educationist vocabularies of competence which were difficult to displace. Troyna's account illustrates that such rhetorics can be mobilised to at least three kinds of end. One, when presented with a specifically anti-racist whole school policy, a position taken by some teachers is to generalise. The specificity of racism is then neutralised by asserting the need to be committed to reject any kind of discrimination, for instance, against women, fat people etc. Secondly, to adopt such policies would indicate an admission of guilt or failure. Thirdly, that in the views of some colleagues anti-racism is irrelevant to the professional domain of certain curriculum areas, mathematics, for instance. A modus operandi of inter-professional subject segmentation and loyalty is the institutional context for mobilising and perpetuating these perspectives. These inhibit the development of broader collective conceptions of professionalism which could incorporate social values for transcending commitments to subject based excellence. Here progressive and comprehensive rhetorical strategies, such as the view that teachers 'are interested in achieving equality of treatment for all pupils', may prove to be a form of foot dragging resistance in defence of esteemed but narrow professional loyalties.

What remains an open question for this kind of analysis, however, is that while the limited success of establishing anti-racist policies and self-critical practices in some schools may be explained in part by non-racially based specific aspects of the social structures of schooling (in this case professional subject loyalties), does this insight lay firm ground for re-appraising the concept 'institutional racism'? It may be that Troyna is here legitimately drawing attention to the place of the indirect and covert structural and ideological features which connect to the perpetuation of this specific kind of inequality. For instance, a parallel might be the indirect consequence of setting and streaming on the part of the institutionalisation of 'clasissm' or 'genderism', which are difficult to avoid in the context of unresolved professional debates about 'mixed ability' teaching. On the other hand, a disingenuous declaration of 'equality of education for all', rather like 'choice for all', can be used to cover more sinister attitudes and ideologies. While defending sectional professional interests it may articulate with racist practices. Troyna's chapter illustrates the fine lines that can be drawn and need to be drawn in analysis of educational policy. There exists through the possibility for subtle collusion with that which is the object of enlightened attention, in this case, racism.

While the work of teachers in comprehensive secondary education in the accounts and analyses of Gordon and Troyna present images, however complex, partial and contradictory, of 'progressive' teacher/pupil relations, William Dubberley's account is a timely reminder of other very real possibilities. It highlights, largely from a one-dimensional perspective of working class pupils and parents, the scope for continuing cultural differentiation both within schools and in the wider local community context. By describing incidents in a coal mining community in Yorkshire during 1985, Dubberley raises again important questions about the resilience of any possible progressive and egalitarian comprehensive ideals where there are local pressures for perpetuating deep social and cultural divisions. What is especially interesting in the light of developing educational policies for secondary education of the 1980's is the very particular and powerful vocationalist perspective in which some lower working class children, and their parents, have on the work of teachers - 'Teachers are paid to teach just as miners are paid to hew coal.'

Implied in Dubberley's analysis is tough-minded parents' technicist view of teachers' work. Their job is to transmit the possibilities for acquiring cultural capital (educational certificates) and this splits the teachers and parents. There is a keen sense of grievance amongst students, especially those who identify themselves as being discriminated against by having opportunities denied through the negligence of the teachers not expecting enough of students. In the view of the students teachers often do not respect either the students or themselves. Here, the critical perspective of working class parents and the 'resistive' activities of children articulate disciplines of their own (self) control. That is to say, using Willis' notion, the pupils' criticisms of teachers realise only 'partial penetration' of the structures of power to which they are subjected. The students hanker for both more equal opportunities as well as the benefits of selective education without appreciating the possible confusion built into such a perspective and without identifying the alternatives the comprehensive approach to education is intended to achieve. To the extent that these attitudes are widespread there is fertile ground for undermining comprehensive ideals and articulating working class discontent about education with a shallow vocational-ism.

At another level, Dubberley's work illustrates the significance for developments in the local politics of education, of differences in occupational cultures, and attitudes to industrial action and work between teachers and working class parents (in this case, coal miners). His observations of moments in the dispute between the Yorkshire miners and the National Coal Board, and simultaneously of the teachers engaged in their action, in dispute over their contract of employment, illustrate the absence of cooperation between these two occupational groups in any sense of broader struggle. While Dubberley concentrates upon the attitudes of the teachers there remains the issue of identifying strategies for cooperation between occupational groups to reinforce and increase their potentially mutual strengths in support of equalitarian approaches to comprehensive education. This is made all the more difficult in the climate of economic privatisation and a further drive towards economic restructuration. This centralised educational control and social and moral transformation aim to profile individualism and obscure the beneficial qualities of collectivism. With elements of human capital theory a crucial part of the common sense of some sections of those who 'fail' in education, failure can be projected onto teachers' shortcomings. This connects with a wider 'common sense' that teachers fail to generate value added to the 'capital' of the lowest forty per cent. Victims blame each other and, by turns themselves while reproducing fetishised conceptions of educational possibilities. A mythical view of teachers' responsibilities emerges which are to include not only preparation of young people for productive paid labour but often and magically, to be creative of paid work itself.

In contrast to Dubberley's chapter on working class children and their parents' relationships with secondary education, Peter Aggleton concentrates upon 'new middle-class' cultural relations and the theme of 'resistance'. It connects with broad debates about class formation and the bases of social transformation - in particular with questions about the possibly contrasting roles of working class and new middle class, or professional occupational groups, in social reproduction and social transformation. While accepting that no general social theory of class formation and action will help us decide on the potential of either in any specific social situation, Aggleton provides a detailed account of new middle class youth - the sons and daughters of, in this case, parents themselves schooled in the 1950's and 1960's. He analyses within the cultural dynamics a very specific group of young people who have moved, at sixteen from school to further education colleges for A level preparation. His account is interesting in the context of progressivism and comprehensive education as offering, like Dubberley's work, insights and challenges regarding students' activity in comprehensive educational cultures and struggles. Aggleton provides us with a vivid portrayal of disaffected middle class youth whose social focus is personalistic rather than collectivist. Using Basil Bernstein's distinction between 'resistance' and 'contestation' he indicates how new middle class personalised culture is at best a contestation of local forms of control in education. It is not resistance which aims at structural transformation in the broader arena of power in society. This personalised and individualist cultural ethos contrasts sharply with Dubberley's images of a more collectivist working class youth and their parents. Aggleton indicates for instance, that the new middle class youth, unlike their own parents, are unlikely to have much sympathy for trade unionism and party politics and for solidarity with 'broad oppositional struggles'. The meaning of their and their parents' commitment to comprehensive and progressive principles in education, is likely to differ considerably from those of the community described by Dubberley. For the latter, what is positive about state provided comprehensive education is the opportunity to acquire credentials for participation in production and to do 'better' than their parents. For Aggleton's new middle class respondents credentials are much less salient than experience for personalised development and fulfilment to participate in the world of symbolic control. In Bourdieu's terms, to realise their personal unit of cultural capital, is the aim. Each of the contrasting class locations and cultural specificities described by Dubberley and Aggleton offers a different route to social and cultural reproduction associated with education and is accompanied by its own partial critique of education. Neither offers much as a basis for a broadly articulated social critique. Each can be mobilized in a particular critique of comprehensive education; on the one hand using individualist rhetoric of 'choice' for the new middle class; on the other, demanding the opportunity to acquire credentials by the working class. Each could well contribute to the continued structure of established powers.

On another dimension, questions of critical cultural differentiation are raised where we consider the place and form of religion in publicly resourced education. Bernadette O'Keeffe's chapter reviews some of these problems within the theme of multi-culturalism, pointing out that hegemony lies with secular humanism and as such tends to undermine the claims of religious ideologies, for instance, to universalism found in Muslim, Christian and other faiths. Thus, as she points out, the Swan Report is unable to satisfy any demand on the question of religious education which requires that values which are 'universally appropriate' be represented as such. The perspective is agnostic in the face of religious pluralities. For Bernadette O'Keeffe it endorses an anti-religious and pro-secular perspective and is fundamentally part of a structure of discrimination against religious observance in education. It cannot go beyond shallow 'tolerance' in order to encourage a deeper exploration of real commonalities of religious values regardless of different forms of expression. This opens up a very difficult terrain for state education. It continues to accept religion as part of the curriculum and claims to be comprehensive, thus providing the opportunity for children to learn and understand the religious traditions of their own faith community. Clearly, to whichever forms of religious observance this can be applied, the secular viewpoint will tend to focus on the dangers of institutional separation of faith communities because it perpetuates the possible deepening of pernicious cultural divisions. The operating policy of educational provision since the 1970's has been an uneasy compromise between those who see the interests of cultural plurality as best being served within the one (comprehensive) school, and the other view which endorses the purpose of safeguarding cultural and particularly religious plurality with equality of esteem by accepting separate religious schools. This is but one dimension of a broader set of issues on the realisation of comprehensive education. The crux of the discussion is about whether there is a stronger likelihood of achieving the comprehensive ideal by having a wide range of 'different but equal' schools available to all, or whether the interests of ethnic minorities and people from disadvantaged sections of the social and political spectrum are to be best served by attempting to strengthen the limited plurality of possibilities currently available within schools. It is unlikely that any real direction can be identified on this in the absence of a clear statement of the social and cultural purposes of education within the broader structure of contemporary society. So-called 'freedom of choice' tends to work to the benefit of those already best placed to take advantage of the unequal distribution of cultural, economic and institutional opportunities available.

For progressive movements in and against the institutional structures and practices of late capitalism to succeed whether in educational terms or elsewhere, they need voices which can articulate their critical perspectives. As at other points in history a radical educational press emerged in the 1970's to work on these projects. In her chapter, Jenny Thewlis charts the rise and demise of this press and illustrates the struggle to provide serious theoretical solutions to the question, 'What is progressive about progressive education?' from several perspectives - from radical libertarian to neo-classical Marxist. The irreconcilability of these solutions partly reflected and partly constituted the explanations for their failure to galvanise forces both within schools - curricular, pedagogic and organisational reforms - and in the wider contexts of social tensions and contradictions during the period. The position of radical professionals in education, based partly at least in the leverage of teacher shortages, gave way to a systematic weakening of collective occupational power. No firm cross-occupational cooperation existed, nor cultural or moral forms, which could go much beyond trade unionism. Thus what was most clearly articulated in mass demonstrations was support for maintaining the present levels and types of provision - a defensive stance undermined by growing social insecurity of rising unemployment and relentless popular right wing press. Here, Thewis' account identifies some of the weakness of political forms associated with education which Dubberley directly describes in relations between schools and many working class parents. As with any political form which claims a professionalist authority in knowledge and training radical teachers must work to build a constituency both within the professional and within 'client' groups and beyond. Cultural and economic dynamics give rise to divisions often difficult to bridge, especially between occupational groups. Where there is an occupational community under pressure, on the one hand, and where within the professions sectionalism occurs, they tend to weaken senses of coherent purpose. The anti-comprehensive movement are currently exploiting this.

For the most part developments in comprehensive education tend to appear to ameliorate the systematic effects of inequality. This is achieved by individualising problems and offering the solution of benign competition for the maintenance of viable harmony and social diversity in which the idea of equality of value for individuals and the cultural differences they practice is simultaneously offered and denied. Systematic differences in opportunity are patterned by social class background and the property relations they are built upon - by cultural differences (often much exaggerated) in terms of race and ethnicity and in gender terms. They are articulated in complex patterns of power and structures of opportunity some of which are described and analysed directly, others tangentially, in the chapters which follow. The scene is probably set for the next few years in British education. A further undermining of comprehensive educational principles will occur. Some of the main modes of institutional transformation will be found in the effects of a 'progressive' rhetoric of 'choice', 'diversity' and competition between schools for student customers. Sharpening of class differences can be expected. Progressive institutional inertia, non-cooperation and exploiting spaces which are internal to education may prove to be the most likely strategic devices of the social democratic bloc in education. The forces for moral control, accompanied by curricular financial centralisation in education have been moving quite quickly, linking as they do to vocationalist models of educational planning and provision. They are profoundly differentialist in implication. Curriculum developments which provide for 'progressivist' individual need fulfilling systems - through complex modularisation, profiling of criterion referenced records of school achievement, and other 'choice enhancing' vocational provisions in schools will keep things very busy in education. But while 'choice' is offered as the basis for equity, the reality is likely to be the continued restriction on the choices of those least able to compete. The consequences will be, to the extent that social forces do not oppose them, a sharpening of differences and deepening of fissures in the social fabric. Given this projection, can education continue the role it once played in ameliorating the consequences of social inequality?

## NOTES

1. We would like to thank the British Educational Research Association for its sponsoring of the conferences at which original versions of several of these papers were presented at the Institute of Education and King's College, University of London.
2. It is important to contrast the treatment of these issues with that of McPherson and Williams (1987) where they have produced evidence of the success of Scottish secondary comprehensive education in social democractic terms, i.e. the gaps between the middle class and the lower classes are being narrowed, while attainment rises generally.
3. ... or any more socially expansive perspective upon adult responsibility for childhood which might encourage 'communal' practices as, say, in certain kibbutz experience.

## REFERENCES

Bullock Report (1975) A Language for Life, London, H.M.S.O.

Cockcroft, W.H. (1982) Mathematics Counts, London, H.M.S.O.

McPherson, A. and Williams, D.J. (1987) 'Equalisation and improvement: Some effects of comprehensive reorganisation in Scotland', Sociology (November 1987)

# 2

## Some Observations on Progressivism and Curriculum Practice

### David Hamilton

Let me begin by declaring my interest. I regard 'curriculum' and 'Progressive' as pivotal concepts in the educational debates of twentieth-century Britain. To consider them in conjunction is, therefore, to reflect upon the major educational initiatives of recent decades.

As an organised force 'Progressives' appeared in British education at the end of the nineteenth century. In 1898, for instance, the London School Board was captured by a 'Progressive' majority. At that time, Progressives were united by two notions. First, that the course of social progress was best promoted, not through the 'survival of the fittest' but, rather, through direct intervention in the organisation of human affairs. And secondly, that responsibility for the management of social interventions should lie with the political state. Thus, the raising of the school leaving age on two occasions in the 1890s not only kept more children from the exploitation of employers, it also brought more children (and their families) within reach of the organs of the state.

In the decades that followed, however, Progressivism broke up into various fractions. The rise of the Prussian military machine and the horrors of World War One damaged the image of the benign, 'positive' state. The notion of intervention was rethought. Some Progressives downplayed the state's remit, transferring its responsibilities to less-powerful institutions such as 'society' and 'the community' (cf. Robert M. Maciver's Community: A Sociological Study (Being an Attempt to Set out the Fundamental Laws of Social Life), 1917). Other Progressives, however, took a more radical stance. They expelled the state from their scheme of things and, instead, began to see 'self-realisation' as the only true guarantee of social progress (cf. Edmond

Holmes' What is and What Might Be, 1911).

Prima facie, then these two Progressive factions stood at a distance from one another. One recognised the steering role of outside agencies, while the other held that, as Edmond Holmes put it, the 'social order' could only be reformed by permitting the unhindered 'growth' of each child's 'natural faculties' (Holmes, 1911, pp. 290 & 291). Historically, it is the early proponents of 'self-realisation' (e.g. Holmes, Homer Lane and Maria Montessori) who are remembered as the Progressive vanguard (see, for instance, Selleck, 1972). Yet, as subsequent critics have repeatedly pointed out (e.g. Dearden, 1968; Sharp & Green, 1975; Gordon & White, 1979; Walkerdine, 1983; and McEnroe, 1986), no educational programme can shut out social pre-suppositions, any more than a teacher can avoid influencing his or her pupils. In short, context free 'self-realisation' is an impossibility.

Accordingly, my own view is that all forms of Progressivism are continuous with each other and, moreover, that all necessarily entail a conception of the overarching 'state'. At the same time, however, I also accept that the Progressives differed among themselves with regard to concepts like 'freedom', 'play', 'interest', 'independence' and 'individuality'. Certainly, these differences created important intellectual and social turbulences within the Progressivism mainstream. Nevertheless, I would suggest that the leading Progressives and their supporters formed a broad consensus. They worked together in schoolteaching, educational administration, educational research, teacher training, the school psychological service, the school meals service, the school medical service (etc.) to fashion a new education system that was, on the one hand, balanced and harmonious and, on the other hand, an agency of social change.

As this suggests, then, 'equality' was not a central concept in Progressive thought. Indeed, there is a sense in which such a notion might be regarded as anti-Progressive. Darwin's original insight - which helped to frame the Progressive ideology - was that (biological) evolution is powered by the differences that exist among members of a breeding population. Thus, the climate that fostered Progressivism also helped to promote a tension between the notion of 'equality' and the notion of 'individuality' (i.e. difference). In the event, it is understandable that the latter became pre-eminent.

Moreover, it was this early twentieth-century climate

that also gave rise to the notion of 'comprehensive' schooling. Here the contrasting label is 'common' schooling. The term originates from the United States (see Rubenstein & Simon, 1969, p. 16) where it was linked to the general reorganisation of Secondary Schooling. In the words of its launching report - The Cardinal Principles of Secondary Education (1918) - the US comprehensive high school was to embrace 'all curriculums in one unified organisation' (see Hamilton, forthcoming, Chapter 6). Here again, differences among learners were emphasised. The purpose of such 'comprehensive' (or 'multilateral') schools was to promote social harmony and social efficiency not social equality. In the words of the British importer of the term - Godfrey Thomson - 'The social solidarity of the whole nation' is 'more important than any of the defects to which a comprehensive high school may be subject' (quoted in Rubenstein & Simon, p. 16).

The fruits of such a broad Progressive consensus are evident in the Consultative Committee Reports issued in the inter-war years by the Board of Education for England and Wales. Self-realisation figured prominently; but so did concern for the efficient placement of pupils into adult society. For instance, the Education of the Adolescent (1926) started from the premiss that all children should have the opportunity of advancing beyond the elementary and primary stage. If 'transplanted to new ground', young adults would be able to 'thrive to a new height' and 'attain a sturdier fibre'. Within the same sentence, however, the Report also endorsed the view that such 'new environment(s)' (viz. 'secondary', 'central' or 'senior' schools) should, 'as far as possible', be 'adjusted' to the 'interests and abilities' of 'each range and variety' of pupils ( p. xix).

Likewise, The Primary School (1931) recommended that the primary school curriculum should - in an oft-remembered phrase - be 'thought of in terms of activity and experience rather than knowledge to be acquired and facts to be stored' (p. 139). Two pages previously, however, it had already issued the prescription that, 'by the age of ten', pupils in a single age group should be 'classified in several sections' (p. 137). Finally, Secondary Education (1939) stated that 'schools of every type fulfil their proper purpose insofar as they foster the free growth of individuality' (p. 362). Yet, elsewhere in its concluding section, the Report also re-affirmed its 'general impression' that the education of boys and girls above the age of eleven-plus 'had ceased to correspond with the actual structure of modern society and with the economic facts of the situation' (p. 353).

The attention given by these reports to the structure of schooling extended, therefore, to a consideration of the social and economic competencies that schools should feed into the labour market. As in the United States, therefore, 'social adjustment' remained a major consideration in the minds of mainstream Progressives. Indeed, 'self-realisation' and 'social adjustment' were, for many of them, merely opposite sides of the same coin.

This brings me to a consideration of 'curriculum'. How, for instance, were Progressives to translate the (new) 'needs' of the labour market into the practices of schooling? Was it simply a matter of syllabus revision? Or were the 'needs of the individual' and the 'needs of society' to be reconciled in new ways? Recently, Malcolm Skilbeck has suggested - in School-Based Curriculum Development (1984a) - that the Progressives chose to make a break with the past. Moreover, he also claims that, in doing so, they changed the basis of modern curriculum thinking:

> In taking the definition of a curriculum away from a course, a subject matter to be covered, towards experiences to be undergone, the Progressives were undoubtedly shifting the emphasis away from the provision of something articulated, definite and preplanned and towards the nature of experience and the process of learning. (p. 26)

There is an important truth in this argument. If transmission theories of learning are, as Skilbeck puts it, 'abandoned'; and if, at the same time, narrow 'reproductive' (i.e. employment-related) functions of schooling are 'rejected', then pre-1900 curriculum theory is seriously devalued. In Skilbeck's view, therefore, a new set of circumstances arose:

> One of the consequences of the Progressives' concerns ... was that the term 'curriculum' itself had to be redefined. A definition was needed that would enable the older programmatic idea of subject-bound content transmitted by teachers in authority to be displaced by the new kinds of programmes that the Progressives were advocating and implementing. (p. 24-25)

There is, however, a problem with this argument. It gives the impression that the Progressives' ideas superseded a cluster of curriculum propositions whose historical significance was in decline. Certainly, the 'programmatic' emphasis in educational thinking already had a long history. As I have argued elsewhere (Hamilton, 1987), it originated in the seventeenth-century Scientific Revolution. At that time schooling in general, and school programmes in particular, came to be seen as crucial elements in the socio-technical instrumentation of the modern state. If the state could acquire control of curriculum planning then, as Jan Amos Comenius argued in the Great Didactic (1632), '(teachers) will not have to select their own subject matter, and work out their own method, but will only have to take knowledge that has been suitably arranged ... (and) pour it into their pupils' (p. 440).

In practice, of course, Comenius' social programme did not come about. Among other things, the state had difficulty in identifying the 'natural' laws of learning (etc.) that would guarantee the success of such policies. To this extent, therefore, Skilbeck's case has some substance: the nineteenth century is not remembered for any kind of social consensus on the management and organisation of elementary schooling. On the other hand, it is also true that, by the end of that century, Comenius-type notions were making a come-back - a state of affairs symbolized by the publication of the first English edition of The Great Didactic in 1896. In those decades, an influential body of social science opinion (discussed in Smith & Hamilton, 1980) advanced the claim that new research into psychology, biology and logic was in much the same position to advance the science of educational engineering as, 200 years previously, works like Newton's Principia (1687) had advanced the cause of mechanical engineering.

The importance of these new notions is that they were regarded as equally 'Progressive' as anything offered by the proponents of 'self-realisation'. Indeed, in my view it is impossible to make a clear separation between these two camps. Note, for instance, Richard Selleck's description of J.J. Findlay, Professor of Education at Manchester University from 1903: '(He) came into prominence as a Herbartian, transferred his allegiance to Dewey, experimented ... with the methods of Montessori and helped to publicize the scientific educationists' (Selleck, 1968, p. 333; see also Hamilton, 1985). And note, too, how inter-war

27

Progressives (e.g. Percy Nunn, Susan Isaacs and Cyril Burt) sought scientific sanction in the writings of Jean Piaget and Sigmund Freud who, in their turn, were strongly influenced by nineteenth-century notions about the 'development', within human beings, of 'normal' or 'natural' behaviour. It is hardly surprising, therefore, that the Consultative Committee argued both for the promotion of individuality and for the positive allocation (or direction) of individuals to their 'true' position in the social cosmos.

Let me now move forward to the 1960s. I believe a similar combination of circumstances engaged the curriculum activists of that decade. That is, a technocratic strand of thought cohabited with a stance more reminiscent of Skilbeck's portrayal of Progressivism. In addition, both were subsumed under a conception of the positive state. One illustration of this coexistence can be found in the work of the Nuffield Foundation Science Teaching Project (founded 1961). The brief drawn up by the Foundation consisted of two seemingly contradictory elements: a statement that the outcome was to be a 'coordinated set of materials' and a corollary that the materials were to be used by teachers in 'any way they saw fit' (Waring, 1979, p. 13).

The Schools Council (founded 1964) had a similar inception. Its philosophy was set out in the opening recommendation of the Lockwood Report (1964). Note the apparent contradiction contained in its first and second sentences:

> We reaffirm the importance of the principle that the schools should have the fullest possible measure of responsibility for their own work, including responsibility for their own curricula and teaching methods, which should be evolved by their own staff to meet the needs of their own pupils. We believe however that positive action is needed to uphold this principle. (quoted in Plaskow, 1985, p. 20)

In the event, the first of these sentences (together with its apparently non-programmatic tone) became a key element in the Council's public persona. Nevertheless, the recently-published valedictory volume on the Schools Council indicates that such rhetoric should be treated with caution. One of the original members of the Council (Arnold

Jennings, see Plaskow, 1985, p. 18) suggests that the stand-point of democratic pluralism was, in part, a device to 'disarm' the local authority and teacher union suspicion that had been directed against the Council's centralist pre-decessor (viz. the Ministry of Education's Curriculum Study Group, founded 1962). And two former Council employees (Freddie Sparrow and Jean Rudduck) draw attention, respectively, to the Council's 'over-concentration' on the production of published materials and to its parallel reliance upon 'big "central team" initiatives' (see Plaskow, 1985, pp. 58 & 152).

Together, these comments suggest that such central-ising and programmatic aspects of the Council's work created the same problem that Comenius had noted 300 years previously in The Great Didactic:

> For more than a hundred years much complaint has been made of the unmethodical way in which schools are conducted, but it is only within the last thirty years that any serious attempt has been made to find a remedy for this state of things. And with what result? Schools remain exactly as they were. (quoted in Silberman, 1971, p. 158; for a comparable modern statement, see MacDonald & Rudduck, 1971)

So what was to be done about this gap? How were the capacities of teachers to be accommodated within the prescriptions of curriculum developers? One immediate, if delaying, response was that greater attention was given to evaluation research - a fact reflected in the 1968 foundation of the Schools Council Evaluators' Group. But the inform-ation generated by evaluation workers proved to be of limited value. It may have assisted individual curriculum projects, but its cumulative effect was merely to confirm what had been known since the field trials of the Nuffield Science Teaching Project. Evaluation studies did not solve the implementation problem; they simply rendered it more visible.

Around the same time, however, two other proposals gained currency: (1) that curriculum development should be directed towards accomplishing greater compliance between goals and outcomes; and (2) that a new model of curriculum development should be constructed - one that fully acknow-ledged the indeterminacy of curriculum implementation.

Let me take these two solutions in turn. The first perspective - greater attention to curriculum compliance -is evident in Professor Jack Kerr's inaugural address at the University of Leicester (The Problem of Curriculum Reform, 1967). Kerr saw his task as finding ways 'to build order' into the curriculum development process:

> The field trials of the new programmes (he continued) might be designed to conform more closely to the requirements of rigorous operational research. Evaluation might be used not just for the terminal assessment of pupil changes but also to produce independent evidence about the effectiveness of each stage of the course as it developed. (1967, p. 5)

Here, Kerr was taking his cue from the experience of science educators (and perhaps, even, from his wartime experiences in the Royal Air Force). The Nuffield Science Teaching Project had, he claimed, evolved a 'standard pattern' (p. 4) that, suitably revised and codified, could 'revolutionize' (p. 5) English education. In short, Kerr believed, like Comenius, that educational change could be 'effectively planned and pre-determined' (p. 24).

Where, then, did teachers fit into Kerr's analysis? At first glance, his position seems unequivocal: 'the message ... which rings louder and clearer than any other is that the reform of the curriculum will not come about without the total involvement of teachers' (p. 21). Yet, as with the Lockwood Report, it is worth examining this rhetoric more closely. What, for instance, is meant by 'total involvement'? And how does teacher involvement fit within the field of 'operational research'? My own impression is that Kerr's model locates the teaching force principally in the 'delivery' department of the curriculum enterprise. Accordingly, responsibility for the 'principles and techniques of curriculum construction and evaluation' (p. 23) remains in other hands. Teachers are, indeed, essential to the curriculum process, but only as components in a sophisticated but pre-given 'system' of 'curriculum improvement' (p. 6) and 'curriculum renewal' (p. 5). At the risk of oversimplification, Kerr envisaged teachers holding more of a curriculum-monitoring than a curriculum-building responsibility.

The second solution to the problem of curriculum

implementation is represented by the work of Lawrence Stenhouse. The gap between curriculum conception and curriculum execution was, from his standpoint, to be bridged in a different way - by moving the locus of conception closer to the schoolroom. Teachers were to be offered an arena where both their creativity and their judgement could be demonstrated and enhanced. Accordingly, the notion of the 'unfinished' curriculum (Bruner, 1966, p. 74) became central to Stenhouse's model for the Humanities Curriculum Project:

> The schools selected as trial schools in 1968 will thus be handling our first trials. Indeed, the word trials, traditional now in curriculum innovation, is probably not appropriate here. A trial suggests the evaluation of materials approaching a finished state, but in fact the teachers in the trial schools will be in a very real sense pioneers who are involved in the process of shaping the (project) material. (1968, reprinted in Stenhouse, 1983, p. 102)

In certain respects, then, the Humanities Curriculum Project exemplified Skilbeck's account of 'Progressive' curriculum practice. It gave an 'enlarged' role to the school; and it replaced the 'precise usage' of 'linear...sequences' of 'learning steps' with a greater 'openness and looseness' of curriculum thinking (Skilbeck, 1984a, p. 25-26). In other respects, however, Stenhouse's thinking differed from the Progressive ideal. It downplayed the importance of the pupil's interests and, instead, gave joint priority to the core values of the humanities and to the responsibility that teachers had in representing these values to their pupils.

To this extent, the Humanities Curriculum Project was knowledge-centred and teacher-centred. It was strong on the production of 'high-quality' materials (Stenhouse, 1983, p. 93); it used the 'evidence' provided by these materials to 'discipline' classroom discussion (p. 111); and it focused its in-service work upon the teacher's task of managing and monitoring the conduct of classroom discussion (p. 133-139). Overall, Stenhouse regarded the Humanities Curriculum Project as 'a vernacular equivalent to the classics' (1979, p. 248). On the one hand, it stressed the importance of discussion and argument in the formation of a civilized citizenry (cf. the role of 'dialectic' in the renaissance university); and on the other hand, it gave great attention to the management and regulation of educational debate (cf. the rules and rituals of the medieval disputation).

Following the completion of the Humanities Curriculum Project in 1972, Stenhouse, his immediate colleagues and a network of participating teachers pushed these ideas even further. Consideration of the technical side of curriculum practice is exemplified by Stenhouse's 1972 paper 'Teaching through small-group discussion: formality, rules and authority' (reprinted in Stenhouse, 1983) and by John Elliott's monograph Developing Hypotheses about Classrooms from Teachers' Practical Constructs (1976); while the emancipatory aspect of curriculum practice is tackled through the idea - raised by Schwab in 'The "impossible" role of the teacher in Progressive education' (1959) - that teaching and learning should be reflective, research-based activities (cf. Stenhouse's An Introduction to Curriculum Research and Development, 1975).

Indeed, Stenhouse elaborated this emancipatory argument even further. He moved from an early nineteen-seventies position of 'no curriculum development without teacher development' (quoted in Stenhouse, 1983, p. 156) to a 1980 position of 'curriculum development is about teacher self-development' (Stenhouse, 1980, p. 255). Progressivism had come full circle: for 'pupil self-realisation' now read 'teacher self-realisation' (cf. Skilbeck's reference to 'teacher self-actualization', 1984a, p. 15).

Curriculum inquiry took on a new tenor at this stage in its history. As Harland (1986, p. 5) has indicated, it was assumed that 'healthy curriculum development' was contingent upon an expansion of the classroom professionalism of teachers. There was even a feeling that, after 10-15 years of centre-periphery development, the 'gap' problem had been solved by giving school curricula back to their rightful owners (cf. Robin Barrow's Giving Teaching Back to Teachers: a Critical Introduction to Curriculum Theory, 1984). But this is an oversimplification of the changes that occurred in the 1960s and 1970s. The property relationships between school curricula and the teaching profession are more complex, especially when taken over the long term. In what sense, for instance, might teachers be said to 'own' the curriculum? Is it more accurate to say that they merely 'possess' the curriculum (i.e. acting as stewards for the ultimate 'owner')? Or, yet again, is it more accurate to say that, for the duration of the Progressive epoch, teachers have merely been curriculum squatters, occupying space they neither possess by convention nor own by dint of a legal title?

These theoretical nuances may seem remote from school life. Yet, in practice, they soon turned out to be crucial. During the late nineteen-seventies, the school-based curriculum research movement underwent a subtle invasion (see Harland, 1986, & Rudduck, in Plaskow, 1985, p. 152). A technocratic vision of school-based curriculum change became more evident - one that included greater official attention to the management of schools. This developmental/managerial combination was not accidental. Schools were to become recognised centres of innovation, but only under the ultimate direction of external agencies. In short, an important redefinition of property rights was in the air. Henceforth, it became important to distinguish school-<u>based</u> curriculum development from school-<u>controlled</u> curriculum development.

This new colonisation initiative appears, in broad terms, to have been launched between 1975 and 1977. In 1975, the Permanent Secretary in the DES (William Pile) speculated whether 'the Government would continue to debar itself from what had been termed the secret garden of the curriculum' (Raggatt, 1985, p. 4). In the following year, the Labour Prime Minister (James Callaghan) gave a major speech at Ruskin College which identified the maintenance of 'proper national standards' and the improvement of 'relations between industry and education' (quoted in CCCS, 1981, p. 218) as components of the educational system in need of overhaul. And finally, 1977 saw the government proceed with three further curriculum-related initiatives: (1) publication of the Taylor Report (which advocated a more even distribution of curriculum power among local authorities, teachers, parents and the community); (2) promulgation of a Green (i.e. consultative) Paper which spoke of harnessing government policies - 'including education' - more securely to the creation of 'national wealth' (quoted in Skilbeck, 1984b, p. 42); and (3) distribution of Circular 14/77 which required local authorities to inform the DES about their curriculum policies and practices.

The last of these initiatives revealed considerable local variation. In response, the government proposed that local authorities should take a more active part in shaping the policies of their schools, albeit after a national 'agreed view' had been established. And it was towards the formulation of this 'agreed view' (Skilbeck, 1984b, p. 30) on educational practices and standards that succeeding DES documents were addressed (e.g. A Framework for the School Curriculum, 1980; The School Curriculum, 1984; and Better Schools, 1985).

The second issue raised by James Callaghan - strengthening the school-industry connection - has also been the subject of a string of publications (e.g. The New Training Initiative (1981), Training for Jobs (1985) and Education and Training for Young People (1985). At one level, these documents relate to a different strand of government thinking, one that focuses on the vocational/occupational arena. Nonetheless, it is equally true that both sets of proposals have been cast from the same political matrix. That is, both embrace a return of the school curriculum to the active stewardship of the state; both presume that curricula should be functionally differentiated; both entail management structures (e.g. national control of INSET) that allow the state's 'will' to reverberate through the school system; and, finally, both see the teaching force as 'licensed agents of the DES' (Harland, 1986, p. 10) or 'state professionals' (see Ozga & Lawn, 1981, p. 18).

Of course, such language is not conspicuous in the official documents listed above. Instead, they echo the 'Progressivism' of the Consultative Committee Reports. First, note how Better Schools regards 'differentiation within the curriculum' as a means of 'meet(ing) more effectively' the 'needs of each pupil according to his ability and aptitudes' (p. 13). Secondly, note its concern with self-realisation: 'learning at school' is for pupils to develop 'lively,· inquiring minds' (pp. 13-14). Thirdly, note how it harnesses curriculum practice to the labour market: the 'linking of education and training ... should have employment as one of its principal functions' (p. 16). And, finally, note how its attention to 'attributes' other than 'skills' and 'knowledge' (p. 36) mimics a 1920s human relations stance towards the productivity functions of education and training.

Indeed, the solution proposed to overcome this last difficulty - viz. a curriculum strongly saturated with social- and life-skills training - is isomorphic with life-adjustment initiatives developed in earlier decades (e.g. following the publication of the Cardinal Principles Report in the USA).

Again, 'self-realisation' enters the argument. Schools are to be reformed so that school leavers can take responsibility for their own careers and life-patterns.

In such terms, a 'child-centred' curriculum is highly functional vis-à-vis the labour market. Youth unemployment is accounted for, not in terms of structural deficiencies in the economy, but in terms of individual deficits. If school leavers are given responsibility for their own education, then they can also be held responsible for their own short-comings in the labour market.

To this degree, child-centredness may be functional for the early (and non-certificated) school leaver. But is it appropriate for pupils whom, it might be claimed, cannot (or should not) be given responsibility for their own education? Here, Better Schools calls a different tune. The teaching force, not the pupil population, is its target population. Teachers are expected both to 'deliver' (p. 88) and to 'mediate' (p. 43) the 'agreed view' of school learning synthesized by the DES. But what does 'mediation' mean in this context? Does it, for instance, revive memories of the 'unfinished' curriculum (à la Stenhouse)? Or does it reactivate a systems-analysis view of teacher profes-sionalism (à la Kerr)? In fact, the combination of 'delivery' with 'mediation' reveals the thinking behind Better Schools. The only modifications it allows to teachers are those which bring the agreed curriculum into line with the 'age, ability and aptitude' of the pupils in their classes. At best, then, the teacher is encouraged to use 'different kinds of language with different pupils' and to 'vary ... the pace of introducing new materials' (p. 43). In short, the 'curriculum mediator' is little more than a 'curriculum monitor'.

Let me draw my observations together. In this paper I have advanced a range of propositions. First, that the roots of Progressivism lie in late nineteenth-century assumptions about the relationship between schooling, state intervention and social evolution. Secondly, that nineteenth-century Pro-gressivism subsequently dissolved into a variety of fractions. Thirdly, that these fractions continued to exert an influence over each other. Fourthly, that all forms of Progressive thinking contain a tension between the role of the individual and the role of the state. And finally, that this tension has remained on the educational agenda until the present day.

Overall, I have sought to demonstrate certain contin-uities in twentieth-century curriculum thinking by criticising a notion of Progressivism which tries to deny these continuities. Accordingly, I remain dissatisfied with Skilbeck's identification of 'two (viz. programmatic and progressive) positions' in curriculum matters and, more specifically, with his conclusion that 'each has something valuable to contribute' (1984a, p. 26). My own stance is rather different. I accept the criticism - made against Progressivism - that self-realisation cannot exclude the penetration of external forces. Further, I regard this penetration as neither random nor amorphous: it is shaped by the pre-given structures of society in the same manner as schooling is shaped by the pre-given structures of the curriculum. To this extent, I believe that all forms of teaching and learning are subject to an external, programmatic influence. Nevertheless, I also accept a contrasting position: that teachers and learners can exert their own influence over a curriculum - structuring it, for instance, according to their past experiences and future plans.

These positions may be separable in an analytic sense. For curriculum practitioners, however, they are indivisible. The problem for them is not a question of 'either/or' but, rather, a question of 'both/and'. Their task, that is, is to devise teaching and learning activities that both reconcile and transcend the two positions outlined by Skilbeck. In short, they have to acknowledge and to confront the fact that they are simultaneously the objects and the agents of the curriculum. Indeed, I would argue that this issue (and neither 'knowledge' nor the 'child') must lie at the heart of any form of schooling that aspires to be truly 'Progressive'.

## NOTE

David Hamilton is a lecturer at the University of Glasgow; European editor of the Journal of Curriculum Studies; and a former President of the British Educational Research Association. He has recently completed a ten-year programme of research, the fruits of which are to be published under the title Towards a Theory of Schooling.

## REFERENCES

Barrow, R. (1984) Giving Teaching Back to Teachers: a Critical Introduction to Curriculum Theory, Brighton: Wheatsheaf.

Bruner, J. (1966) Toward a Theory of Instruction, New York: Norton (original edition, 1966).

CCCS (Centre for Contemporary Cultural Studies) (1981) Unpopular Education, London: Hutchinson.

Comenius, J.A. The Great Didactic (1632), London: Adam & Charles Black, 1896.

Dearden, R.F. (1968) The Philosophy of Primary Education, London: Routledge.

Elliott, J. (1976) Developing Hypotheses about Classrooms from Teachers' Practical Constructs, Grand Forks: North Dakota Study Group on Evaluation.

Gordon, P. & White, J. (1979) Philosophers as Educational Reformers: the Influence of Idealism on British Educational Thought and Practice, London: Routledge.

Hamilton, D. (1985) 'Progressivism reconsidered', History Workshop, issue 20, pp. 195-198.

———— (1987) 'The pedagogic juggernaut', British Journal of Educational Studies 35, 18-29

———— (forthcoming) Towards a Theory of Schooling.

Harland, J. (1986) 'The new INSET: a transformation scene' in TVEI Working Papers, No. 2, 4-15

Holmes, E. (1911) What is and What Might Be, London: Constable.

Kerr, J.F. (1967) The Problem of Curriculum Reform, Leicester: Leicester University Press. Reprinted in J.F. Kerr (ed.) (1968) Changing the Curriculum, London: University of London Press, pp. 13-38.

MacDonald, B. & Rudduck, J. (1971) 'Curriculum research and development: barriers to success', British Journal of Educational Psychology, 41, 148-154.

McEnroe, F. (1986) Psychoanalysis and Early Education: a Study of the Educational Ideas of Sigmund Freud (1856-1939), Anna Freud (1895-1982), Melanie Klein (1882-1960), and Susan Isaacs (1885-1948), Ph.D. thesis, University of Glasgow.

Ozga, J.T. & Lawn, M.A. (1981) Teachers, Professionalism and Class: a Study of Organised Teachers, London: Falmer.

Plaskow, M. (ed.) (1985) Life and Death of the Schools Council, London: Falmer.

Raggatt, P. (1985) 'It's no secret any more: curriculum policy in public view' in P. Raggatt & G. Weiner (eds) Curriculum and Assessment: Some Policy Issues, Oxford: Pergamon, pp. 1-7.

Rubenstein, D. & Simon, B. (1969) The Evolution of the

Comprehensive School 1926-1966, London: Routledge.

Schwab, J.J. (1959) 'The "impossible" role of the teacher in Progressive education' reprinted in J.J. Schwab (1978) Science, Curriculum and Liberal Education: Selected Essays, I. Westbury & N.J. Wilkof (eds), London: University of Chicago Press, pp. 167-183.

Selleck, R.J.W. (1968) The New Education: the English Background 1870-1914, London: Pitman.

———— (1972) English Primary Education and the Progressives, 1914-1939, London: Routledge.

Sharp, R. & Green, A. (1975) Education and Social Control: a Study of Progressive Primary Education, London: Routledge.

Silberman, C.E. (1971) Crisis in the Classroom: the Remaking of American Education, New York: Vintage Books.

Skilbeck, M. (1984a) School-based Curriculum Development, London: Harper & Row.

———— (ed.) (1984b) Readings in School-based Curriculum Development, London: Harper & Row.

Smith, J.V. & Hamilton, D. (eds) (1980) The Meritocratic Intellect: Studies in the History of Educational Research, Aberdeen: Aberdeen University Press.

Stenhouse, L. (1975) An Introduction to Curriculum Research and Development, London: Heinemann.

———— (ed.) (1980) Curriculum Research and Development in Action, London: Heinemann.

———— (1983) Authority, Education and Emancipation, London: Heinemann.

Walkerdine, V. (1983) 'It's only natural: rethinking child-centred pedagogy' in A. Wolpe & J. Donald (eds) Is There Anyone Here from Education, London: Pluto, pp. 79-87.

Waring, M. (1979) Social Pressures and Curriculum Innovation: a Study of the Nuffield Foundation Science Teaching Project, London: Methuen.

# 3

## Implications for Progressivism of Recent Changes in the Control and Direction of Education Policy

### Roger Dale

It is as difficult as ever to pin down very precisely what is to be understood by 'progressivism' in education. Some years ago I suggested that the strongest thread uniting those brandishing the progressive label was their opposition to an industrial model of education, whether that applied to the process or the products of the education system (see Dale 1979a). This still holds good, but is even less adequate as a definition at a time when the recrudescence of the industrial model in a virulent form has made it clear that the 'anti-industrialism' includes far more than 'progressives'; it includes, indeed, many who would be quite opposed to progressivism in other areas, for instance such academic purists as Enoch Powell. While its anti-industrialism is a particularly important feature of progressivism in the context in which this book is written, then, it does not represent the essence of the progressivism which the existence of this book at least implies is under threat. The other crucial aspect of progressivism is its child centredness, the assumption that the direction of education cannot be imposed from outside, but must emerge, with the help of skilled teachers, from the child.

Central to both these definitions of progressivism is that they assume and require a certain autonomy of the education system; the emphasis on child centredness and the key role of the skilled teacher in enabling the child to develop, in particular requires a wide autonomy for teachers, who should be free to exercise their skills for the benefit of the child alone. In the remainder of this paper I want to examine the implications of recent changes in the form and direction of education policy for the conditions, especially of professional autonomy, which progressivism needs to survive. I shall compare the form and direction of education policy at the time of the Plowden revolution, which may be taken as the high point of state-endorsed progressivism, with that of the present day. I shall first of all consider how the form and direction of education policy are themselves shaped by the structure and ideology of the education system.

## THE STRUCTURE AND IDEOLOGY OF THE EDUCATION SYSTEM

The structure and ideology of the education system set limits to the form and direction of education policy by controlling both the relative capacities of the various parts of the education system, and the possible mandate(s) to which education policy must respond. In short, they determine the scope of education policy (for an elaboration of the idea of the scope of the education system, see Dale et al. [1988]). The structure and ideology of the education system which held at the time of Plowden is well known. The Education Act of 1944 led to a balance between the three partners in the management of the education system, national government, local government and the teaching profession, such that

> power over the distribution of resources, over the organisation and context of education was to be diffused among the different elements and no one of them was to be given a controlling voice ... the DES was not given strong formal powers to secure the implementation of its policies because it was assumed that both central government and local education authorities were managed by men of good will whose main concern was to improve the service and whose reflective judgements remained untainted by the intrusion of party ideology. (Bogdanor 1979, pp. 157, 166)

The implications for the nature and direction of education policy of this basic structure depended on how it was interpreted. Two features notable by their absence were of critical importance. First, while central government did have potentially crucial powers under the act, there was, as Kogan points out, 'a curious lack of connection between these powers, used vigorously by the centre, and any overt policies for changes within the school' (1983, p. 62). Second, with the exception of the comprehensive issue education was not nationally or locally infused by party political contestation. The consequence was that both local government and the teaching profession had considerable latitude for taking or influencing educational policy initiatives. It will be recalled, for instance, that even the alternative models of comprehensive education set out in Circular 10/65 were themselves based on existing, locally derived schemes, while the kinds of progressive initiatives of concern here were set up equally in Conservative Leicestershire and Labour West Riding. Seeing education as a professional rather than as a political matter also meant that a major influence over what was taught in schools rested with the teaching profession -as the events over the setting up of the teacher-dominated Schools Council rather than a central government intervention into the curriculum demonstrate (see Manzer, 1970). Indeed, the decade of the 60s represented the apogee of teacher professional autonomy, with control not only of the Schools Council, but also of the Certificate of Secondary Education in the hands of the teaching profession. Teachers had autonomy both in the 'strong'-policy formation - as well as in the 'weak'-policy implementation - sense, and if this was, as I have suggested, a 'licensed' autonomy, the terms of the licence were comparatively loose (see Dale 1979b).

This structure and ideology were associated with particular economic, political and social circumstances. For at least two decades after 1944 economic growth and full employment could be assumed. This produced increasing investment in education; it also depreciated links between education and the economy. In such a situation, as Kogan puts it, 'the prevailing principles of the governance of education could be those of evolution, interaction, de-centralization, and letting things grow at the base, rather than central preconstruction and installation. Innovation and change would be innate rather than externally-fostered, spontaneous rather than pre-structured, although encouraged by national policies which gave maximum discretion to the prime institutions' (1983, p. 60). To put it more broadly, there was what Claus Offe calls a 'conjunctural' mode of political rationality where demand inputs are treated as given. Because of this, 'the only thing that can and must be rationalized by a "good" policy maker is the efficiency and effectiveness of outputs. Conjunctural policies would seek to maximize the adequacy of response to problems as they emerge and appear on the agenda: the concomitant expectation is that such problems and demands will remain within a range of manageability defined by existing capacities of state action and their continuing improvement' (Offe, 1981, p. 125).

The last phrase highlights a further feature of the conditions under which the post-1944 structure and ideology of the education system flourished, i.e. what Samuel Beer calls 'collectivism', 'that thrust of policy ... toward control over the economic and social order as a whole [whose] agents may be Tory or socialist [and whose] social inclinations accordingly more or less egalitarian [but who] have in common a readiness to assume overall responsibility' (Beer 1982, p. 10). Allied to this was a 'civic culture of deference' consisting of attitudes towards political behaviour that were widely held at all levels of the polity. Embodying hierarchical and organic values, these attitudes strongly supported structures of action which mobilized consent for their respective goals among their constituents' (op. cit. p. 209). Of course there was resistance to these attitudes at all levels of the system, but with shared political commitment the possibility of economic and social improvement, and especially with the strong leadership of the local authorities by Sir William Alexander, and of the teachers by Ronald Gould, the conditions of success of the post-1944 structure and ideology of the education system outlined by Bogdanor seem to be met. As he puts it 'Were any element in the system to seek to use its power to the full, the system could not work. Mutual constraint, as in the Hobbesian universe, is the precondition of success, and the war of all against all would make progess in education impossible. There must, therefore, be limits on the degree of politicization of the education service if it is to operate successfully', while this sytem worked best 'when only a small number of interests were involved whose rank and file were content to defer to elites, and could, therefore, be relied upon to act "sensibly" ' (1979, pp. 158, 161).

This structure and ideology enabled the development of education policies of a form and taking a direction highly conducive to the development of progressivism. Funding was adequate and growing (a key consideration for an approach which being highly teacher-labour intensive, tends to be very expensive). Teachers' formal freedom to develop progressive ideas in their own schools was given substance and encouragement by the ability of local authorities to sponsor and support such developments; this enabled a shift from individual progressive teachers, or progressive enclaves, to 'progressivism' as an officially promoted policy in some authorities. And finally, the incipient movement was given massive official endorsement by the Plowden Committee (significantly, composed of the Great and the Good, above party, to be relied upon to act 'sensibly' and to keep its 'demands within a range of manageability defined by existing capacities of state action and their continuing improvement'). Thus while it is undoubtedly true that the 'Plowden revolution' was a bottom-up, grass roots affair, it is also true that it could scarcely even have penetrated the grass roots let alone become a quasi-officially endorsed philosophy for primary education without an education system with a structure and ideology in which it could develop. Though, obviously, these were not the only conditions under which it could have developed, it is the central argument of this chapter that they depended in turn on a set of economic, political and social conditions, which no longer exist, and which have been replaced by conditions much more hostile to the development of progressivism, even if not necessarily eliminating the possibility of individual, or even enclave, progressive practice. In the following section I will discuss these conditions, their effect on the structure and ideology of the education system, on education policy and on the implications for progressivism.

## FROM RUSKIN TO ROTHERHAM

If Prime Minister Callaghan's Ruskin College speech in 1976, and the flurry of activity associated with it - the Yellow Book, the Great Debate and the Green paper - was a crucial watershed in the development of the structure and ideology of the education system, it was because it was preceded by signs of acute breakdown in the economic and political conditions that had sustained it since 1944. The post-war boom was already moving into decline by the end of the 60s before being given a further brisk heave down the slope by the oil crisis of 1973. If unemployment was not yet at catastrophic levels, it was beginning to rise at a rate without precedent in the last thirty years. Declining economic performance quickly created strains in all areas of society associated with the economy. Not the least of these consequences was that the education system's credibility ceased to be taken for granted. The anti-progressive critiques of the Black Papers, originally derided and disregarded by the majority of the education profession, came to be taken more seriously, as they both contributed to and benefitted from the growing politicization of education. This developing question of, and discontent with, the education system came to a head in 1975 and 1976 with the William Tyndale affair, which, I have argued elsewhere (see Dale 1981) added to the dominant critical theme of falling standards (which had already been responded to in part in the setting up of the Bullock Committee on English language teaching in 1972, and the Assessment of Performance Unit in 1974), the theme of the negative consequences of excessive teacher autonomy.

The series of papers, speeches and events that led up to the Green Paper Education in Schools picked up and reinforced these themes, and laid down an agenda that has framed discussion of secondary education throughout the succeeding decade. That agenda had four main items: declining standards; inappropriate curriculum (knowledge, skills and attitudes); ineffective and misguided teachers; and insufficiently strong and direct links to economic needs. The form of the response to this agenda made it clear that the whole of the existing structure and ideology of the education system, and not only the teaching profession, were part of the problem as much as of the solution. And so we witnessed continuing attempts by the DES to abandon the tripartite consensus and to take the lead in making education policy. It did this initially through bringing all the pressure at its disposal to bear on local authorities to move towards a core curriculum. However, there were limits to DES action - Stewart Ranson has described the various means they employed to overcome the constraints on their mode of operation (see Ranson 1985).

Another key feature of the DES response in the post-Ruskin decade was the attempt to clip the teachers' wings. This was demonstrated in the termination of the Schools Council and its replacement by the Secondary Examinations Council and the Schools Curriculum Development Committee, both with membership nominated by the Secretary of State. It is clear too in the attempt to monitor initial teacher training much more closely through the newly-created Council for Accreditation of Teacher Education. And it is particularly evident in the stress on stronger 'management' of teachers. LEAs are now required by the DES to manage their stock of teachers (see Walsh

1986), while courses in management for Heads and would-be Heads have been heavily promoted and supported by central government.

These attempts not only to address the issues - especially of curriculum and teacher quality and accountability - directly, but also to begin to rebuild the structure and ideology of the education system to fit it better for its new priorities, may be regarded as the first phase of the government's response to the Great Debate. The nature and outcome of the third phase - which is based on an imposed settlement of teachers' salaries, and the very much greater central control of the curriculum indicated in Kenneth Baker's speech to the North of England Education Conference at Rotherham at the start of 1987 - is not yet sufficiently clear to permit further discussion. The second phase includes the changes referred to in the title of this chapter and includes the more direct central intervention in the education system contained in the MSC's entry to the scene, and especially in the setting up of TVEI in 1983. Before going on to discuss those interventions and their consequences for progressivism in detail, however, I wish to set out what seems to me to be the crucial change in economic, political and social conditions which underly the developing structure and ideology of the education system.

## RECENT CHANGES IN THE FORM AND DIRECTION OF EDUCATION POLICY

### (a) The Underlying Conditions

There is little need to do more than mention the increasingly steep economic decline Britain has undergone over the past two decades and more, or the enormous increase in unemployment, especially of young people, associated with it. It has had major consequences for the structure and ideology of the education system, both directly and indirectly. Directly, it has had two implications, greatly reduced funding for education, and an insistence that education contribute much more to economic recovery through the provision of young people with appropriate knowledge, skills and attitudes - as we shall see below, these two elements came together in some of the policies advanced under phase two of the response to the Great Debate.

Indirectly, economic decline has been responsible for a

change in the mode of political rationality from that of Offe's conjunctural mode to what he calls the structural mode, which 'follows the imperative of keeping output constant, that is, at levels that are considered reasonable or affordable, while channelling demand inputs in a way that appears compatible with available resources. The variable to be manipulated and balanced, in this case, is not policy outputs, but the system of interest representation and the modes of resolution of conflict. The standard of a 'good' policy here, to put it in the simplest terms, is not to satisfy demands but to shape and channel them so as to make them satisfiable' (op. cit.). Hence, for instance, rate-capping. Not only curtailment of funds, and the compelled fitting of demands to them, but the concomitant drastic undermining of local authority power and control it entails (and which is being dramatically extended in the third phase) are aspects of this mode of political rationality which have been increasingly evident in this second phase. However, the implications of this mode of rationality for the structure and ideology of the education system are not exhausted by 'brute' measures like rate-capping. In the long term such strategies as categorical funding (to be discussed at length below) represent a much more finessed employment of structural political rationality.

Other, more overtly 'political', changes entailed by the Thatcher government's response to economic decline have had important implications for the development of progressivism and comprehensivism. One of the most notable of these has been the erosion of the 'new middle class' political constituency which provided fertile soil for the growth of progressivism and comprehensivism in the 1960's. The whole of the public sector - with the exception of defence, never likely to be very fertile ground for progressivism - has, of course, suffered from cuts in government spending. However, two other associated sets of factors have also contributed to the undermining of the progressive constituency. One is the ideological attack on it, contained not just in the promotion of a structural mode of political rationality, but also in the pervasive thrust to 'privatize' almost any and every public body or institution (a thrust represented in education first by the Assisted Places Scheme and more recently and more directly in the proposals for privately funded City Technology Colleges). The other important factor in the erosion of the progressive constituency has been the fragmentation and neutralization of the formal political influence it might have commanded, brought about by the SDP's split from the Labour party. All this means that there is no longer a natural constituency outside the education service to which progressivism and comprehensivism might appeal. The increasing dominance of the structural mode of political rationality also helps explain the declining influence of the teaching profession on education policy. It was in any case being eroded 'passively' due to a number of factors, such as falling rolls and numbers of teachers (and loss of union 'muscle' consequent on this), fewer resources, restricted opportunities for professional development and promotion, which all depressed the morale of the teaching profession. This process has, though, been reinforced by the 'manipulation ... of the system of interest representation and the modes of resolution of conflict', which Offe sees as characteristic of this mode of political rationality. What this means is that teachers are denied access to decision-making fora and procedures they took for granted under the post-1944 structure of the education system. This was presaged in, but is by no means confined to, the abolition and replacement of the Schools Council. For instance, like the local authorities they were told nothing about TVEI before its announcement - though unlike the local authorities they were not subsequently invited to discuss how it might be implemented. The further 'manipulation ... of the mode of resolution of conflict' entailed in the abolition of Burnham and the imposition by central government of a salary settlement in the latest phase of the response to the Great Debate emphasise the spread of this form of political rationality. Finally it should be noted that these changes have not occurred without protest and bitter resistance from teacher unions; but the nature as well as the purpose of this resistance has been shaped by the effect of changed political conditions on the structure and ideology of the education system. The nature of 'the employer' has changed (from being seated essentially in local government to being seated in central government) and so has the employer's ideology, and these key changes in the structure and ideology of the education system have profound effects on the form and direction of education policy and its effects on the possibilities of progressivism.

## (b) Changes in Funding, Orientation and Pedagogy

What I am calling here the second phase of the central

government's response to the agenda set by the Great
Debate begins with the introduction of the Technical and
Vocational Education Initiative. For while school rolls
continued to fall, while funding for education was still at
best static, while the DES continued to pressure and
persuade local authorities and schools to conform more
closely to the programme laid down in the Green Paper,
unemployment, especially among young people was
beginning to rise inexorably. And the rise in youth unemployment was paralled by the rise in the fortunes of the
instrument the government chose first to try to overcome
it, and later to try to disguise and mitigate its worst
effects, the Manpower Services Commission (MSC). From
relatively humble beginnings as a retraining agency set up
by a Labour government, the MSC has grown massively,
through its programmes aimed at youth unemployment,
chief among which were the Youth Opportunities
Programmes (YOP), and, later, the Youth Training Scheme
(YTS) [on the growth of the MSC and its programmes see
CCCS (1981), Benn and Fairley (1986), Cohen (1984)]. What
lay behind TVEI, then, was a diagnosis based on the Great
Debate/Green Paper, but sharpened and channelled by (a)
the rapid rise in youth unemployment, (b) the apparent
relative failure of the existing educational government
machinery to commit the education service effectively to
the goals stated in the Great Debate/Green Paper and (c)
the apparent relative success of the MSC's programmes to
combat youth unemployment, not only in their content, but
also in the whole approach to the problem.

The Technical and Vocational Education Initiative[1]
(originally known as the N [New] TVEI) was announced by
the Prime Minister, Margaret Thatcher, in the House of
Commons on November 12, 1982. She announced that 'in
response to the growing concern about existing arrangements for technical and vocational education for young
people expressed over many years, not least by the National
Economic Development Council', she had asked 'the
chairman of the Manpower Services Commission together
with the Secretaries of State for Education and Science, for
Employment, and for Wales, to develop a pilot scheme to
start by September 1983, for new institutional arrangements
for technical and vocational education for 14-18-year-olds,
within existing financial resources, and, where possible, in
association with local authorities'.

The TVEI scheme emerged as

a pilot scheme; within the education system; for young people of both sexes; across the ability range; voluntary. Each project must provide a full-time programme; offer a progressive four-year course combining general with technical and vocational education; commence at 14 years; be broadly based; include planned work experience; lead to nationally recognised qualifications. Each project and the initiative as a whole must be carefully monitored and evaluated. The purpose of the scheme is to explore and test ways of organising and managing readily replicable programmes of technical and vocational education for young people across the ability range. (MSC, 1984)

A central feature of the scheme is that local authorities sign contracts with MSC for the delivery of the project outlined in their application; participation in the scheme is voluntary for LEAs, schools and pupils. LEA projects were all drawn up to meet the same guidelines, though in the event they differed considerably from each other.

What the MSC provided as their side of the contract was unprecedently large amounts of money, to be used exclusively for the purposes outlined, and with the pupils named, in the contract. The fourteen local authorities in the first round of TVEI received between them £51.5m to finance the five year pilot scheme. The forty-eight (second round) local authorities whose TVEI schemes started in 1984, received £94.5m between them and the twelve (third round) who started in 1985 received £24m between them over the five year pilot period; a fourth round of possibly twenty-eight more authorities will take up TVEI in 1986, funded at the same £2m average as the second and third rounds, considerably less than the initial fourteen authorities received.

While early fears about its divisiveness and excessive vocationalism have not been borne out, and however liberal the interpretation of its guidelines, TVEI still represents an attempt radically to break away both from the existing content of the curriculum - in essence to place the vocational rather than the academic at the centre of educational gravity - and to transform the process of educational change by altering the structure and ideology of the education system which was still making DES in many ways impotent and where the teaching profession was still a key influence on the pace and direction of educational change. It is certainly not the case that 'anything goes', and an extensive monitoring, auditing, advisory and evaluation apparatus ensures TVEI accountability and adherence to the contract.

The money that TVEI brought was clearly a necessary condition of its success. So, too, was the contractual agreement between the MSC and the local authority which bound the latter to use the money for purposes agreed by, and with the pupils identified to, the former, and this clearly represents the most obvious departure from orthodox patterns of curriculum change.

All the three aspects of the second phase that I will refer to here are at least partly rooted in TVEI, but much the most important of them is the form of funding it introduced and served to pilot. The difference between TVEI funding and the form of educational support that typified DES education policy making is summed up very neatly in another distinction drawn by Claus Offe, that between what he calls 'allocative' and 'productive' types of state activity. (The differences between MSC and DES are much more fully spelled out in Dale et al., 1987). Offe's distinction is well summarized by Jessop.

> Allocation involves the use of state resources to secure the general framework of economic activity and/or to provide general public services in accordance with general consitutional or legislative codes which effect the prevailing balance of political forces. Production involves direct state-sponsored provision of material resources as a precondition of crisis-avoidance or crisis management where there is no general code that can be applied and decision rules must therefore be developed in order to determine more effective action by case. Offe then argues that, although rational-legal bureaucratic administration may be appropriate to the allocative activities of the state, it is inadequate to the demands of state productive activities insofar as they are orientated to the attainment of particular objectives rather than the general application of pregiven rules. (Jessop 1982, pp. 110-11)

It is through the mechanism of such 'productive' state

activity as that prefigured in TVEI (significantly because it represents a manipulation of the system of interest representation under the auspices of the corporatist MSC rather than the democratic/bureaucratic DES) that the response to the two main implications for education of economic decline - reduced funding and changed orientation - shape the new structure and ideology of the education system. The shift to the new structure and ideology is complete, of course, when what was originally set up as a form of 'productive' state activity becomes routinized and incorporated under the system it helps bring into being, as a form of 'allocative' state activity - we can see this clearly in the shift from TVEI to TRIST to GRIST, to which we turn now.

I have argued elsewhere (Dale, forthcoming) that under the conditions in which it was introduced TVEI has had a greater impact on the process of educational change than on the content of the secondary school curriculum. Certainly the process aspect and its central principles of categorical funding, bidding and contractual agreements has been much more rapidly and more thoroughly institutionalized than any of the curriculum changes that might be attributed to TVEI. In the situation where funding of even the essential educational core was under pressure, where there had been no funds for development, where LEA budgets were being squeezed by rate-capping and where the morale of the service was at a very low ebb, MSC found a large number of takers when it invited LEAs to bid for money under the conditions laid down for TVEI, even in the climate of hostility and apprehension that was engendered by the manner of its announcement and introduction (see Dale 1985). The experience of TVEI in practice has apparently done nothing to put LEAs off applying for inclusion. Far from it; there are now very few authorities, indeed, who have not applied to take part, with even the ILEA, originally vehemently opposed to the scheme, now seeking to enter. It appears, then, that this system of categorical funding has proved sufficiently attractive both to the funders (as demonstrated in the decision to extend TVEI for another ten years), and to the funded, to justify its more widespread use. The term categorical funding is Janet Harland's; she defines it as

> used to facilitate a policy where policy makers or
> their initiating agency have neither, under existing

conditions, the statutory right nor the means to implement desired changes without the cooperation of those who have both. They do however have the resources and proceed to use the normal processes of contract to implement their policies ... As refined and practised by MSC policy implementation via categorised funding has several distinct stages:

1. A policy is developed

2. funds, generous enough to attract those who can and may deliver are made available (this is particularly potent, of course, when local providers have recently felt themselves starved of resources)

3. voluntary cooperation is invited in exchange for a share of the resources

4. acceptance of the resources is equated with acceptance of policy - and also with the ability to deliver. (Harland, 1985, pp. 2,3)

Central to this process are the bid for funding and the contract between the funding body and the recipient authority. The bid has to be prepared with great care in order to meet the appropriate guidelines and in the knowledge that it will be the basis of a formal contract, which itself can be expected to be closely monitored and audited.

As stated above, this process is now in the course of becoming institutionalized. The first step in this process was the creation of the TRIST (TVEI-Related in Service Training) programme, which disbursed £25m of government money in less than two years to local authorities to provide - again on a contractual basis - in-service education of teachers in certain clearly defined areas associated with TVEI (all LEAs, not just those in TVEI, were allowed to bid for TRIST funding). This programme has been followed by the similarly named and similarly structured GRIST (Grant Related in Service Training). This programme, administered now by the DES (and thus now the 'normal' rather than an 'exceptional' form of policy implementation) has become the major form of support for in-service education of teachers, replacing the existing 'pool' arrangements from 1987. Here too, local authorities bid for funding for in-service training under certain specified headings. Once again, it is not the content but the form of this programme that is important. Potentially any area of education could be funded under GRIST (and the first list of approved areas is by no means confined to the technical and vocational), but the process of bid and contract has quite altered the relationship between the three partners to the educational consensus of the post-1944 period. Under this arrangement, LEAs and teachers become the agents of central government rather than its partners; they 'cooperate' with central government on terms laid down by central government rather than being consulted by it. LEAs and teachers have no formal access to policy making where it involves drawing up the bids of priority areas. The limited funding available to these programmes means that LEAs may be in competition with each other for the funds - and this can extend down to competition between schools, departments within schools, and even between teachers.

The major changes in the orientation of the education system have already been alluded to. What appears to be intended is a shift in the dominant orientation from a teacher controlled, academically justified curriculum to an externally controlled, vocationally justified curriculum as the norm for most pupils. Trying to pin down the dominant orientation of the education system is a notoriously difficult enterprise, but it is useful to approach it by first examining the dominant vocabularies of motive and then analyzing how, and how far, they are institutionally embedded within the education system.

Looking for dominant vocabularies of motive for educational policies and practices is best done through considering what practitioners find it necessary to justify not doing. Thus in the heyday of the Plowden revolution, teachers would explain all their actions in terms of a progressive vocabulary of motives and be apologetic and almost shamefaced about any apparent deviations from what they perceived to be the progressive line (see Sharp and Green, 1976, where it is also made clear that this progressive rhetoric did not necessarily bear much resemblance to the teachers' practice). By contrast, what all the pressure from central government from Education in Schools in 1977 to Working Together in 1986 has established as the dominant vocabularies of motives are the vocational rather than the academic, the instrumental rather than the expressive, the extrinsic rather than the intrinsic; it is now necessary to justify not making subjects, teaching, etc.

53

vocationally relevant. One difference from the previous era is that this tends to be done not apologetically, as a regretful refusal of an invitation, but rather defiantly, as a principled refusal to comply with a requirement.

The institutional bases sustaining progressivism as the dominant vocabulary of motives in primary education were teacher training and certain local education authorities. Though Plowden was heavily officially endorsed, without these institutional bases it could never have become the dominant orientation. Vocationalism is not yet as fully embedded in the system as progressivism was but it has already a number of key institutional bases. In-service training, as has already been mentioned, is one, and some inroads are being made into initial teacher training under the auspices of CATE with the requirement to acquaint all students with the nature of industry. It is embedded, too, in the aims of TVEI. Though, as I have argued, there is little evidence as yet that TVEI has had a major impact on the secondary school curriculum, it does stand as clear evidence of the official preference and objective. The final area of institutionalization of the vocational vocabulary of motives I will mention is the Review of Vocational Qualifications. Though its immediate focus was on post-16 educational and training qualifications, the decision not to include GCE 'O' level and 'A' level examinations in the review can only contribute to a widening of the gulf between the academic and the vocational, and the possibly increasing confinement of the academic to providing entry to higher education.

If the recent changes in funding and orientation just outlined are fairly obviously inimical to the development of progressivism, the same cannot be said about recent changes in pedagogy. On the surface, at least, much of what is being proposed and promoted has clear affinities with, and may even seem to draw on, progressivism. The main source of this new pedagogy is the Further Education Curriculum Review and Development Unit (FEU) and in particular its seminal publication A Basis for Choice (often referred to as ABC). While the FEU's explicit focus is on the further education sector, it has had an impact on schools especially through the medium of CPVE - which is derived from ABC - and through its influence on TVEI practice. Its principles can be stated fairly briefly. The best source is probably an address given by George Tolley, chairman of the FEU from 1977 to 1982 and since then Director of the Open Tech and Head of Quality Branch at the MSC. The address is entitled

The New Curriculum: Towards the Primary of the Vocational. In it, Tolley states:

> What was wrong, and what is wrong, can be characterised in three statements about our education system:
> - Notions of excellence have over-ridden and displaced notions of competence.
> - The content of learning has over-ridden the process of learning.
> - Examinations have assumed an importance transcending purpose, values and goals in education.
>
> Underlying these three statements characterising education in the U.K. are three fallacies:
> - Learning is a matter of training the intellect and only the intellect.
> - Knowledge is understood and extended through a study of subjects.
> - Performance in written examinations is a valid indicator of future personal potential. (Tolley, 1985, p. 96)

Later in his article Tolley puts forward four priorities for change, (i) providing 'opportunities for young people to do as well as to think, to make as well as to explore ideas (ii) reforming examinations so that they enable pupils to demonstrate competence rather than to recognise knowledge (iii) changing teacher attitudes and practices to secure much greater emphasis upon learning rather than teaching, and upon the application of knowledge rather than its isolated study (iv) changing attitudes and practices in industry in favour of the recognition of competence'.

It is possible to draw up a rough list of the characteristics of the 'new FEU pedagogy'. It contains, as Tolley indicates, an emphasis on teaching skills rather than teaching knowledge. It emphasises the application of knowledge rather than abstract book learning. Records of achievements permitting a wide range of personal achievement and qualities to be registered are preferred to reports on academic progress. There is a stress on students being able to negotiate the curriculum that is of most use to them rather than their being bound to follow the intrinsic demands of the pursuit of particular subject knowledge. Associated with this is an emphasis on courses constructed with particular targets in view, rather than the teaching of subjects according to their own logic and boundaries. As Tolley puts it, 'We need a new map of knowledge which breaks down the artificiality of "subjects" as they are now known and experienced within the school (and higher education) curriculum, but nowhere else are they experienced in this form. The teaching of "subjects" is an artificial necessity created by the closed circle of academic education. The application of knowledge over-rides and ignores the subject classification that rules curriculum. If it were not so we should live in a strange world' (ibid, p. 98).

None of this would be entirely unacceptable to progressivism. Even more in tune with it are the precepts of 'vocational preparation' for the young unemployed (see Farley, 1983). The curriculum and pedagogy of vocational preparation is said to derive neither from academic requirements, nor from the claimed requirements of the specific jobs young people are either already in or are training for, but from the personal needs of the young people themselves. Indeed, the personal and the subjective are at the core of ABC itself.

The parallels with progressivism are somewhat strained, however, when we ask who is this new pedagogy for? and what is it for? The answer to the first question is rather clear. It is for those who will not get large numbers of GCE or even CSE passes. The relevance of the academic curriculum for the academic streams is not challenged. It reinforces the academic-vocational distinction, backing up the Review of Vocation Qualifications by providing a separate curriculum and pedagogy for the non-academic which it hardly seems to be suggested might enjoy parity of esteem. So what is it for? Certainly at the level of vocational preparation the key criterion appears to be preparing young people for potential employee status in general rather than for the particular jobs that do not exist. Its aims, as stated by Farley, are (i) to give young people basic skills, experiences and knowledge, (ii) to help them assess their potential and to think realistically about jobs, employment, etc., and to optimize their employability (iii) to develop an understanding of the working and social environment and (iv) to help them become progressively responsible for their own development.

More broadly, we have to ask what young people are being encouraged to choose from, what kinds of competencies and skills they are to be encouraged to pick up, to what ends their knowledge is to be applied and organized. The answers to these questions are distinctly inimical to progressivism, being rooted almost entirely in the industrial model in opposition to which it may be defined. Choices are limited by supposed vocational (if not occupational) requirements. Personal and social skills and competencies (the very idea of which is quite alien to progressivism) are as central in the FEU pedagogy as manipulative or mechanical skills. The purposes of learning are extrinsic to education rather than intrinsic to it, and instrumental rather than expressive.

The whole ABC/FEU enterprise has been likened to those of the Human Relations school of industrial relations.[2] (see Avis, 1983 esp pp. 27-8). As Avis puts it, 'ABC recognises student resistance to traditional education and attempts to defuse this in the same way as the human relations school attempts to colonize the space of worker resistance' (p. 20). The superficial progressivism conceals a harsh instrumentalism aimed at both 'cooling out' and 'cooling down' those suffering worst from economic and educational shortcomings.

This has been a rather harsh catalogue of the implications for progressivism of recent changes in the funding, the orientation and the pedagogic content of recent changes in education policy. The implications for comprehensivism seem no more promising. Central to these changes, for instance, is a divisiveness quite inimical to the comprehensive concept. This divisiveness is clearly evident in the separation of the academic and the vocational in the Review of Vocational Qualifications. As important are the creation, encouragement and funding of specific courses designed with specific 'ability levels' and assumed occupational destinations in mind. CPVE is a clear example but the Foundation Programme of Pre-Vocational Studies proposed for 14-16-year-olds by CPVE's begetter, the Joint Board for Pre-Vocational Education, appears likely to be in the same mould. Contrary to some impressions TVEI is not a course of the same kind; participating schools are formally obliged to recruit pupils from across the ability range. However, RVQ's academic/vocational split on the one side, and the ability/destination specific courses on the other, are producing a great pressure towards a trilateral stratification of the comprehensive school to which TVEI is not always able to remain immune. So, ironically, some TVEI schemes are being squeezed towards reluctant fulfilment of unfriendly predictions that TVEI was for the middle ability group.

## Progressivism and Recent Changes

The implications of the recent changes described above are not confined to the arrival of greater obstacles to the fully comprehensive school, rather than a multilateral school. As with progressivism, the vocabulary of motives has changed. Though multilateralism may have been the reality of much 'comprehensive' education, it was not a reality that could easily be owned up to, or justified. Now the position is rather different. Proponents of comprehensivism have been placed on the defensive. Stratification is justified as a means of advancing both the school and the pupils it serves. As Stephen Ball puts it, 'comprehensivism is in effect by-passed and rendered silent in the new discourses of vocationalism and efficiency and structural priorities have usurped its policy relevance' (personal communication).

## IMPLICATIONS FOR TEACHING

I want to examine, finally, and briefly, the effects of these changes on teachers' work, since the possibilities for progressivism are so clearly dependent on teacher autonomy. An immediate reaction to the foregoing discussions might be that they demonstrate the validity of the teacher deskilling thesis. Professional autonomy is being eroded passively and actively. Bodies with less interest in education as a good in itself are moving to a potentially dominant position in some LEAs, schools and departments, who become accountable to them as well as to their traditional chiefs. It is, though, worth looking briefly at the impact of these recent changes, which if they were not actually coordinated, nevertheless bear a powerful overall coherence - a coherence derived in part from a conception of teachers as (in the short term at least) being as much a part of the problem as of its solution - on a small set of aspects of teachers' work situations.

It has, for instance, been argued above that the dominant vocabulary of motives has changed from progressive/liberal/expressive to instrumental/vocational/extrinsic. But as Sharp and Green demonstrated so well, vocabularies of motive should not be taken as accurate guides to practice. They are as likely to be used as legitimate and effective screens to justify whatever is going on behind them, and there is evidence from reports on some TVEI schemes, for instance, that teachers are already learning how to construct screens made up of 'instrumentalist' vocabularies of motive to protect continuing 'expressive' practices. A second aspect of teachers' work where changes have been brought about is the pastoral area where it has been suggested that under externally funded schemes with contractual accountability, teachers have been changed from general advisors to 'agents of referral' (see Shilling 1986). Third, teachers' curriculum and pedagogic work is being pushed in the direction of courses and away from subjects - a shift hastened by if not wholly brought about by, the increasing popularity of modular curricula. One major implication of this shift is the possible erosion of a major bastion of teachers' identity and autonomy, the subject department and the single subject examination, in which were encapsulated many of the very features of the education system to which Tolley is so opposed.

The remaining aspects of teachers' work situations to be discussed are of particular importance in considering the new structure and ideology of the education system. The consequences for the role of LEAs of much more central government assertiveness and exercise of power and control are beginning to become clearer and were briefly alluded to above. The consequences for the teaching profession have not yet emerged so clearly. Indeed, this issue can be seen to be at the heart of the acrimonious disputes between teachers, their employers and their pay masters over the past three years and more. While that dispute is about levels of payment proper for professional teachers, it is also equally importantly about bringing the teaching profession into congruence with the new structure and ideology of the education system. It is clear that their autonomy is moving from 'licensed' to 'regulated', but the terms of the regulation are not yet finalized. It is relevant to mention three aspects of this move. The first relates to control where the key question is how far the notion of contractual duties implies a shift from professional to managerial accountability and control and what the consequences of that may be. There is a real tension here, for as Walsh puts it, 'The notion of professionalism is inevitably bound up with concepts of the autonomy and self-control of occupational groups; in contrast, management involves dependence and control' (Walsh 1986, p. 124). And if, as Walsh argues, educational expansion mutes those conflicts, its contraction and re-orientation are likely to exacerbate them. The second issue, appraisal, raises rather similar questions. Though there is something of a bias towards evaluation and management in the notion of 'appraisal', the activities it involves can as well be made to serve professional development through mutual support. So, while it obviously does have an important place on the agenda of regulating teacher autonomy, how far it is to be locally controlled, informal, mutual and voluntary, and how far nationally controlled, formal, external and compulsory remains to be decided. And finally, what are the likely consequences of these changes for teachers' 'collegiality'? Is a form of collegiality based on assumptions (not always borne out!) of solidarity, co-operation, mutual support (or at least non-interference) and universalism of treatment - likely to survive intact the introduction of forms of funding which are extremely competitive and offer encouragement to personal (or group) entrepreneurship within the relevant unit of the education system?

These questions are still open. Teacher autonomy has been, and seems likely to be further regulated. But whether it will be curtailed to the point where progressive teaching becomes difficult or impossible to practise is not at all certain.

## CONCLUSION

In discussing the development of progressive education in this country some time ago, I listed a number of conditions which seemed crucial to its success. These were favourable economic conditions, pervasive ideological support, licensed autonomy for the teaching profession, hegemony in key institutions of the education system, such as teacher training, and compatibility with teachers' work structures and practices. This paper has suggested that only the last of these - which may be the most crucial - has up to now survived the changes in economic, political and social conditions, the shifts they have brought about in the structure and ideology of the education system, and the policy changes created under that structure and ideology. However, these work structures and practices are themselves currently being threatened and undermined by central government moves to bring the teaching profession into congruence with the new students and ideology it is seeking to impose upon the education system.

## NOTES

1. This section draws heavily on Dale (1985) and Dale (1986).
2. This point was also made by David Hamilton in discussion of this paper when it was first presented.

## REFERENCES

Avis, James (1983) 'ABC and the New Vocational Consensus', Journal of Further and Higher Education 7, 1, 23-33.

Beer, Samuel (1982) Britain Against Itself: The Political Contradictions of Collectivism, London: Faber.

Benn, Caroline and Fairley, John (1981) Challenging the MSC: on Jobs, Education and Training, London: Pluto.

Bogdanor, Vernon (1979) Power and Participation Oxford Review of Education, 5, 2.

Centre for Contemporary Cultural Studies (1981) Unpopular Education: Schooling and Social Democracy in England since 1944, London: Hutchinson.

Cohen, Gaynor (1984) 'Youth Training: Search for a Policy' in Jones C and Stevenson J (eds) The Yearbook of Social Policy, London.

Dale, Roger (1979a) 'From Endorsement to Disintegration: Progressive Education from the Golden Age to the Green Paper' British Journal of Education Studies 28, 3, 191-209.

——— (1979b) 'The Politicization of School Deviance: Reactions to William Tyndale', in L Barton and R Meighan (eds), Schools, Pupils and Deviance Duffield: Nafferton, 95-112.

——— (1981) 'Control, Accountability and William Tyndale, in·R Dale et al. (eds) Education and the State: Volume II Politics, Patriarchy and Practice, Lewes: Falmer.

——— (1985) 'The Background and Inception of the Technical and Vocation Education Initiative', in R Dale (ed.) Education, Training and Employment: Towards a New Vocationalism, Oxford: Pergamon 41-56.

——— (1986) 'Examining the Gift Horse's Teeth: a Tentative Analysis of TVEI', in Walker and Barton (eds) Youth Unemployment and Schooling, Lewes: Falmer

——— (Forthcoming) 'Buying Change: Britain's Technical and Vocational Education Initiative', Curriculum Inquiry.

——— et al. (1988) 'TVEI: A Policy Hybrid?' in D Reynolds

and A Hargreaves (eds) Milton Keynes: Open University Press.

Farley, Mick (1983) 'Trends and Structural Changes in English Vocational Education', in K Watson (ed.) Youth, Education and Employment, London: Croom Helm.

Harland, Janet (1985) 'TVEI: a Model for Curriculum Change', Paper presented to BERA conference, Sheffield.

Jessop, Bob (1982) The Capitalist State, Oxford: Martin Robertson.

Kogan, Maurice (1983) 'The Case of Education', in K Young (ed.) National Interests and Local Government, London: Heinemann, 58-75.

Manzer, Ronald (1970) Teachers and Politics, Manchester: Manchester University Press.

Manpower Service Commission (1984) TVEI Operating Manual, London: MSC.

Offe, Claus (1981) 'The Attribution of Public Status to Interest Groups', in S. Berger (ed.), Organizing Interests in Western Europe: Pluralism, Corporatism and the Transformation of Politics, Cambridge: Cambridge U.P. 123-58.

Ranson, Stewart (1985) 'Contradictions in the Government of Education' Political Studies, 33, 1, 56-72.

Sharp, Rachel and Green A (1972) Education and Social Control, London: Routledge Kegan Paul.

Shilling, Chris (1986) 'Implementing the Contract: the Technical and Vocational Education Initiative', British Journal of Sociology of Education, 7, 4, 397-414.

Tolley, G. (1985) 'The New Curriculum: Towards the Primacy of the Vocational', Economics, 21, 3, No 91, Autumn.

Walsh, Kieron (1986) 'Managing Contraction', in S Ranson and J Tomlinson (eds) The Changing Government of Education, London: Allen and Unwin.

# 4

# Progress and Control in Scottish Secondary Education Policy

## David Hartley

## INTRODUCTION

The central concern of this paper is the management of consent and the emerging institutional forms which facilitate it. I shall argue, first, that pupils in Scotland's secondary schools who are perceived as less than manageable will tend increasingly to be exposed to a pupil-centred, progressive pedagogy of the type widely advocated during the 1960s. What is attractive about this pedagogy is that its rhetoric has a superficially democratic appeal in that it appears to provide for the imputed needs of the individual, not, as will be argued here, to the preservation of social harmony and the curbing of structural criticism. Second, it will be argued that teachers themselves - though not all - will require to be managed into practising the new pedagogy to which officialdom wishes low-achieving secondary pupils to be exposed. ('Officialdom' is defined throughout here as the Scottish Education Department (SED) and its advisory councils to which appointment is made by the Secretary of State. It accords with Humes' (1986) definition of the 'leadership class' in Scottish education.) The management strategy in 'eliciting' the compliance of teachers will broadly accord with the tenets of 'industrial psychology' and the human relations school of management which provided an agreeable antidote to the authoritarianism of Taylorism in the late 1920s, especially in the USA. This managerial style now operates under a nomenclature which includes phrases such as 'collaboration', 'participatory staff development' and 'consultation'. In short, all this represents an emerging isomorphism (DiMaggio and Powell, 1983) in the forms of collaborative control in education: that is, a non-directive and collaborative pedagogy in the classroom; and a similar collaborative strategy on the part of officialdom when trying to persuade teachers to implement the new progressivist pedagogy for low-achieving and possibly disruptive pupils in the third and fourth year of secondary education.

In secondary education, this learner-centred pedagogy was first advocated in 1963 in the Brunton Report (SED, 1963), the counterpart to the Newsom Report (Central Advisory Council on Education, 1963). Its focus was the less-than-average pupil who was at the point of transition from school to work. Hitherto, his/her motivation had been regarded as poor, and the curriculum to which he/she had been exposed was perceived as irrelevant. A new pedagogy, one which was 'active' and 'participatory', was recommended, together with a more practical curriculum (SED, 1963: 37-39). Implicit in the pedagogy is the notion that this kind of pupil is a 'concrete', not an abstract, thinker; one who prefers the 'physical', not the 'mental'. (Indeed, there is a strong current in pedagogical literature which points up these two cognitive styles [Shapin and Barnes, 1976; Nasaw, 1979].) The emergence of this less didactic pedagogy may have been the SED's attempt to incorporate those pupils whose commitment to schooling was seen as less than firm, and whose acquiescence in the work ethic was doubtful (SED, 1963: 9-10):

> It is not perhaps surprising that to many of the pupils school, especially if they have as yet achieved little joy or success in it, becomes positively irksome. If interest is to be maintained and enthusiasm aroused at this stage in school life it appears essential that the secondary school should take account of this outward look and the approach to adulthood and employment.

Concern is voiced forcefully at a later point in the Brunton Report (SED, 1963: 52):

> As a consequence, many of these boys and girls lack a sense of security; this becomes as often as not the key to the whole pattern of their behaviour, the background to their thoughts and actions, and lays them open to the less creditable influences of modern society. It also forces them often into undesirable kinds of group associations,

leading into the gang with its conventions, loyalties and which can be quite anti-social.

Among the examples of the SED's curricular response to the 'needs' of these pupils was an integrated science programme (SED, 1969) which advocated a progressivist pedagogy. Here was a clear example whereby pedagogical rhetoric was justified through an appeal to the educational needs of the pupil but whose undeclared rationale was to incorporate the pupil into a value system not to his liking (Millar, 1981). The response of teachers, however, was to continue as before: the innovation did not take hold during the 1970s (Hamilton, 1982).

In the early 1980s, the 'problem' of the 'young person' of less-than-average academic achievement again came to the fore. The concern was not so much to ensure his/her compliance in the school (though this remained important), but more to prepare him/her psychologically for the impending attenuation between school-leaving credentials and employment. No longer was the latter a necessary consequence of the former: the possibility of longterm unemployment was to be made a real, but legitimate, post-school destination for some pupils. The urgency with which officialdom acted seems to correspond with unemployment statistics which were almost inconceivable in the 1960s. Whereas in the mid-60s the rate of employment in Britain was actually falling (in November 1965 it stood at 1.5 per cent [Central Statistical Office, 1965: 5]), between April 1980 and April 1982 male unemployment for 16-19-year-olds rose from 11.6 to 26.3 percent for males, and from 10.5 to 20.6 percent for females (Central Statistical Office, 1983: 190). The confident assertion in the Newsom Report that new technologies would not lead to de-skilling and very high rates of unemployment (HMSO, 1963: 5) seems very empty in the 1980s. Further, the structure of occupations had also changed since the 60s: between 1961 and 1980 in the UK, manufacturing jobs had fallen from 8,540,000 to 6,808,000, whilst those in the service sector had risen from 10,382,000 to 13,379,000 (Central Statistical Office, 1983: 55). Two implications of these trends arise: first, the high levels of youth unemployment require to be legitimated; second, the expanding service sector will need communication and social skills to levels which hitherto had been lacking in the school-leaver. The vanguard of the SED's solution to these two requirements took the form of social education. That is, the government now sought to make manifest as part of the formal curriculum what hitherto had comprised the hidden curriculum and to call it 'social and vocational skills'. In order to transmit these skills, a new, learner-centred pedagogy was advocated. Before dealing with this, the policy documents on social education in Scotland are now set within the framework of the SED's educational policy since 1965. What sets them apart from those in England is the heady pace at which the centralisation of educational policy in Scotland has occurred. For example, a national structure for curriculum and assessment has been adopted and is currently being implemented (SED, 1977ab); courses in further education have been rationalised into a national, modular framework (SED, 1983); INSET provision has similarly fallen to central control (Hartley, 1985a); and critics like Pickard (1985) and McPherson (1985) have raised well-founded suspicions that educational research in Scotland will itself be more circumscribed by the SED. Set against these general developments, the nature and development of the multidisciplinary course Social and Vocational Skills (SVS) is now introduced.

## MANAGING THE PUPILS

### The Re-Emerging Progressivism

The thin end of this progressivist revival in the 1980s comprises those subjects referred to in the 1977 Munn Report as the 'social subjects' 'mode of activity'. The Munn Report recommended a national core curriculum for the third and fourth years of Scottish secondary education (SED, 1977). It was based on Hirst's 'forms of knowledge', renamed as 'modes of activity', one of which, relevant here, was the 'social subjects'. A further report provided for a school certificate for all school-leavers whereby a three-tier structure of assessment was recommended for each 'mode of activity': 'credit', 'general', and 'foundation', the last being for the least able pupil (SED, 1977b). These reports are analysed by McIntyre et al. (1978). The progressive pedagogy is represented at secondary level by the 'social subjects', namely Contemporary Social Studies (CSS), Health Studies (HS), and Social and Vocational Skills (SVS). They share a number of characteristics: they are not offered to the most able pupils; they are multidisciplinary; and all advocate, to differing degrees, a new pupil-centred pedagogy. Of these subjects, Social and Vocational Skills (SVS) has loomed largest in the SED's priorities, a matter to be discussed shortly. For this reason, the implementation of SVS has been evaluated more fully by the SED than CSS and HS, and it is accordingly given the greater emphasis here. The piloting of SVS has been examined by Currie and Weir (1985), and that of CSS, HS and SVS by Munn and Morrison (1984).

During 1983 and 1984, a number of documents about social education were published in Scotland. The first, Social Education in Scottish Schools: a position paper, was published by the Consultative Committee on the Curriculum (1984). Two other documents (Scottish Education Board (SEB) 1984(a) (b)), both published by the Scottish Examination Board, contained guidelines and arrangements for 'Social and Vocational Skills' (SVS) and for 'Contemporary Social Studies' (CSS) in the third and fourth years of secondary school. Social Education in Scotland was prompted by a recommendation in the earlier publication (CCC, 1983) An Education for Life and Work, which was produced by the Project Planning Committee for the 'Education and the Industrial Society Project'. Its initial impetus, therefore, was related to the needs of the 'industrial society', a fact which serves to underpin the notion that social education is for rather than about 'industrial society'. Of interest, too, is that in the Scottish Examination Board (SEB)'s paper Arrangements in Social and Vocational Skills at Foundation and General Levels in and after 1986 there is a conceptual shift from the more abstract concept of 'social education' in the title of the CCC's paper to the more practical concept of 'social and vocational skills' in the SEB's document. More than this, the SEB's declared rationale was lifted, word for word, from the DES-funded Further Education Unit's publication Developing Social and Life Skills: strategies for tutors (FEU, 1980: 5). The Scottish Examination Board (SEB), however, replaced the FEU's term 'life skills' with its own 'vocational skills', thereby bringing social and vocational skills into a clear association within the official nomenclature relating to secondary education, not, as with the FEU, further education. On the surface, this may seem innocent enough, but it may reflect the growing strength of the MSC-led industrial lobby on education policy in Scotland, especially when it is realised that since 1977 the SED has reported to the same minister as does the MSC, namely the Under Secretary of State for Scotland in charge of Industry and Education. This means that, as the SED (1983: 14) put it,

> Because he has combined responsibility for the education service and the MSC, the Secretary of State is uniquely well-placed to ensure an integrated approach to the whole field of education and training for the 16-18 age group in Scotland.

Moreover, SVS came as something of an afterthought to the 1977 Munn Report on the curriculum (Currie and Weir, 1985: i):

> This new course assumed a considerable importance for the SED who wished to see a credible course emerge as quickly as possible, restoring some of the education service's reputation in the vocational field. (emphasis added)

A similar sentiment was expressed by Munn and Morrison who noted (1984: 1-2) that SVS's development had been 'accelerated' in comparison to the development of the other multidisciplinary courses.

As stated, the Scottish Examination Board's Arrangements in Social and Vocational Skills at Foundation and General Levels in and after 1986 was published in 1984, and it has already been noted that the rationale behind SVS was extracted from an FEU publication. The SEB state (1984: 8):

> The course in Social and Vocational Skills seeks to draw together these strands into a coherent course which identifies and develops the range of life and social skills necessary for pupils to make their way in·society, while the vocational intent is to foster those skills and attributes which will make a pupil more employable. At one and the same time the course is firmly rooted in practical work and the realities of economic survival, yet ascends to touch our humanity at higher levels - self-assurance, ability to collaborate, caring for others.

The course was only piloted at the lowest 'foundation' level of the new Standard Grade recommended in the 1977 Dunning Report (SED, 1977b), and there are no plans at present to offer it to the most able 'credit-level' secondary pupils. The SEB has laid down guidelines for SVS, namely that three 'themes' must be covered: 'work', 'community' and 'home'. Suggested 'pupil experiences' for SVS have also been published (SED, 1985). Implicit in the two non-work themes is the notion that, for some pupils, paid employment may not be a reasonable expectation for them to hold. Nonetheless, unemployment should not, so the rhetoric runs, be regarded as anything but propitious: it is simply an 'alternative' which can lead to other worthwhile lifestyles:

> The emphasis should be on vocational preparation in the broad sense and <u>not on training for specific jobs or occupational groupings.</u> While it is right and proper that the main emphasis should be on paid employment, <u>a realistic appraisal of prospects, at least in the foreseeable future, has to take account of the possibility of some pupils not gaining employment on leaving school.</u> The theme, therefore, should also consider the alternatives to conventional paid employment such as self-employment, further education and voluntary work. (emphasis added) (SEB, 1984: 8)

The SEB's SVS course appears to offer no political analyses of the 'day-to-day situations' (which by its own admission could include unemployment) with which the young must 'cope'. Nor does the optional course, Contemporary Social Studies (CSS), appear to offer such an analysis, particularly to the lowest-achieving 'foundation-level' pupils. In the multidisciplinary courses, and particularly in the case of SVS, there is a very strong emphasis on a pedagogical style which emphasises the 'self':

> .. to enhance personal qualities such as self-awareness, self-respect, confidence and initiative, so that pupils develop their abilities in respect of self-adjustment and self-evaluation, taking reasoned judgements and drawing reasoned conclusions, and <u>coping</u> with day-to-day situations [emphasis added]. (SEB, 1984: 6)

A number of inferences may be drawn from this concern with the 'self'. There is the implication that the 'self' of such pupils needs 'enhancing' in a compensatory fashion. This is virtually tantamount to a deficit thesis - an attitudinal and presentational deficiency in these (mainly working class)

69

pupils. This represents, therefore, an instrumentalization of the expressive order of the school (Vallance, 1973; Hartley, 1985). Social and Vocational Skills will provide the self with a portable repertoire of presentational skills which will suit the emerging service sector. More than this, because SVS also includes 'home' and 'community' skills, as well as emphasising self-assessment and evaluation, the young person will have been given the requisite coping skills which will perhaps cause him to think that his unemployment is not an adversity, but is an opportunity for personal development in domains other than the wage economy, a point more fully discussed by Moos (1979). Indeed, the SED now questions quite openly the traditional relationship between schooling and employment for less well-qualified pupils:

> Opportunities for less well-qualified pupils, already decimated by the reduction in semi-skilled jobs, are further eroded. Fundamentally, education and careers education in particular must face questions such as: is the traditional work ethic still relevant; is job satisfaction still a priority or is any job in fact, better than none? [emphasis added] (CCC, 1986a: 26)

If this individual deficit thesis is the only explanation of unemployment offered to the young person, then it is difficult to square this with courses which purport to enable the young person to understand 'industrial society'. In this respect, therefore, it can be suggested that SVS and CSS provide, albeit subliminally, a form of anticipatory legitimation of under- and unemployment for those most likely to face it, and they provide it in such a manner that may leave unanalysed the structural determinants of youth unemployment itself. If all goes according to plan, therefore, the education system achieves a twofold aim: first, it provides industry with a young labour force with the appropriate demeanour and dispositions; and second, it fulfills its aim of 'social education' by facilitating the integration of the young into institutions other than the wage economy.

## A SPECULATION

There now appear to be moves afoot in Scotland which will regard the low-achieving 14-18-year-olds as a homogeneous category which requires a distinctive educational provision.

The elaboration of this speculation requires the description of a number of procedures. In Scottish secondary education there is only one examination board, the Scottish Examination Board (SEB), which administers the 14-16 Standard Grade, the counterpart to the GCSE in England. The examining board for non-advanced further education is the Scottish Council for Vocational Education (SCOTVEC), which validates the 16+ National Certificate for 16-18 year-olds. The National Certificate curriculum is modular (some 2,000 in 1986). Normally, the less-able 14-16-year-old would follow the 'foundation' courses in the Standard Grade, and then proceed to work, to YTS or to full-time 16+ National Certificate modules. Thus, this group of less-able 14-18-year-olds now straddles the secondary/FE divide. The speculation has been aired (Hartley, 1987) that the SED may seek to provide a single institutional educational provision for that group. Already, post-16 school pupils can take SCOTVEC modules, but now the SED is actively considering the possibility of SCOTVEC 16+ National Certificate modules being taken by pre-16-year-olds in schools. This would produce two consequences. First, there would be a commonality of pedagogy - a progressivist one - for the low-achieving 14-18 year-old, perhaps in a separate institution. Second, there would be a similar modular curricular structure, a matter already receiving official attention (CCC 1986b: 111). If the latter were to occur, it would effectively lead to the post-16 examining body, SCOTVEC, taking over some of the 14-16 Standard Grade examining board's (the SEB) responsibility for the current 'foundation' level of the Standard Grade (Munro, 1986). The bureaucratic elegance of this rampant rationalisation would serve to undermine further the comprehensive ideal in Scotland. Moreover, it would also neatly fit TVEI's 14-18 provision, which, though it purports to apply to all ability levels, in its first two years has tended to be confined to the less able (Tenne, 1986). And finally, it would tighten even more the centre's hold on the system. All this will require the consent, commitment and action of teachers who hitherto had not been well inclined to change from their preferred didactic and subject-centred pedagogy. This is not to say that all teachers have eschewed pupil-centred pedagogy, but, as Weston (1984) points out, the majority of secondary teachers appear to have done so. We shall argue now that just as dissaffected pupils (Gow and McPherson, 1980) may be more subtly controlled by the new pupil-centred

71

pedagogy of SVS, so too may their teachers be guided, through 'collaboration' with the SED, into adopting that very pedagogy to which the SED wishes problematic pupils to be exposed.

## MANAGING THE TEACHERS

### Collaborative Staff Development

Educational innovations which are imposed are likely to wither; innovations which are negotiated are more likely to bear fruit. Recent policy statements on staff development indicate officialdom's support for these assertions. Both the OECD (1982: 59) and the Scottish Education Department's National Committee for the In-Service Training of Teachers (NCITT, 1984) agree that a 'collaborative model' of staff development is preferable to a centre-periphery model. In Scotland, this means consultation, or 'collaboration', but only between contiguous strata of the educational bureaucracy, and is typical therefore of a human relations management strategy in which, in the last analysis, the needs of officialdom will prevail over those of teachers. The SED's advisory committee, the NCITT, does recognise the merits of both 'personal professional staff development' and 'centralised staff development':

> 3.11 The strength of personal professional development is that it generates enthusiasm and commitment among teachers who are doing things which they themselves have chosen. Its weakness is that teachers may not be channelling their energy and enthusiasm in directions which seem important to· their local authority. It therefore does <u>not guarantee that the most important needs of the school or of the authority are being met</u>. (emphasis added) (NCITT, 1984: 10)

On the other hand,

> 3.13 The strengths of centralised staff development are that it can channel resources into the areas of greatest needs and that <u>it is relatively easy to organise and control</u>. (emphasis added) (NCITT, 1984: 10)

In the end, however, the SED's advisory committee sees the former as only 'in relation to' the latter (Hartley, 1985). The SED's new collaborative, consultative staff development strategy only permits the discretion of teachers within the broad parameters of its educational policy: central government defines the premisses and sets the agenda for action; the teachers 'develop' professionally within that framework. This general view of staff development provides the basis for the SED's particular strategy for implementing the Social and Vocational Skills course at issue here.

The SEB's 'guidelines' for SVS form the uncontested basis for its implementation. At the outset, there was a conscious attempt to remove the distinction between 'them' (those at national level who devised the curricular innovation) and 'us' (the teachers) who were to implement it. The Scottish Education Department, the Scottish Examination Board, the schools and the researchers were to be seen as 'full partners in the development process. At the national level, SVS was said to have demonstrated the effectiveness of a genuinely collaborative model of curriculum development' (Weir and Currie, 1985: 17). This strategy for curricular implementation at a national level marked a departure from previous practice because,

> from the beginning, the Scottish Education Department took the wise decision to involve the researchers in the policy-making team and encouraged the researchers to feed their findings in, on a continuous basis, to the various stages of the development. (Weir and Currie, 1985: 17)

Nevertheless there is some evidence that teachers were less than forthcoming about collaboration. Approximately forty teachers were involved in Weir and Currie's development-research programme between 1981-84, only eight of whom admitted to volunteering to work with the research team. The majority of the others faced a strategy of 'guided volunteering' (Currie and Weir, 1985: 56). 'Guided discovery' for problematic pupils and 'guided volunteering' for teachers neatly encapsulate the ismorphism in the forms of control which are being enacted in Scottish secondary education for pupils of low academic standing and their teachers.

How collaborative was all of this? First, the national guidelines in the Scottish Examination Board's (1984) document were taken as given in the collaborative exercise:

the broad structure and the subject (SVS) were taken as agreed, and so too was its 'target', namely 'non-credit' pupils. The general policy, therefore, was assumed at national level, and only some details of implementation were negotiable. Second, it was further assumed at national level that teachers would accept in principle the fact that an interdisciplinary course (Social and Vocational Skills) was educationally sound and professionally acceptable to them. The changes for teachers, however, were to be profound:

> The conventional autonomous role of the subject specialist, hidden inside the classroom, delivering curriculum elements devised by experts, was con-fronted by an alternative collaborative role of the teacher of no specific subject expertise working in a common endeavour with a team of colleagues, often in full view of the rest of the school or the community at large, and together building a course from their own (and their pupils') imagination, supported by only the barest of national guidelines. (emphasis added) (Currie and Weir, 1985: iii)

But 'the barest of national guidelines' is a massive under-statement. It is true that in terms of content there was to be minimal direction from the Scottish Examination Board as long as the content 'filled in' the pre-defined 'themes' of 'work', 'home' and 'community' skills. There was to be no consultation about the pedagogical style to be adopted by teachers:

> The teaching should be pupil-centred. The teacher should create a climate in which pupils can take increasing responsibility for their own learning and their own actions. This requires the teacher to adopt the role of facilitator rather than simply a purveyor of knowledge. (emphasis added) (SEB, 1984: para 6[A])

The declared official rationale behind SVS was to give pupils 'self-esteem' and 'self-confidence'; to help them develop 'tolerance, perseverance and initiative which will serve them in different contexts both in and out of school', to help them 'assume the mantle of responsibility'; and to 'help pupils grow in a systematic way in maturity, autonomy and responsibility' (SEB, 1984). It was the hidden curriculum of

SVS which, for the SED, was crucial. That being so, it did not figure as a subject for debate with classroom teachers. Put another way, the details of the formal curriculum were negotiable, albeit within the government's parameters; those of the pedagogical style were not. For the SED, the new subjectivity and demeanour of the pupil may have been more crucial than the assessable skills which he was to be 'taught'.

## CONCLUSION

The foregoing has pointed to both an emerging progressivist, pupil-centred pedagogy for low-achieving pupils in Scottish secondary education, and a corresponding change in the ways in which their teachers will 'collaborate' with central government on the implementation of that pedagogy. This correspondence constitutes an embryonic isomorphism in the organisational field of education and is defined here as 'consultative centralism': that is, educational bureaucrats at the centre (and those whom they co-opt [Humes, 1986]) will decide both policy and the parameters of content, after which teachers will merely be 'consulted' in order to ensure their 'collaboration'. Even educational research policy is beginning to be constructed in this manner. For example, Kirk (1985) states that:

> (research) will be more responsive to the professional needs of teachers and others: it will be concerned to effect improvements in teaching, learning and assessment at all levels of education; and it will be collaborative, seeking to secure the active involvement of practising teachers and others as partners in the research enterprise. (emphasis added)

The correspondence represents the initial stages whereby the consent of pupils, teachers and perhaps even researchers may be tacitly structured by officialdom. Nevertheless, it has an appeal. First, it can be said that pupils will feel better able to cope with a schooling which emphasises their participation rather than their passive tolerance. This pedagogical style - what Hargreaves (1974) has called the 'reformist' style - has had considerable appeal for many teachers and pupils, and it is no purpose of this paper to denigrate it per se. But this pedagogy should be seen in relation to the formal curriculum which it transmits. If this pedagogy transmits knowledge which, as in the case of Social and Vocational Skills, offers little analysis of the 'day-to-day situations' which the young person faces, then it matters little whether or not that pedagogy manifests 'participation', 'integration' and 'experiential learning'. Moreover, this pupil-centred pedagogy has little chance of being applied to the more academically inclined pupils who are taking the 'credit-level' courses in the Scottish Standard Grade, despite rhetoric to the contrary. In short, therefore, there is an emerging 'apartheid' in the hidden curriculum of the Scottish secondary school, a trend which logically flies in the face of comprehensive schooling. Moreover, this pupil-centred pedagogy for the less academic may run counter to the management regime in work settings where creativity is curbed and worker discretion is minimal. Given this, it may be expected that the MSC will wish to see steps taken to effect an accord, or correspondence, between the management regimes of classroom and workplace for those likely to face routinised labour (Seale, 1984). But this would serve only to re-introduce that very same didactic pedagogy which had proved so unsatisfactory in the first place. Second, teachers, having been consulted - regardless of the issue - may see this as an enhancement rather than an erosion of their professionality. If, however, their views are merely noted, or ignored, then they will come to regard 'collaboration' with greater suspicion, if not antagonism. [In their attempts to implement SVS, the SED had originally permitted a good measure of discretion to those teachers who had accepted its parameters, but later the SED reverted to more central control. The SVS teachers, however, quickly formed a national association to counteract the SED's move (Munn, 1986).] However, the consideration which seems crucial to all of this collaboration is to ask what its purpose is.

It may be legitimation. In a society which claims to be democratic and scientific, the questioning of the natural and social worlds is the necessary precaution against authoritarianism and dogmatism. Those who hold power and authority in a scientific democracy must have their legitimacy conferred by consent. Once coercion is required, legitimate authority is foresaken - the minds of the dominated have been lost (Weber, 1922). However, the management of consent, rather than its imposition, must be such that it both 'elicits' compliance and furthers the illusion that the discretion of the individual is being increased, not reduced. Consultative centralism offers a means to these ends. That is, officialdom defines the agenda and priorities and others participate in the consultative 'machinery' in order to 'choose' the appropriate means of effecting the ends themselves.

This raises the wider question - which cannot be fully dealt with here - of who sets the priorities and agenda in education, and to what extent education can claim 'relative autonomy' from the needs of capitalism. In referring to the state educational bureaucracy in Scotland (the Scottish Education Department), it is not being implied that officialdom alone is the instigator of policy. Nor is it being advocated that the SED comprises an ideological consensus on the ends of education, although there is little to doubt the view that it contains a view, not expressed, that supports a liberal democratic notion within capitalism. But there is little evidence that in recent years the SED has been able to withstand pressure from the vocationalist lobby in Scotland. The degree of institutional autonomy which Salter and Tapper (1981) had attributed to the DES in England - albeit before 1980 - does not square with occurrences in Scotland. This accord between the SED and industrial concerns in Scotland is most manifest in further education and, as the substance of the present paper suggests, in the education of the low-achieving school-leaver, all of this being facilitated by the administrative structure which combines the institutions of education and industry under a single Secretary of State. Whilst it is conceptually difficult to imagine an education system being entirely bereft of autonomy, it can be said that, at the level of policy, its margin for autonomy in Scotland has lessened considerably since 1977. This is especially so of the education of the low-achiever who may later become marginal to the wage economy. It is he who must be re-socialised into thinking that his future adversity constitutes an opportunity for 'personal and social development' by learning how to cope with, not criticise, his plight. Moreover, the SED, aided and abetted by the MSC's TVEI programme, appears to be moving rapidly to provide a separate educational provision for the low-achieving 14-18 year-old. This provision will have all of the hallmarks of progressivism, and it will be justified on educational terms (ie it meets their needs), but its impetus is clearly political (ie it purports essentially to re-school and re-socialise a group which has the capacity to provoke social unrest).

However, although the very rapid rationalisation of courses in further education and the quick but careful introduction of SVS both attest to the success of the vocationalist lobby at the level of policy, it remains very much problematic whether, at the level of practice, these policies will be implemented in the manner desired, despite 'collaboration'. Nevertheless, the SED appears optimistic and has produced a panoply of measures ranging from teacher-produced newsletters, conferences, curriculum advice support teams and 'action-research' projects which co-opt teachers into managing and 'researching' 'their own' innovations.

Finally, consultative centralism poses risks both for officialdom and those whose interests it (willingly or not) furthers. First, it spawns a plethora of 'position papers' for consultation and discussion about aspects of education which hitherto had been beyond public consideration. For a political philosophy which purports to 'roll back the state', the paradox of burgeoning bureaucracy may become difficult to argue away on 'efficiency' lines alone. Second, officialdom runs the risk of inviting opinion which it would rather not hear, let alone have publicly reported. Containing the content of consultative exercises as the areas for consultation expand rapidly may prove very difficult. Failure to do so, however, would compel officialdom to resort to 'undemocratic' pronouncements in order to ensure its policies remained unaltered. That done, its position as the final arbiter would be exposed for all to see.

## REFERENCES

Central Advisory Council on Education (England) (1963) Half Our Future, London: HMSO.

Central Statistical Office (1965) 'Economic Trends'. Economic Trends, December (146).

—— (1983), untitled Social Trends, 13, 190.

Consultative Committee on the Curriculum (1983) An Education for Life and Work, Scottish Curriculum Development Service, Jordanhill College, Glasgow: CCC/SED.

—— (1984) Social Education in Scottish Schools, Dundee College of Education: CCC/SED.

—— (1986a) More Than Feelings of Concern, Dundee College of Education: CCC/SED.

—— (1986b) Education 10-14 in Scotland, Dundee: CCC.

Currie, B. and Weir, D. (1985) The Responsibility of the

Teacher: Social and Vocational Skills at Foundation and General Levels, Glasgow: University of Glasgow (Vocational Initiatives Unit).

DiMaggio, P. and Powell, W.W. (1983) 'The iron cage revisited: institutional isomorphism and collective rationality in organisational fields'. American Sociological Review, 48, 147-160.

Further Education Unit (FEU) (1980) Developing Social and Life Skills, London: Further Education Unit.

Gow, L. and McPherson, A. (1980) Tell Them From Me, Aberdeen: Aberdeen University Press.

Hamilton, D. (1982) 'Handling innovation in the classroom: two Scottish examples'. In Challenge and Change in the Curriculum, Horton, T. and Ragatt, P. (eds), Hodder and Stoughton, Sevenoaks.

Hargreaves, D.H. (1974) 'Deschoolers and the New Romantics'. In Educability, Schools and Ideology, Flude, M. and Ahier, J. (eds), Croom Helm, London.

Hartley, D. (1985) 'Social education in Scotland: some sociological considerations.' Scottish Educational Review, 17(2), 92-98.

———— (1985a) 'Bureaucracy and professionalism: the new hidden curriculum for teachers in Scotland'. Journal of Education for Teaching, 11(2), 107-119.

———— (1987) 'The convergence of learner-centred pedagogy in primary and further education in Scotland: 1965-1985'. British Journal of Educational Studies, June.

———— (1987) 'Re-Schooling Society? 14-18 in Scotland'. Scottish Educational Review, 19(2).

Humes, W. (1986) The Leadership Class in Scottish Education, Edinburgh: John Donald.

HMSO (1963) Half Our Future.

Kirk, G. (1985) 'A better forum for research'. Times Educational Supplement (Scotland), (990), 2, 6.

McIntyre, D. et al. (1978) A Critique of the Munn and Dunning Reports, Stirling: Stirling University Department of Education.

McPherson, A. (1985) 'Infidels in the citadel'. Times Educational Supplement (Scotland), (989), 20-21.

Millar, R.H. (1981) 'Curriculum rhetoric and social control: a perspective on recent science curriculum development'. European Journal of Science Education, 3(3), 271-284.

Moos, M. (1979) Government Youth Training Policy and its Impact on Further Education, Birmingham: Centre for Contemporary Cultural Studies.

Munn, P. (1986) 'Teacher perceptions of school-based curriculum development: some evidence from multidisciplinary courses'. Scottish Educational Review, 17(2), 82-91.

Munn, P. and Morrison, A. (1984) Approaches to Collaboration in Scottish Secondary Schools in Multidisciplinary Courses, University of Stirling Department of Education.

Munro, N. (1986) 'Scotvec moves into schools'. The Times Educational Supplement Scotland, November 21, (1046), 1.

Nasaw, D. (1979) Schooled to Order, New York: Oxford University Press.

National Committee for the In-Service Training of Teachers (1984) Arrangements for the Staff Development of Teachers, Edinburgh: SED.

OECD (1982) In-Service Education and Training of Teachers: a Condition for Educational Change, Paris: OECD.

Pickard, W. (1985) 'Rumblings stir the world of research'. Times Educational Supplement (Scotland), (970), 3.

Salter, B. and Tapper, T. (1981) Education, Politics and the State, London: Grant McIntyre.

Scottish Education Department (1963) From School to Further Education, Edinburgh: HMSO.

———— (1969) Curriculum Paper 7 - Science for General Education, Edinburgh: HMSO.

———— (1977a) The Structure of the Curriculum in the Third and Fourth Years of the Scottish Secondary School, Edinburgh: HMSO.

———— (1977b) Assessment for All: Report of the Committee to Review Assessment in the Third and Fourth Years of Secondary Education in Scotland, Edinburgh: HMSO.

———— (1985a) Social and Vocational Skills - Pupil Experiences, Edinburgh: SED.

———— (1983) 16-18s in Scotland: An Action Plan, Edinburgh: Scottish Education Department.

Scottish Examination Board. (1984a) Standard Grade Arrangements in Contemporary Social Studies at Foundation and General Levels in and after 1986, Dalkeith: SEB.

Scottish Examination Board. (1984b) Standard Grade Arrangements in Social and Vocational Skills at Foundation and General Levels in and after 1986,

Dalkeith: Scottish Examination Board.

——— (1985b) Standard Grade Contemporary Social Studies: specimen question papers, Dalkeith: SEB.

Seale, C. (1984) 'FEU and MSC: Two curricular philosophies and their implications for the Youth Training Scheme.' The Vocational Aspect of Education, XXXVI(93), 3-10.

Shapin, S. and Barnes, B. (1976) 'Head and hand: rhetorical resources in British pedagogical writing, 1770-1850'. Oxford Review of Education, 2, 231-254.

Tenne, R. (1986) 'TVEI students and subjects studied: the first two years'. Employment Gazette, August 94(7), 306-310.

Vallance, E. (1973) 'Hiding the hidden curriculum'. Curriculum Inquiry, 38, 5-21.

Weber, M. (1978) Economy and Society, vols 1 and 2, Berkeley: University of California Press, original 1922.

Weir, D. and Currie, B. (1985) 'In search of vocational standards'. Times Educational Supplement (Scotland), March 22, 17.

Weston, R. (1984) 'Reviewing compulsion: pupil perspectives on the fourth year experience'. In Fourteen to Eighteen: The Changing Pattern of Schooling in Scotland, Raffe, D. (ed.), Aberdeen University Press, Aberdeen.

# 5

# Community and the Limits of Social Democracy:
## Scenes from the Politics

### Steve Baron

In this paper I want to locate the practices of 'community' in the politics of education in the period from the 1960's to the 1980's. In order to do this I will first outline what I understand to be the salient features of the politics of the period. I will then analyse the three major arenas in which 'community' was elaborated, the area comprehensive school, the community college and the community primary school. I will then offer a critique of these practices and the political context from which they took their sense and suggest that they were especially vulnerable to the New Right critique which is currently restructuring British schooling. I will conclude with a reassessment of the 'community' tradition in the light of these arguments and changed circumstances.

The period in question was dominated by the 'social democratic' settlement in education; its holding sway during the 1960's and early 1970's and its being discredited during the later 1970's and 1980's.[1] The roots of this settlement were quite distinctive - a coming together of certain elements of the Labour Party, the teacher unions and some of the leading figures of the emerging Sociology of Education.

The social democratic repertoire within the Labour Party developed significantly during the long years of opposition during the 1950's with the search for a new educational strategy. Having abandoned, to all intents and purposes, anti-state politics in education (and wider fields) during the inter-war period and having gained universal secondary education, of sorts, the Labour Party needed a new policy direction. With a seemingly impenetrable ideology of affluence to counter and a felt crisis of working class 'community' one central political issue began to be articulated as the problem of reducing class both in the sense of cultural divisions and in the sense of inter-generational mobility. This configuration constituted the first partner of the social democratic alliance.

In this context the emerging 'Sociology of Education', the second partner of the alliance, provided powerful intellectual support for the Labour Party. In Britain this sub-discipline emerged largely through documenting, meticulously and repetitively, the inequalities of opport-unity for the access of boys to Grammar Schools as structured by Father's Occupation and the nature of local provision. Implicit in these definitions of the problems were solutions in terms of restructuring the institutional form of schooling and in terms of interventions into the lives of specific class fractions to make them more amenable to education.

Teacher unions provided the third partner in the alliance which was to dominate the politics of schooling during the 1960's and early 1970's. Educational reform had been one of the themes of the change in popular feelings which has become known as 'war radicalism'. In response to a shortage of teachers the Emergency Training Scheme had been set up towards the end of the war to recruit 12,000 trainee teachers within a year. It received 57,300 appli-cations and accepted 17,800 people. It was this generation of teachers who struggled through the 1950's for teaching to be recognised as a 'profession' on a par with the other 'professions'. This claim to professional status was grounded in expert knowledge of the curriculum, its organisation and transmission.

The resultant social democratic repertoire was charact-erized at a global level by the motifs of social justice and economic modernization to be achieved by the lowering of inefficient class barriers and the installation of a technological meritocracy. Education was central to this strategy - the site where class was actively to be dismantled and talent promoted. The main reform of schooling proposed by the alliance as necessary to achieving this was, of course, the introduction of the comprehensive secondary school. This repertoire gained some dominance in the politics of the late 1950's, flourishing in the mid-1960's, but it was discredited in the mid-1970's with the onslaught of the New Right. At first the critique was limited to a marginal group in the Right but, with a deepening economic and social crisis in the 1970's (let alone a leadership coup), it became the orthodoxy of the Conservative Party and, in the glare of lights at Ruskin College in 1976, the Labour Party. The social democratic repertoire was exhausted, if not quite exorcised, by the weight of its own overambitions and contradictions. The New Right agenda was a populist one - the return of education to people (in the form of 'parents') both in terms of (market) control and in terms of the common-sense structuring of curricula both overt and hidden.

## COMMUNITY AND THE COMPREHENSIVES

At first sight 'community' played little part in the debates over the introduction of comprehensive schooling. Pedley, in what was treated as the official manifesto for supporters of comprehensive schooling (Pedley 1966), surveyed the provision of rural comprehensive schools in the terms of Henry Morris[2] as providing, potentially or actually, centres for their surrounding communities. This form of comprehensive schooling he effectively dismissed from the contemporary debate as it 'owes little or nothing to educational, social or political theories. It has been a matter of hard economics and practical efficiency' (Pedley 1966 p.47). As I will argue later this was to misunderstand, severely, the nature of Morris's innovations.

Pedley's concern was with establishing comprehensive schools in the towns - 'a much more stormy course ... where large, efficient, selective schools were entrenched' (Pedley 1966 p.62). Here 'community' faded into the background as Pedley revolved the debate around size, internal organisation and standards. Symptomatically, as we shall see later, community appeared in its absence in the case study of Kirkby. 'Kirkby is not only a working class area but very largely a slum clearance area. There is indeed something like a common culture here, but it is far from comprehensive. Socially it is a one class town ... Fundamentally, Kirkby's problem is lack of roots and social stability ... the need not only for a community centre, but for leadership from such a centre, is very great' (Pedley 1966 p.72). The results of the efforts of the teachers of the local school were held to be 'giving the people of this one class town what they need more than anything else: hope, self-respect, the real prospect of a long, hard, rewarding climb to a satisfying individual and communal life' (Pedley 1966 p.73).

Pedley clearly held out hopes for the relationship between comprehensive schools and the community - the L.C.C. experimental schools were not truly comprehensive for Pedley as 'the two way flow, often involving people other than parents, which marks the real neighbourhood community, is missing ... in terms of rounded social life it lacks something when compared with a place where school and community are balanced and integrated' (Pedley 1966 p.78). Indeed he argued that 'as a concept the comprehensive school is above all a school for the community' (Pedley 1966 p.132). Pedley took as his definition of the comprehensive school the Ministry of Education definition: 'schools intended for all secondary pupils in a district'. The lack of selection for such a school was the 'real point of the argument' in that it generated a 'mixed, balanced, healthy, natural community' (Pedley 1966 p.79), 'diversity within a greater unity' (Pedley 1966 p.112).

These points, declared central, were never really developed in his argument. His view of this reciprocal relationship between school and community revolved around two issues - around teacher professionalism and the relationship between teachers and parents, and around the W.E.A. and adult education. In both of these formulations Pedley was boldly suggestive but no more. Despite the centrality of teacher professionalism to the politics of comprehensive reform Pedley was forthright in defining at least aspects of it as a problem - 'it is dangerous and a sign of inner weakness, for adults to seek to maintain their prestige by extending the authoritarian role unchanged from infants to adolescents. The adolescents of today are the parents of tomorrow' (Pedley 1966 p.133). In part Pedley's solutions were modest - PTA's in the 50% of schools without one, in part they were extremely bold - the need for 'questioning the existence of categories like "C stream (parents)" at all' (Pedley 1966 p.136).

The field of adult education provided 'a wonderful opportunity' (Pedley 1966 p.133) for the comprehensive school in Pedley's view. Here he was quite explicit in his view - the W.E.A. needed to abandon its role of 'purveyor of middle class culture to would-be intellectuals' (Pedley 1966 p.133) and to fulfill its historic role as a repository of 'social and political (non-party political) wisdom' (Pedley 1966 p.134).[3] This role was not to be limited to the provision of classes but it should intervene in the internal workings of the school - 'the promotion of a classless, communal culture

85

is a practical possibility: not, I repeat, a flat common culture, but one whose basic values (such as truth, tolerance, courage, justice and beauty) would be accepted by all, one leading to lives rich in purpose and variety' (Pedley 1966 p.134).

This educational/political configuration is confirmed if we look at Circular 10/65, the instrument of comprehensive reform. 10/65 was promulagated to provide guidance for local authorities on how to reorganize secondary education on comprehensive lines 'to raise educational standards at all levels' and to 'preserve all that is valuable in grammar school education' (Department of Education and Science [hereafter D.E.S.] 1965 p.1). Over half of the Circular was devoted to describing six main forms of comprehesive organisation which have 'emerged from experience and discussion' (D.E.S. 1965 p.1), two of them not even comprehensive. This discussion was purely organisational - the age and methods of transfers with nods in the direction of problems of buildings and staffing.

One paragraph was devoted to 'The School Community' in which the school was defined internally as a community reflecting an external community. The comprehensive school 'aims to establish a school community in which pupils over the whole ability range and with differing interests and backgrounds can be encouraged to mix with each other, gaining stimulus from the contacts and learning tolerance and understanding in the process' (D.E.S. 1965 p.8). To establish this Authorities should define catchment areas so that 'schools are as socially and intellectually comprehensive as is practicable' (D.E.S. 1965 p.8) - to fail to do so would mean that 'fewer of the pupils come from homes which encourage educational interests (and) schools may lack the stimulus and vitality which schools in other areas enjoy' (D.E.S. 1965 p.8).

The relationship between 'community' and comprehensive reorganisation was paradoxical. In one sense community was given very cursory treatment in the politics of the time - it was thoroughly subordinated to questions of institutional definition and selection and, where community was treated, proposals were scarce and vague. On the other hand there was an uneasy recognition that community was a new organizing principle of the education system replacing psychometry. As selection by 11+ was to die so selection by area was to grow with all the implications of neighbourhood differences in 'character' and 'interests'. Judgments of social pathology replaced the I.Q. test as the mediation between education and inequalities of race, class and gender. I will discuss the consequences of these half-conscious evasions later.

## COMMUNITY COLLEGES

If community played a somewhat hidden role in comprehensive reorganisation it had no such modesty when it came to specifically 'community' innovations. Harry Ree, in his review of community education (Ree 1985), identifies three major phases of community education in Britain -Morris's original Cambridgeshire Village Colleges, the post-war building of Community Colleges and the post-Plowden creation of community primary schools.

Contemporary community education traces its heritage back to inter-war Cambridgeshire and the introduction of Village Colleges by Henry Morris during his long tenure as Secretary for Education. The bare bones of his innovations are well known: the provision of well equipped centres which function not only as schools but as the sites for various statutory and voluntary agencies (Morris 1984). Beyond this we enter the realm of the 'holistic concept of education' and its manifest interpretations (Poster 1982 p.29). In the post-war years, but increasingly in the 1970's, such centres spread throughout the country often hand in hand with comprehensive reform. Poster estimates that by 1980 there were 250 Community Colleges half of which were concentrated in four Local Authorities - Cambridgeshire, Devon, Cumbria and Leicestershire (Poster 1982 p.15). Although relatively small in number the Community Colleges have made a considerable impact on practices in wider fields.

These colleges were characterized by a selection from a number of consistent themes. Firstly there was great emphasis on providing facilities far beyond those found in normal secondary schools and on encouraging use of these by non-pupil populations. This perhaps found its clearest expression in self-conscious show piece colleges such as the Stantonbury Campus in Milton Keynes or the Abraham Moss Centre in north Manchester where designs for international standing were elaborated. This impulse did have an impact in less publicised spheres so that 'shared use' has become a blanket policy in Authorities such as, for example, Birmingham. Community Colleges conceived their role as extending beyond 'shared use' - nothing touches a more raw nerve in a Community Educator than to suggest otherwise. Consistently through the field ran aspirations to new functions for education - from 'the village college would lie athwart the daily lives of the community it served' (Morris 1985 p.154), to 'it is partly to do with lifelong education, partly to do with people becoming involved in the provision for their own needs' (Watts 1977 p.106) or the Devonian 'education is too precious to be confined to children and adolescents' (Poster 1982 p.33).

In the weak form this represented no more than the location of traditional adult education in shared use facilities. More common was the search for new forms of knowledge and organisation by which the college could become a, or, more usually, the, focal point for the community - an expression and transformation of the community. Concomitant with this impulse to widen the boundaries and functions of the traditional school were new management structures. At the level of the Local Authorities this often involved bodies crossing traditional boundaries both in terms of different statutory bodies and in terms of different departments within any one authority. Internally Colleges developed a variety of uneasy structures attempting to unify or coordinate their diverse activities within the constraints of current legislation.[4] Few went as far as the Stantonbury Campus with its Director, single management team and central governing body.

Community Colleges also provided perhaps the most consistent articulation of progressivism and comprehensivisation. The Leicestershire Colleges were an integral part of the Plan to create a new pedagogy for 11 - 14 year olds while Countesthorpe College represented perhaps the most consistent attempt to apply progressive ideas to secondary education (Watts 1977 & Leicester Mercury passim). Here democratic relations between staff and students, inter-disciplinary team teaching, resource based learning with new definitions of knowledge and new forms of certification were explored in a very public way. Other Community Colleges followed a less thoroughgoing programme but the tendency was clear.

## THE COMMUNITY PRIMARY SCHOOL

The third arena in which 'community' was elaborated by the politics of the social democratic alliance was the community primary school. This development stemmed from the proposals of the Plowden Report of 1967 (Central Advisory Council for Education (England) [hereafter, Plowden] 1967 Vols. 1 & 2) - perhaps the high point of this educational politics. The terms of reference were all-encompassing 'to consider primary education in all its aspects and the transition to secondary education' (Plowden 1967 Vol. 1 p.iv) and the Report similarly voluminous. The Report was an impassioned argument for more resources to be directed to the primary sector in order, in famous phrases, to 'provide a perfectly ordinary, well staffed school' and to bring 'a system designed for "other people's children" up to the standard which "a good and wise parent" would accept for his own children' (Plowden 1967 Vol 1 p.460).

In defining the priorities of this ambitious programme the Central Advisory Council used two criteria - educational and social need, and cost-benefit with the former given priority over the latter. 'Absolute priority' (Plowden 1967 Vol 1 p.436) was given to only one proposal - the creation of Educational Priority Areas to cover 10% of the child population by 1972/3. These areas were where schools were caught in 'vicious circles' (Plowden 1967 Vol 1 p.50) of low expectations, poor facilities, poor (by implication) teachers and educational failure. 'Schools play a central part in the process, both causing and suffering multiple deprivation' (Plowden 1967 Vol 1 p.50) whereas 'schools exist to foster virtuous circles' (Plowden 1967 Vol. 1 p.37).

To break these vicious circles the Council recommended 'positive discrimination' in favour of those deprived areas - 'the first step must be to raise the schools with low standards to the national average; the second, quite deliberately to make them better. The justification is that the homes and neighbourhoods from which many of their children come provide little support and stimulus for learning' (Plowden 1967 Vol. 1 p.57). These schools were to benefit from additional resources and support. The major reform of the schools themselves was that the concept of the community school should first be explored in the context of the Educational Priority Areas. The logic of this proposal was derived from the National Survey conducted for the Report and its regression analysis which concluded that 'the variation in parental attitudes can account for more of the variation in children's school achievement than either the variation in home circumstances or the variation in schools' (Plowden 1967 Vol. 2 p.181). The community school, at first in the E.P.A.'s, but certainly not to be restricted to them, was to be part of the solution to this problem - 'a school open beyond the ordinary school hours for the use of children, their parents and, exceptionally, for other members of the community' (Plowden 1967 Vol. 1 p.44). This was in addition to the Minimum Programme for all schools - Welcome Meetings, Open days, Teacher Meetings, Information Packs and Reports.

The consequent E.P.A. programme of action-research in Deptford, Birmingham, Liverpool, the West Riding and Dundee was rapidly followed by cognate innovations in many Authorities with areas of 'multiple deprivation' particularly where special funding from central government was forthcoming. It also provided much of the groundwork for later programmes which were less specifically educational and more comprehensive in scope - from the Community Development Projects ('the project that got away'[5]) to the Inner City Partnership Programme.

## COMMUNITY AND THE LIMITS OF SOCIAL DEMOCRACY

We thus have three, somewhat disparate, scenes from the politics of the mid-1960's through to the mid-1970's although clearly these innovations continue in the changed circumstances of the 1980's. How are we to come to terms with them? I want firstly to suggest that each of the articulations of 'community' with education occupied a strategically important place in the politics of social democracy. I then want to offer a critique of each of them before suggesting that, together, they marked many of the boundaries of social democracy in its attempt to serve both popular interests and capital simultaneously.

Community provided the hidden ground for comprehensive reorganisation - little analyzed but heavily loaded with expectations of reaching the pluralist heaven of a just and efficient capitalism. The Community Colleges provided show cases not only of comprehensive reorganisation and progressive secondary schooling but also of the facilities of the newly coordinated Welfare State. The E.P.A. community school represented an acid test of social democratic politics - an explicit attempt to breach class reproduction (but only marginally the reproduction of gender based and racial oppressions). As has been noted elsewhere 'Halsey's own progress along the road to Balsall Heath provided a courageous case of social democratic policies taken to the edge' (Centre for Contemporary Cultural Studies 1981 p.178).

It is important to recognise the strengths of these propositions before any critique is offered. The community and comprehensive proposals were and are important. They denied the legitimacy of assigning children at 11 on the basis of IQ tests to future locations in production and, to a lesser extent, reproduction. They asserted education as a collective, social activity with responsibilities to, and demands from, a wide public. The connection between schools and social structure was placed as central to the politics of education. The reforms were to expand the practice of education considerably - wider constituencies were to be canvassed, new forms of knowledge were to be explored, new relations to other social sites were to be formed and even new forms of government were to be tested. While important questions can be raised about the extent to which these proposals were ever implemented and about the coherence of them given a flourishing and expanding commercial sector I want to focus on their inherent weaknesses and the ambiguities which often converted them to their opposites.

A central weakness of the social democratic politics of education in the 1960's and 1970's was its overloading of the education system with contradictory expectations. In the social democratic repertoire education was to play multiple roles - it was to be the source and transmission of the new technology which was to modernize British capitalism, simultaneously it was to be an agent of social reform pulling down archaic class barriers by allowing talent to rise and by the creation of the 'classless, communal culture' for which Pedley hoped (Pedley 1966 p.134). These contradictory impulses were held together by the problematic of mobility - the friction free rise and fall of talent. Implicitly assumed were that the 'needs of industry' provided the datum mark for education, that they were simply definable and that education could (and should) 'meet' them. Also assumed were that education could locate individuals in production and reproduction accurately while creating a common culture in which the necessity of these different locations (and life experiences) was universally accepted so that class became a vestigial trace in the common culture of a functionally differentiated society.

In the context of a crisis ridden mode of production increasingly deskilling its mass labour force or expelling it

91

from production these assumptions were individually and collectively fragile. The 'New' sociology of education of the 1970's can be read as diverse essays on these themes: why education is more determined than determing, how pupils come to, and experience, school with cultural identities rooted in the realities of a society structured by class, gender and race, how schooling, in part through the mechanisms of the hidden curriculum, (re)locates pupils in the social structure. This overloading of the education system with contradictory expectations was not carelessness but necessary to the coherence of the social democractic politics <u>as a whole</u>. In trying to satisfy the conditions for renewed capitalist accumulation while, at the same time, seeking social justice and some form of equality the social democratic alliance was invariably pulled in opposite directions. The education system was <u>the</u> site where these tensions could be brought together and focussed and where they could be held to be resoluble. Rarely had a social institution been held to have such a capability.

In this constellation the practices of 'community' provided an important case of the limits of social democracy through the magical resolution of structural conflicts. Although differences within the community were sometimes recognised there was scarcely any sense that these differences were resistently rooted in the social structure and that they were often, implicitly or explicitly, antagonistic. In common with the rest of the social democratic repertoire conflicts were held to be resoluble being rooted in attitudes - class was a state of mind to be transformed into the common culture, race was a difference to be overcome by assimilation, racism an ignorance to be combatted through discussion while differences of gender did not appear on the agenda (being natural). These evasions were not passive but an active principle of the system. The assumption of social unity not only tended to conceal the antagonisms of British society but it also allowed the active resubordination of subordinate groups. By inspecting each of the arenas in which community was elaborated we can see this principle in operation.

As I suggested above 'community' provided the hidden ground for comprehensive reform replacing psychometric selection with selection by catchment area. As the New Urban Sociology has begun to demonstrate spatial organis-ation is substantially structured by the conditions for the realization of reproduction of labour power (Castells 1977).

The articulation of the schooling system with the other elements of this system suggests that the 'comprehensive' school intake may be at least as effective in the class structuring of schooling as was psychometric selection. 3,489 Estate Agents cannot be wrong. The problem of catchment area was, of course, not entirely ignored by the politics of social democracy. In 10/65 we find the Secretary of State urging authorities 'to ensure, when determining catchment areas, that schools are as socially and intellectually comprehensive as is practicable' (D.E.S. 1965 p.48). In part this was a pluralist hope that simple mixing would decrease conflict, in part this was predicated on a pathology model of working class culture in which contact with middle class cultures would improve attitudes. The ambiguities of this position were neatly expressed in 10/65 - 'But particular comprehensive schools will reflect the characteristics of the neighbourhood in which they are situated; <u>if their community is less varied and fewer pupils come from homes which encourage educational interests</u>, schools may lack the stimulus and vitality which schools in other areas enjoy' (D.E.S. 1965 p.8, emphasis added). Clearly stimulus and vitality were thought to be in short supply while variety was a directional practice.

Pedley's analysis of Kirkby cited above contained an identical ambiguity - Kirkby had a communal culture but it was a one class culture ('it is far from comprehensive' [Pedley 1966 p.72]) and, here is the rub, being not only a working class but also a slum clearance area this common culture did not give the people hope, self-respect nor a satisfying individual and communal life. The problem of one class catchment areas, inexplicably, does not seem to have spread up the coast to, say, Crosby, Formby or Southport. Comprehensive reorganisation with its area based catchment policy can thus be seen as falling from the avowed, mistaken ideal of justice <u>and</u> efficiency under capitalism into a covert system which more certainly secured a class structured schooling system predicated on the pathology of the majority.

The Community Colleges, as showpieces, highlighted other weaknesses in the social democratic repertoire. Above all the Community Colleges represented the top down nature of the politics of the time - there was little evidence to suggest that the formation of these Colleges originated in popular pressure for an extended practice of education and much to suggest that they owe their origin to high policy making by the local Authority and often by national and international bodies. Mason's analysis of the context of the Abraham Moss Centre makes depressing reading - an enormously expensive project which manifestly failed to understand anything of the dynamics of the area to be served: the results, 2% of adult education enrolments being from the area and the disorganisation of existing community groups and facilities (Mason 1978). Community Colleges in new towns were part of this 'planting' style of politics on a grander scale. This politics, of necessity, tended to emphasize the provision of facilities at the expense of considerations of the relationship between such a community institution and its constituencies. The aim of community colleges to become a focus for the community was rarely matched with a detailed analysis of the 'community' - its diversity, its cultures, its spontaneous philosophy (Gramsci 1971), its existing centres of organis- ation - and how an implanted institution could intermesh with these.

These points can perhaps best be made by a comparison between the work of Henry Morris and the Community Colleges which traced their lineage to his work in Cambridgeshire. The continuity was one of superficial institutional form - as I have suggested elsewhere Morris's Village College proposals were a specific response to a specific political context (Baron 1987). They connected with, and satisfied, popular pressure for access to full secondary education for all some twenty years before this became national policy. The Village Colleges enabled Morris to consolidate his wresting of control of schools from the Church and to provide basic communal facilities in rurual areas. They threw a cordon sanitaire around the city of Cambridge in an attempt to stem the loss of 'able' children to city schools. Above all they represented an attempt by Morris to fill the vacuum of leaderhip in the countryside being left by the decline of the power of the Parson and Squire - Morris was determined that a new democratic institution and not commercial capital should fill this vacuum.

While many questions can be raised about Morris's analysis of inter-war Cambridgeshire, particularly his reliance on a nostalgic organicism, the level of his analysis is clear. In this there was little continuity between the Village College and the Community Colleges - a few admini- strative changes, shared use and aspirations to be a communal focus were all that hold together Morris's carefully planned, radical policies of the 1920's and the rather glossy Community Colleges. It is highly significant that Morris, once retired from the education service, sought to develop community centres not only in schools but also in a pub and in a centre for the arts.

The community primary school provided the third arena in which social democratic politics elaborated 'community'. From the inception in the Plowden Report these were pivoted around the pathology of the local community - initially the families of 10% of the child population but with ambitions for greater coverage. At the community level the pathology was one of the loss of community - in part connecting with the real disorganisation of many long established working class areas by the post-war redevelopments, in part a version of the Golden Age myth providing a niche for free floating social angsts. At the level of individuals the pathology was ascribed to attitudes or culture. The Peaker regression analysis firmly identified parental attitudes to education as the major problems these schools faced. It took little work to extend this model to whole cultures - as the proposal document of one major initiative telegrammed 'West Indian families often very strict with corporal punishment regularly inflicted, Asian families are withdrawn, following their own culture, have serious communication problems, Irish are restless, violent, nomadic, undernourished and poorly clad.'[6]

The community primary school, based on such analyses, developed various practices to link home and school. Home-school liaison teachers developed extensive home visiting programmes the results of which could be shared with other agencies at local area meetings. Parents (and others) were invited into the ambit of the school to participate in a variety of activities, to use facilities and to form local organisations. In addition to this surveillance, attempts directly to reform the local culture were developed. Particular attention was given to altering the local child-rearing practices especially in the preschool years on the basis of versions of the cycle of deprivation argument through vehicles such as preschool groups, toy libraries and summer play schemes. The 'mother' provided the rarely analysed reference point for these reforms of childrearing but the 'mother' was also an object of reform herself - from English classes to bring Asian women into the public realm, to afternoon groups in kerb crawling districts to take women out of the public sphere.

Community education through the primary school also had its hidden curriculum - the representation of a constituency to itself. The constituency was represented as united - a community but a community united in need for intervention. The professional-lay division, with all its micro-physics of power, was propagated while the community was represented as being organised around acceptable 'leaders' - classically the priests of various religions - to the exclusion of unacceptable 'leaders'.

How then are we to come to terms with 'community' in the political constellation of social democracy? At one level community initiatives must be seen as vehicles for state reform quite independent of any external reference to empirical populations. In the era of corporate management, its proposal, its adoption and sometimes its subsequent rejection, community initiatives were test beds of state organisation developing new forms of intra-departmental management structures and inter-departmental coordination quite independently of any impact on specific areas.

More important for present purposes is that 'community' in the politics of social democracy was, above all, an ideology. By ideology I understand two very specific features: the concealment of antagonisms (in this case antagonisms of class, race and gender) and the outcome of these concealments being to the advantage of dominant groups. 'Community' served to secure two major advantages for dominant groups in social democracy - the less fraught reproduction of labour power and the more intrusive control of specific subordinate groups. 'Community', supremely, was an ideology of social unity - the common weal to which all could subscribe and contribute. In global terms this served to disqualify notions of the necessary nature of the conflicts of contemporary Britain - the constant resort to attitudinal explanations (and solutions) concealed the resistant material bases of conflicts. In more specifically educational terms the assumption of community (even if underlying different empirical communities) allowed notions of classless culture and national needs to drive educational policy.

Such unities are common features of ideologies and represent the elevation of specific historical formations to the status of universals. Here community was more than a simple concealment but a positive mechanism for the resubordination of subordinate groups. The area base of school intake lay education open to spontaneous structuring by class based housing processes - the covert re-creation in many areas of secondary moderns and grammar schools. The concern in the comprehensive reforms to 'preserve all that is valuable in the grammar school education for those children who now receive it and make it available to more children' (D.E.S. 1965 p.1) allowed the invisible structuring of curricula (both overt and hidden) by assumptions based on specific class, racial and gender relations to the detriment of non-sponsored cultural forms without even the resonant, individualized hope of the 'scholarship boy'.

Community initiatives were important concealment mechanisms in themselves - allowing the state, with remarkable agility, to represent itself as being on the side of the people and, simultaneously, as an efficient controller of areas of crisis. The provision of facilities, spectacular in the cases of the purpose built Community Colleges, represented the state as benevolent provider while community interventions into areas of crisis were heavily laden with expectations of managing social tensions. It is in terms of the functions of community initiatives in providing new forms of social control that the nature of the social democracy of the era becomes most clear. Hall et al. (1978) have described the politics of the time in terms of the growing crisis of hegemony - the progressive disintegration of mechanisms for securing the spontaneous consent of people to the current social and economic organisation. They trace how economic, political and ideological forces coverged to produce a 'cause célèbre' of violent crime in the 'Handsworth Mugging' and how on the back of this moral panic new forms of coercive social control were developed.

I suggest that the tendency represented by the community primary school constituted a parallel history to that of the Handsworth mugging - from shotgun duels in the streets of Rochdale to pathological family forms in Birmingham the history is constant:[7] the need to intervene in the reproduction of a specific class fraction, the under-class, to make it conform better to state defined forms. While the panic about mugging developed a repertoire for controlling the 'depraved' largely through coercive means so the community primary school developed a repertoire for the control of the 'deprived' largely through ideological means - the denigration of subordinate cultures, their close surveillance and direct or indirect intervention to re-formulate them into closer conformity with state defini-tions.

Such politics were deeply unpopular in two senses - they failed to build upon and organize popular experiences of education and they tended to resecure, with whatever fragility, the subordination of the majority to the current relations of production and forms of reproduction. The flow of the politics was from the top downwards - 'community', in a real way, was an imposition on actual populations and indifference or hostility followed. Target populations were quite insultingly identified and subjected to an often gross form of 'professional' power play. The logic of operation of community based initiatives, whatever the good intentions of the reformers, was often towards resecuring the class structure with its racial and gender based inflections.

The assault by the New Right on this social democratic form of educational politics accurately exploited these weaknesses with less liberal intent - in many ways the New Right of the 1970's and 1980's would not have been possible without the social democracy of the 1950's and 1960's. The New Right placed itself on the side of the individual against the state (while centralizing in a manner inconceivable even to the managerialism of social democracy) - teacher power was to be diminished, parent power was to be increased, expert knowledge was not to be trusted, sturdy common sense was. Social engineering through education was neither possible nor desirable whereas the natural competition of abilities was both.

At a minimum these themes had significant references in popular experiences of the community based reforms of social democracy in action - the re-creation of downgraded schools for working class areas without the individualized hope of grammar schools, the planting of expensive but alien institutions in areas of poverty, the insulting interventions of ill thought-out para social work etc. At a maximum the New Right repertoire began to settle a new set of educational definitions which could be taken as common sense - schooling was about individual competition for places in the labour market with the lines of the race being unambiguously defined by the needs of the economy and a definition of the national culture. The tendency was clear - the systematic definition of education as the servant of Capital, training and classifying individuals for 'their' places in the relations of production and reproduction.

Where does 'community' stand in this new political configuration? While this paper has been critical of the social democratic community initiatives, indeed I have suggested that they are collapsing under the weight of their own contradictions, the articulation of 'community' (whether we use the specific word or not) with education is of crucial importance. As the New Right is restructuring education away from being a collective concern for the development of potentials and for the realization of an equitable social structure so the community tradition represents an important counter. Here I have space for no more than the sketching of a few directions for such a counter politics.

A simple return to the social democratic repertoire provides no way forward - as I have suggested the politics were incoherent, the practices tended to their opposites and the effects provided the ground for the New Right. The unitary nature of the concept of 'community' was a central weakness and any renewal of the community tradition will need to start from an analysis of the differences within constituencies, their oppositions and the bases of these oppositions. If education is not to be 'an escape from reality, but an enrichment and transformation of it' (Morris 1984 p.29) then it will properly become the site of, and contributor to, conflicts. If education is to develop human potentials then the identification of education with the contemporary structures which necessarily inhibit potentials will properly be broken.

The implication of this is that state provision will rarely provide the starting point for community initiatives. Rather than the 'planting' style of politics of social democracy a renewed community tradition will need to work up the politics. Rather than assuming that communities in crisis are at best voids, at worst internally pathological, starting points can be found in the spontaneous organisations which make life social and in making 'coherent the principles and the problems raised by the masses in their practical activity' (Gramsci 1971 p.324). This depends on understanding organisations as something other than institutions.

While the logic of this analysis is away from seeing the state as the ground for community education the state in the form of the school penetrates social life in a fundamental way and is one of the major stakes in the enrichment and transformation of reality. Here an education which serves its constituencies will start from an understanding of how its constituencies are located in the social structure and how schooling serves to resecure these relations. These issues can then provide the raw material for curricula both overt and hidden. The Public Schools have been doing such for more than a century (without transformational intent).

The New Right agenda provides the ground for such a guerilla war against reproduction as it represents a paradigm of capitalist training with little disguise. Education for industry, the denial of any difference in the position of minorities, the sharp differentiation of pupils, the populist appeal, the simple moralism or the attempt more firmly to locate women in the home all provide more fertile ground for a community education, whether in school or not, than did the arid statism and professionalism of social democracy. In such an education the realities of the crisis of British capitalism, of oppressions based on class, gender and race, of increasing state control as they are experienced and as they structure local areas can become overt topics of education, challenge and transformation.

This, rather than showpiece facilities, is, I suggest, the legacy of Henry Morris.

## NOTES

1.  This analysis follows that presented in Centre for Contemporary Cultural Studies, (1981) Unpopular Education, London, Hutchinson.
2.  Classically Morris, Henry (1924) The Village College, Cambridge, Cambridge University Press, reprinted in Morris, Henry (1984) The Henry Morris Collection, Cambridge, Cambridge University Press, and Ree, Harry (1985) Educator Extraordinary, London, Peter Owen.
3.  Other interpretations of the W.E.A., past and present, do exist.
4.  Management models flow all over Poster 1982.
5.  Interview with a Senior Official of Birmingham M.D.
6.  Personal communication from a major project.
7.  Interviews with officials of the relevant LEA's.

## REFERENCES

Baron, Steve (1987) 'Community Education: from the Cam to the Rea', Paper presented to the International Sociology of Education Conference, Westhill, January 1987 in Barton, L. & Walker, S. (eds) (forthcoming) Politics and the Process of Schooling.

Castells, Manuel (1977) The Urban Question, London,

Arnold, 1977

Central Advisory Council for Education (England) (1967) Children and their Primary Schools, Vols. 1 & 2, London, HMSO.

Department of Education and Science (1965) The Organisation of Secondary Education: Circular 10/65, London, Department of Education and Science.

Gramsci, Antonio (1971) Selections from the Prison Notebooks, London, Lawrence & Wishart.

Hall, Stuart, et al. (1978) Policing the Crisis, London, Macmillan.

Mason, Tim (1978) 'Residential Succession, community facilities and urban renewal in Cheetham Hill, Manchester'. New Community, 10, 3, pp. 78-87.

Morris, Henry (1984) The Henry Morris Collection, Cambridge, Cambridge University Press

Pedley, Robin (1966) The Comprehensive School, Harmondsworth, Penguin.

Poster, Cyril (1982) Community Education: its Development and Management, London, Heinemann Educational Books.

Ree, Harry (1985) Educator Extraordinary, London, Peter Owen.

Watts, John (1977) The Countesthorpe Experience, London, George Allen & Unwin.

# 6

# Progressive Education, Oppositional Spaces and Gender

## Tuula Gordon

## INTRODUCTION

This paper considers contradictions between democratic schooling and radical teaching and learning by discussing what scope progressive education offers anti-sexist work, and what difficulties are posed by the progressive framework. It is based on my research activities in a progressive secondary school, which took place over a period of several years. The research (Gordon 1985 and 1986) focussed on possibilities and limitations for radical teaching and learning within progressive schools, and considered shifts in these over time by relating them to a discussion of restructuring. This question was developed through the concept of oppositional spaces[1] - if formal education is located within capitalist, patriarchal and racist social relations and structures, and schools are a microcosm of these social relations, can radical work within schools be worthwhile? And are there any specific issues to be raised in discussing progressive education and radical work?

To consider these questions, I shall formulate a framework of formal education as state schooling, and try to pin down the rather 'elusive' concept of progressive education.

Progressive schools are based on a child-centred ethos, and the intention is to treat students as unique individuals, and to realise their potential as far as possible. Thus such schools lack many gender related features described in feminist literature on education, such as differentiated registers, seating arrangements, structured channelling of subject choices etc. (Deem 1978, David 1980, Sharpe 1976, Wolpe 1978, Barrett and McIntosh 1979). In Greenfield College,[2] the progressive school where my research activities took place, the school ethos expresses concern for equality, discussion, participation and autonomy. The teachers include liberals and pragmatists, and feminist, socialist and libertarian radicals. It is interesting to consider how questions of sexism and anti-sexism are raised within this framework.

An underlying assumption in the discussion is that women are in a subordinate position in power structures. Patriarchy has been used as an analytical concept to describe this; Hartmann (1979) gives a useful definition. She focusses on patriarchy as a set of social relations among men which have a material basis: the control of women's labour power by men. However the subordination of women is defined, it is integrated into the structures of our society; schooling is located in these structures, and contains the social relations embedded in them. Hence questions of limitations and possibilities for anti-sexist work are related to a broader question of oppositional spaces within formal education.

I shall not reconsider old questions of whether schools are determined or determining in any abstract way. But it is practically and politically important to consider whether positive radical action in schools is possible. I will return to this discussion by looking at Greenfield College, and sexism and anti-sexism within it, focussing both on the possibilities and limitations for critical action, by considering curriculum, interaction, relationships, school ethos and democracy. But first I want to clarify the concepts of progressive education and 'oppositional spaces'.

## PROGRESSIVE EDUCATION

Progressive education in the state educational system was 'endorsed' in the sixties (Sharp and Green 1975, Dale 1979) in the context of expansion of education. With this expansion coincided an optimism about the economy and about the contribution of schools towards it. More practically, there was a need to attract more teachers, in particular male graduates. A DES recruitment campaign emphasised teaching as a professional career with scope for decision making, job satisfaction etc. At the same time within progressivism teachers were presented as non-authoritarian facilitators with expert pedagogic knowledge, facilitators of learning, who interpreted particular situations and the needs of particular students, on the basis of their professionalism.

103

The ideal-typical characteristics of progressive education include:

- mixed ability, flexible, vertical groupings which work together and/or individually in an open plan classroom under a team of teachers;
- the day is 'integrated', the curriculum is problem- or concept-based;
- a wide range of resources is drawn upon;
- the teaching-learning is child-centred, based on the students' interests, needs and skills;
- the teacher is a guide and supporter in the students' pursuit of learning;
- academic learning is balanced by social, emotional and creative learning;
- decisions in the school are made by all those involved in it.

This is an ideal-typical construction, which serves as a methodological starting point; not all schools labelled progressive contain all these features, and schools labelled as traditional may contain some of them.

Thus it makes sense to specify progressivism further, by considering specific theoretical, educational and political strands within it; these are 1) a libertarian strand, 2) a liberal strand, and 3) a socialist strand.

1. Humanitarian libertarianism developed in independent, fee-paying schools outside the state system. It stemmed from a disillusionment with society and emphasised the potential of children, to be realised in a free, individualised environment. Anarchist libertarianism developed in state schools, emphasising equality, critical analysis of society, anti-authoritarianism and individualism, combined with a class perspective.
2. There are two tendencies within the liberal strand as well: the child-centred and the society-centred. The former emphasises the needs of children, and genuine learning for intrinsic rewards. The latter also contains assumptions about the needs of society and ways of meeting them. A common thread is that in an industrial, complex, technological society traditional methods are no longer appropriate. Schools need to introduce skills of research and retrieval of information, and promote flexibility and an ability to cope

with rapid social change. The needs of society provide the starting point, but lead to child-centred approaches.

3. The socialist strand adopts aspects of the child-centred approach, curriculum innovation, non-authoritarian teacher-student relations and informal teaching methods. This adoption occurs within a socialist framework. There is a distinction to be made between socialist teachers concerned with trade union action and/or wider political struggles, who consider innovative work in schools misguided because of limited results, and those emphasising the need to develop ways of teaching and relating to pupils in their own schools, or through forging links with other teachers in other schools, or with the trade union movement. Many of the latter teachers as well as the former are critical of what they consider 'bourgeois' progressivism.

## OPPOSITIONAL SPACES

To consider the implications of these strands, we need to note schooling as state schooling. A distinction between state form and state apparatus is made (Holloway and Picciotto 1977, London-Edinburgh Weekend Return Group 1980). The state is one aspect of the social relations of capital; it is a particular surface form of these relations, and is stamped by their contradictions - the state form is an abstraction embodying the capital relation. The state apparatus is the machinery of the state. The theoretical implication of this distinction is that though there is a relationship between state form and state apparatus, this is not constant, but dynamic, full of contradictions and complexities, and variable over time. 'Oppositional spaces' are located within the disjunctures of state form and apparatus. During a period of restructuring, which may begin in the sphere of production, but has impact on social relations outside that sphere and on the state, necessitating a tighter relationship between form and apparatus, spaces are eroded.

The practical implication of the distinction between form and apparatus is that it is possible for radical groups and individuals to work within the state in the oppositional spaces. Its importance is further evident, when we consider the period of restructuring of state schooling, as characterised by the Great Debate in the latter half of the seventies. Jones (1983) argues that spaces within progressive education were overemphasised, and limitations were noted. But they were nevertheless considered significant within the context of restructuring, and the potentially increased fragility of social relations during a period of rapid social change, as headlines such as 'Marxist mindbenders in the classroom' (Evening News 20.9.1977) and the events surrounding the William Tyndale school[3] illustrate.

During restructuring there has been concern about these spaces for 'radical' teaching, even though such teaching has been located within the narrow confines of professional autonomy where teachers as 'experts' were making decisions. Anti-sexist work, here, is considered radical. I am not asking to what extent progressivism has privileged questions of sex-gender, but by focussing on possibilities and limitations for radical anti-sexist work in one school I want to raise the following questions: 1) how persistent are sexist processes in schools; and 2) what implications are there for critical action within schools in relation to sexism.

I operate with two underlying assumptions: it is important to consider what the spaces might be, because they are being restructured, so that their regeneration will be possible. Secondly, anti-sexist work, in order to be effective, must engage with the raw materials that students bring into the situation. Formal teaching cannot reach students and their restrictive sex-gender stereotypes if the ways in which these are reinforced and/or re-created by their immediate realities are not considered. Traditional, formal education does not perceive students as members of class, gender, race etc., but as units brought together in groupings such as forms, houses, year groups etc. Within progressivism the aim is to consider students as concrete persons with their own particular characteristics. This individualisation poses difficulties for anti-sexist work, whilst also affording scope for it in important ways. I shall now return to Greenfield College to illustrate this.

## GREENFIELD COLLEGE

Greenfield is a comprehensive upper school, with participatory democratic structures, concern for curriculum innovation, non-authoritarian teacher-student relations, and an emphasis on the autonomy of individual students.

Progressive education contains various strands, as we noted above. Indeed we can find differentiated approaches among teachers in Greenfield. This is also reflected in the views of students when they are asked about sexism and anti-sexism in their school:

> I bet there's no equality in other schools. I mean if you just take this school there is equality, to a certain extent anyway. They let the girls do metalwork if they want to, but you don't get girls doing it, you know. (Stuart)

But other students shift the onus from structures outside the school to the processes within the school:

> Duncan [a teacher] is nice to us. And the boys - he's not very nice to the boys at all in our class. He's always pestering them and ... if they don't wanna do a subject, he makes them do it ... but if any of us didn't want to do something then he'd just say fair enough. (Brenda)

### The School Ethos

Liberalism was strong in the school in the early seventies. Along with libertarianism it contains an emphasis on 'human beings' and 'individuals'. Group characteristics such as sex-gender, race and class are not given a great deal of consideration in the school ethos and organisation. This means that many salient sexist features are missing, as Stuart notes above, and also, that policies in relation to groups are difficult to conceptualise.

Thus when we look at subject choices for example, as mentioned above, despite the lack of channelling procedures, overall the choices of girls and boys are differentiated. Because of the emphasis on the autonomy of individual students to control their own learning situations, overall policies to tackle such differentiation are difficult. But as individuals, students who do choose to cross gender-lines are generally given a great deal of encouragement in their work, and support in difficulties that they encounter.

The emphasis on autonomy is communicated to students through negotiations about their own work and development in the school, and the students are often active in maintaining that ethos. In a discussion one girl told her friend 'they won't let me give up science' - because of the flexible timetabling there is scope for students to have their timetables tailormade and they are able to drop subjects. But in this case teachers were reluctant to allow a girl to give up science, with the result that her timetable would be further sex-typed. 'Just give it up' was the advice that her friend in tune with the personalised ethos of the school gave her.

The question of liberalism is important, because it is such a strong response in schools vis-à-vis sex and gender. In the context of an experimental curriculum unit taught in some London schools in connection with a research project on 'Girls and Occupational Choice',[4] male teachers in one school initially refused to have any of their mixed classes separated by sex, as they felt that this would damage their attempts to integrate boys and girls together. When lessons were observed, it was noted that in discussions loud boys dominated and gradually took over.

The difficulties of integration were indicated in a mixed group discussion on sexual morality in Greenfield. Boys made loud and defensive jokes, whilst girls tried to explore issues that had been raised by a film. In the end the girls' voices could not be heard, and they stopped talking. But it would have been a brave girl anyway who would have expressed liberal views about sexuality in front of the embarrassed boys quick to resort to categorisations (slags etc.)

These observations lead us to consider femininity and masculinity in the interactions in the school.

### Femininity/Masculinity

Expressions of masculinity and femininity contain tensions and contradictions in Greenfield, which to some extent are specific to it as a progressive school. I shall illustrate this by first looking at a male deputy principal called 'Hacker'. The name was initiated in the football field; the image created had been effective, as Hacker explains:

> I can stop kids who are known as very tough in the local district, and ... they are quite meek and mild ... Now the idea that I actually lay a hand on a kid is absolutely commonplace in the district. I mean OK I break up fights and I may do that very aggressively ... but that is as far as it would go, but the reputation exists. And let's face it, if a kid is bullying I will have him in here for a large number

of hours and when they come out psychologically they might be in a pretty beaten down state.

This indicates a masculine 'tone' of control; men pose themselves as an incipient physical threat to boys. And female teachers find themselves in difficult positions when they are unable or unwilling to emulate that tone. An example is given by Sarah,[5] a woman teacher, who recounted an evening in the school disco/concert:

> I was the only woman [teacher] there, and I'd come partly because I wanted to hear it, and the bouncers were Tom, Rob and Phil [male teachers]. And particularly Bill was extraordinarily heavy. I really objected to it, because if he sets the tone at that level, there's nothing I could do. I cannot maintain a heavy tone, because I'm not going to heavy kids. Physically I'm not capable of it ... Sharon runs discos, Jill does, and they're little ... It's really easy for certain men to fall into that trap without thinking about it - being an incipient physical threat.

It has been suggested that there are two models of a teacher, that of a mother (in the primary sector in particular) and of a father (in the secondary sector in particular) (Bernstein 1975, David 1978, Deem 1978). In Greenfield College the model of the teacher as a mother has some significance in the caring relationships formulated between teachers as tutors, and their students, whereby the tutors spend a great deal of their timetable with their students, and try to get to know them as whole persons in order to build on their interests and in order to help them in their difficulties as obstacles to learning, and through concern for their social and emotional development. But it may be useful to add a further dimension though, of teachers as young uncles able to relate to the concerns of the students, but particularly those of the boys, as Jill, a teacher, explains. She notes that in her team teachers were more tolerant of boys' 'inane' discussions than those of the girls:

> The girls start behaving in a way that those characters behave in magazines, you know, sobbing about this boy who doesn't love me anymore. I

> mean I find it pretty difficult to take, but I'm
> prepared to tolerate it, I find football just as
> offensive, and I'm still prepared to tolerate
> football conversation ... Not one of the men
> actually ever will talk to the girls about something
> that they got as a problem, particularly if it's what
> they would consider to be trivial ... Yet they will
> always relate to the boys about football.

Thus men related to boys' culture, but find it difficult to relate to girls' culture. Some women teachers also find girls' culture difficult to deal with in terms of its emergent femininity and concern for romantic love.

Similarly conflicts among the boys tend to be loud, whereas girls' conflicts are quieter and less obvious. But when girls did deviate, were disruptive and difficult, they received more attention than boys (Davies 1978 has made a similar observation). Lesley, a girl student, one of the 'lasses', notes that 'the teachers are more lenient with the lads when they're fighting or they're arguing or something like that'. Discussions with girls who had been considered 'difficult' indicated that they experienced the control in the school as tighter than boys who had not lost the sense of scope for making their own decisions: 'you do what you wanna do in this school'.

But I noted that the model of a teacher as a mother has some resonance in Greenfield as well. Even the dreaded Hacker recounts its influence:

> In many ways [I had] a very sort of masculine,
> aggressive approach ... As I saw teachers whose
> work I respected taking a very gentle approach
> with students, and some of these were men
> teachers, and that was very successful, I have
> changed my own ideas in a way from that sort of
> rather aggressive approach that I had. People laugh
> about that in the school, as I am seen as pretty
> aggressive, having gone into teaching very starry-
> eyed indeed and having some of that starry-
> eyedness knocked out of me, and I brought that
> with me here, and I began to realise that in fact
> probably I had slung too far in one direction and
> the whole thing of getting through to students
> required a very soft approach.

This process can be difficult for men, as students have their particular expectations. Thus a male teacher who worked hard with a group of disruptive boys - he talked to them, tried to understand them and empathise with them - prompted these boys to ask another teacher whether he was a homosexual.

Teachers were observed to shift between the mother/father models; these shifts reflect contradictions, and the short-term effectiveness of the male model. For example a student, Joanne, describes Trevor, a teacher:

> He ... doesn't shout that often, but when something really gets him mad, he gets dead mad and he goes to them and picks them up and throws - well not throws them around - just puts them down where he wants them to sit because he's been telling them for about ten times, and it shuts them up.

The ethos, organisation and relationships therefore have some openness and flexibility to enable exploration, but contradictions and tensions exist. We are constantly dealing with both opportunities and limitations.

## A Democratic School

Before making some comments about the significance of Greenfield College as a democratic school with particip- atory structures open to teachers and students, I must add that as the process of economic restructuring has developed, new structures with new forms of management are being introduced in the school with the backing of the local education authority.

Democracy in the school has been confined to the sphere normally occupied by a headteacher. Thus it has obviously been faced by constant difficulties, not the least because it was not formally recognized by the local education authority. But though there were differences in the orientations of teachers, the democratic structures were considered an important feature of the school, and were seen to relate to the curriculum, pedagogy and teacher- student relationships. In short democracy was considered integral to the school ethos by a majority of the teachers.

When concern about sexism was voiced in the school, the clear policies and positive action on sex-gender were

111

considered to be lacking, a girl student, Tina (with encouragement from her female tutor) used the democratic structures to try to initiate changes. She called a meeting, and found that despite the concern expressed about sexism, it was not necessarily high on the priorities of the majority of teachers. Thus she had to postpone her meeting several times before an open slot appeared and no subsequent meeting was called to coincide with it. Teachers and students detailed problem areas, and made suggestions for changes. But no policies were formulated, and thus suggestions were partially implemented.

The democratic structures, then, provided possibilities for action, but, again, limitations were contained in them, in that action was not consistently enforced. As the framework of restructuring encroached on the school further, even feminist teachers doubted the possibility of fitting anti-sexism into the curriculum, not merely because of recalcitrance of many of the men teachers, but also because of developments in formal education which diminished scope for action. Thus Sarah notes:

> the trouble is what one needs to argue now is the whole thing that you have got to have positive discrimination in favour of girls ... an argument like that is streets ahead of most of them who are way back in the old idea of treating boys and girls identically and equally, you know you have got such a hell of a long argument ... we are trying to just keep where we are in terms of education cuts etc.; to tackle the problem of sexism as well just seems too much like hard work.

The discussions on sexism, and the difficulties in initiating positive action, led to the formation of a women's group in Greenfield. Initially the group included teachers and students, but tended to assume a somewhat patronising air, where teachers tried to pass their concerns about sexism to the girls, and did not discuss sexism as a process affecting them all regardless of age. The students decided to form a group of their own, which disintegrated when those girls who were closely involved left the school. The teachers' group continued, and on a different basis they initiated girls-only activities outside the school hours. The women's group itself has become an important forum responding and commenting vocally on a range of issues within the school. For example the new proposals for management structure were considered to strengthen male domination, because of the model of a 'manager' constructed, which seemed to draw predominantly on masculine qualities, so that women teachers would be less appropriate for these positions.

I have focussed a great deal on internal limitations, tensions and contradictions in the school. This is to counteract the powerful liberal view that schools can and should pursue a policy of integration and equal opportunities, and if these fail, the problems are really located outside the school, in the gender-typed socialisation that students receive, and bring to school as particular expectations and orientations. Paying attention to sexist structures externally diverts attention away from considering the ways in which sexist processes are replicated and indeed reinforced inside schools. But there is no doubt that these external processes do impinge upon schools that try to tackle sexism. When women teachers in Greenfield organised women's peace day activities, and painted their faces with peace symbols, this led to complaints by students about indoctrination, and parental complaints which are difficult to deny for a progressive school dependent on parental support in order to develop their pedagogy in the context of professional expertise.

Liberalism in Greenfield is declining. Many teachers veer towards pragmatism, and consider their work in more limited terms as a job than as a vocation. But in some respects teachers have also become radicalised. There is more preparedness to see sex-gender as a category on the basis of which it is possible to search for positive policies, though this is counterposed by demoralisation about the situation in Greenfield, and about the wider difficulties faced by state schooling.

In discussing the school ethos, I discussed problems posed by individualisation, by the concern to consider all students as unique entities with their particular character- istics, interests, aptitudes and needs. I shall now focus on some positive aspects, and will reflect on how, if combined with a feminist perspective, there may be some strengths which can be utilised in anti-sexist work. To consider these issues I shall now concentrate on curriculum.

## Curriculum

The school ethos emphasises the autonomy of students, and

the need for them to actively organise their own learning. Close relationships between teachers and students are the aim, so that mutual negotiations are possible. Work tends to be individualised, and group work occurs on an informal basis; in fact efforts to introduce more structured group work run into difficulties, because the students have internalised the school ethos, and want to make their own choices about work.

In this context there is an emphasis on creativity, personalised orientation, joint exploration and discussion between teachers and students. Teachers try to approach students openly, and are also prepared to enter the personal arena themselves - for example a teacher who encouraged creative autobiographical work among her students presented her own autobiography through photographs and captions displayed on the classroom wall.

Feminists have emphasised that the personal is political. Indeed while the individualisation in Greenfield College, and the emphasis on personalisation may remain shallow, tying students to their own preoccupations rather than extending them, it can also provide scope for connections to be made between personal and political structures, between the private and the public. But this approach can contain difficulties as well. I shall illustrate by discussing Gwen. She was working on a comprehension sheet on a kibbutz, and as she asked several questions to clarify the points, we entered into a long discussion which moved considering the ethos and organisation of kibbutzim to the Nazism and racism as a background to the formation of Israel. Gwen got interested, and decided to do a project on this 'topic'. Her interests were somewhat vague and broad, and her tutor found it difficult to pin them down. In his efforts to do so, after Gwen had acquired information from kibbutz representatives, he directed her attention to a letter written by a kibbutz inhabitant, and wrote down questions which focussed on the writer's perceptions and feelings, which did not satisfy Gwen's concern for information (she had asked me whether this project would be for 'brainy people'). Fairly soon the project was dropped, and Gwen moved on to work on costume and dress. Her tutor Trevor explains:

> that raised a lot of important questions and started
> from something in which she was herself interested
> - that preoccupation with dress that that sort of

girl's got, and actually worked that through to something that was really perceptive, and I think that was valuable.

But Trevor also remarked that

If you talk to Gwen the chances of her expressing any view on political matters are very remote. She would have decided that that was something for brainy people.

Gwen's project on dress may have encouraged her to consider matters important to her, but little challenge was provided for her gender-specific socialisation and personal concerns which were focussed on and underlined in a way that did not encourage links with the broader political questions that Gwen was interested in, and had opinions on, but which she did not consider to be her proper concern.

But it is not impossible to develop connections. Rita's work in team was largely personalised, and this led her tutor to doubt whether she should go on to sixth form despite her good examination results, because such work would not be possible there. Rita decided to stay on, and commented after about a year that her earlier personalised focus had been important, because 'I wanted to find out more about myself and people around me', but now she was interested to 'probe deeper into history, geography, and sociology'. The move from one approach to another seemed important to her, and in the process she adjusted and developed her own conceptions, and she expressed amazement at her earlier naiveté when studying a transcript of an interview that had been conducted during the previous year. She had become more radical, and questioned many of her earlier views, including her racism, and association with traditional femininity, of which she had become much more critical.

Within humanities many girls were engaged in projects that considered issues important to girls and women, ranging from abortion to girls and education, cultures and teenaged girls and boys etc. The value of non-traditional career strategies which do not take account of people's lives, and their powerful immediate realities is open to question. In Greenfield girls may choose feminist projects, use feminist literature, and develop or strengthen an anti-sexist stance. There is an emphasis on personalisation, their work is discussed, they are encouraged to actively reflect on issues, and to try to re-create knowledge. Thus these girls are more likely to touch on the powerful immediate realities of their lives here than within a more formal teaching-learning situation. But, as many women teachers have commented, the girls do not alter their lives and behaviour. Perception does not necessarily give power. Marilyn, a girl determined to have a job and 'work like any man' still fears that she will 'end up cooking the dinners', and notes that the concern indicated by teachers for the behaviour patterns of students was somewhat misplaced. She begins by describing a student, Tina, whose campaign against sexism in Greenfield we discussed earlier:

> She's so strong in her attitudes ... maybe if all the teachers were the same as her, it would be inbuilt in them to change things, then it would happen. But the women teachers are going to come to school and argue about sexism, and they're still going to go home and cook the dinner. It's just the way it is, whereas for Tina it's more clearly from the inside; it's her whole life.

But when we reflect on Marilyn's comments, we may also remember the difficulties experienced by women teachers who took action on women's peace day (above).

I want to make a further point by considering the critical potential of creative writing. Creative writing is considered, by the English-trained child-centred teachers, to form the backbone of learning in Greenfield. Educationally it is connected to theories of learning which emphasise the motivation and involvement of the learner, in order for the learning to transform her/him through personal impact. Politically it is linked to thinking emphasising the importance of the individual and stresses the need to develop the ability of students to take control of their own lives and futures. Frith, at a Socialist Teachers' Conference in 1978, has argued that state realism ought to be encountered by radicals by focussing on fantasies. Walker-dine (1984) raises questions about providing alternative but essentially realistic information to counter sexist images. She explores girls' literature, and powerful fantasies they engender, and the real needs they meet. More realism cannot serve the same function, and cannot touch girls in the same way. She argues for the exploration and creation of alternative fantasies. Thus the concern within progressivism not to focus too closely on academic learning in a narrow way, nor to concentrate the exploration of alternatives merely in critical Social Studies or similar realism, has potential to provide a framework which facilitates the questioning of reality, of what is natural, of what is inevitable.

## CONCLUSION

The progressive teaching/learning situation has advantages for work on gender which is informed by feminist theory, politics and commitment; it can give scope for exploration, as indicated, by connecting personal to political structures, through fantasy, through social relationships and friendship groups. But the child-centredness and the emphasis on autonomy also mean that there is an attempt not to impose on the girls, but to start from their situation, to consider their futures, the way they see them, and the way they want to construct them.

When considering oppositional spaces vis-à-vis gender in progressive education, the framework of wider economic and political restructuring must be remembered. Greenfield College is a somewhat demoralised place, because of the difficulties posed by the external and internal situation; questions of sex-gender are not centrally focussed on, and a great deal of the energies of the teachers are diverted to their trade union work. But there have been attempts to consider what anti-sexism might mean in such a school, and the questions have been posed in a way that is different from traditional, formal schools. These efforts, though contained with limitations which have received emphasis in this paper, should not be belittled. We can explore the possibilities within them in order to develop them, or at least to keep them ticking over so that further work will be possible in future. The CCCS Education Group in Unpopular Education (1981) under a heading 'looking for education' considers several examples. One of the negative examples suggests that 'innovative and radical education has sometimes emerged in state schools, but only sporadically and briefly' (pp. 260-261). Despite the problems of such attempts, and the often narrow professional confines within which they are located, they nevertheless provide signif-icant information and experiences that can be built upon and such attempts should not be dismissed too lightly.

I conclude with a note on a Greenfield student, Lesley,

who was one of the lasses, considered difficult and disruptive, with domestic problems, yet bright and alert. Her reports from a previous school already indicated that if her interest could not be captured, she would give up. And indeed by the time she came to Greenfield, she had largely done so. Julie, her tutor, said that she very quickly decided that Lesley was in a mess and that examinations did not matter as much as concern for her social development and support for her emotional difficulties when she ran away from home etc. This seemed somewhat shocking, when counterposed with Lesley detailing her ambitions for life in the fifth year (in an interview) 'I keep saying that I'm not going to get married and be a little suburban housewife in a semi-detached house and things like that.' Initially when Lesley left school she went into hairdressing. Julie explains her strategy and her reactions:

> What's happened, i.e. that she's not taking much in the way of exams was always what I expected would happen. Didn't expect to do miracles with her, and didn't particularly care. In a sense if she scraped together a few O-levels it wouldn't have made any difference, because she wouldn't have coped with the sixth form. So her formal education was always fairly irrelevant, once it was clear what sort of state she was in. And it always would have been, unless she'd been very, very different. She would have had to have been enough of a worker to stop at the sixth form for formal education ever to have mattered very much, being as she was as able as she was. I mean what's she going to do if she gets four O-levels - she's going to go- and work in a bank, so what, you know. She might as well be hairdressing, really.

Julie was aware of the traps that were around; indeed Lesley would have entered the female job market anyway, and Julie felt that there was actually something that the school could offer her, by supporting her through considering her particular situation. I met Lesley a year after she left school. She talked about readjustments she had made, when I showed her a transcript of an earlier interview. She focussed on marriage and children - she was now working as a secretary.

I must have grown up so much to realise that that's probably what's going to be in store for me anyway. You know, I'm not clever or anything ... and now I've not got any qualifications to say yeah I'm going to be managing director of such a firm ... I think you come down to earth a bit and you realise that you can only do so much, there's only so many opportunities open for you. I mean if I wanted to I suppose I could be a career girl, or whatever. I could go to nightschool for so many years, and learn whatever, but, you know, I'm quite happy as I am at the minute.

Lesley had a boyfriend, and was planning to set up a home with him, and this was quite important to her. But when I spoke to her three years later, the relationship had ended, she had got a new job in a large firm, and was fairly quickly promoted, to seemingly quite a responsible administrative position, which involved travelling etc. She enjoyed her job, exuded confidence, and was delighted about her new flat where she was living on her own.

Through determination she seemed to have got much nearer to the kind of situation she had described in her fifth year. I leave open what the role of the school was, including her tutor, who was able to take a personal interest in her, was able to get to know her, and able to adjust her strategies accordingly, in a way that might seem quite dangerous to those concerned with equal opportunities, labelling, self-fulfilling prophecies etc. But it is certain that the case of Lesley raises questions about what the possibilities and limitations of a progressive, flexible situation might be. It also indicates the importance of considering the scope for an approach which does not only develop curriculum initiatives, but includes relationships, styles of learning, indeed the whole ethos of the school. Hence the dissolution of the democratic structures as an integral part of that ethos further indicates that we are unable to discuss oppositional spaces without also discussing wider restructuring. But if we are to develop meaningful, broad and effective anti-sexist strategies, we must not ignore work that has been ongoing in schools, and we can usefully discuss the possibilities and limitations contained within progressive education. Despite the contradictions and tensions we need to suspend disbelief in order to develop our effectiveness.

## NOTES

1. This term was initially used by Donald (1978).
2. The name is invented, as are all the names of teachers and students.
3. See Ellis et al. (1976) and Gretton and Jackson (1976).
4. See Chisholm and Holland (1986) and Holland et al. (1985).
5. 'Sarah' also introduced the term 'tone of control' to me.

## REFERENCES

Barrett, M. (1980) Women's Oppression Today, London, Virago

———— and McIntosh, M. (1979) 'Christine Delphy: towards a materialist feminism', Feminist Review, 1

Bernstein, B. (1975) Class, Codes and Control, vol. 3, London, Routledge and Kegan Paul

Chisholm, L. and Holland, J. (1986) 'Girls and occupational choice: anti-sexism in action in a curriculum development project' in British Journal of Sociology of Education, vol. 7, no. 4

Dale, R. (1979) 'From endorsement to disintegration: progressive education from the Golden Age to the Green Paper' in British Journal of Educational Studies, vol. 27, no. 3, October

David, M. (1980) The State, the Family and Education, London, Routledge and Kegan Paul.

Davies, L. (1978) 'Deadlier than the male? Girls' conformity and deviance in school' in Barton, L. and Meighan, R. (eds) Schools, Pupils and Deviance, Nafferton, Nafferton Books

Deem, R. (ed.) (1980) Schooling for Women's Work, London, Routledge and Kegan Paul

———— (1978) Women and Schooling, London, Routledge and Kegan Paul

Donald, J. (1978) 'Media studies: possibilities and limitations', paper presented at the CSE (Conference of Socialist Economists) conference

Education Group, Centre for Contemporary Cultural Studies (1981) Unpopular Education, London, Hutchinson

Ellis, T. (et al.) (1976) William Tyndale: The Teachers' Story, London, Writers and Readers Publishing Cooperative

Gordon, T. (1986) Democracy in One School? Progressive Education and Restructuring, Barcombe, Falmer Press

———— (1985) 'Progressivism and the changing educational climate: a case study of a progressive school in Leicestershire', PhD thesis, University of London

Hartmann, H. (1979) 'The unhappy marriage of Marxism and feminism' Capital and Class, no. 8

Holland, J., Blackman, S.J., Gordon, T. and the teaching team (1985) 'A woman's place: strategies for change in the educational context', GAOC Working paper, no. 4, Sociological Research Unit, University of London Institute of Education.

Holloway, J. and Picciotto, S. (1977) Capital, crisis and the state', Capital and Class, no. 2, Summer

Jones, K. (1983) Beyond Progressive Education, London, Macmillan

Lahelma, E. and Viljanen, K. (1985) 'Report on equal opportunity work in Scandinavia' (in Finnish), Education Ministry, Helsinki.

London-Edinburgh Weekend Return Group (1980) In and Against the State, London, Pluto Press

Sharpe, R. (1976) Just Like a Girl: How Girls Learn to be Women, Harmondsworth, Penguin.

———— and Green, T. (1975) Education and Social Control, London, Routledge and Kegan Paul

Walkerdine, V. (1984) 'Some day my prince will come' in McRobbie, A. and Nava, M. (eds) Gender and Generation, London, Macmillan

Wolpe, A.M. (1978) 'Education and the sexual division of labour' in Kuhn, A. and Wolpe, A. M. (eds) Feminism and Materialism, London, Routledge and Kegan Paul

# 7

## Points and Posts: A Case Study of Teacher
## Careers in a Comprehensive School

### Robert G. Burgess

School teaching is often regarded as a female occupation. Certainly, there is evidence that large numbers of women have been recruited to teaching (cf. Deem 1978, Burgess 1986, Department of Education and Science 1983). But what positions do men and women hold in teaching? The picture is not easy as teaching is such a diverse occupation covering a variety of institutions and age ranges. Furthermore, teachers are divided by age, experience, qualifications and sex (Lacey, 1977; Sikes, Measor and Woods 1985). On this basis, sociologists have recently turned their attention to critically examining the stereotypes associated with the view that teaching is a female profession (Acker 1983; Kant, 1985; Davidson, 1985).

A major strand in this research has consisted of an analysis of teachers' lives and careers (Ball and Goodson 1985). Much of this research in Britain and the USA has relied heavily upon interviews in which teachers have reconstructed their career histories with the result that the presentation is static rather than dynamic. But these presentations of teacher careers are not placed in the context of discussions about posts, scale points, job interviews, employment opportunities, falling rolls and redeployment. In short, analyses that are currently available fail to come to terms with the dynamics of teachers' work and teachers' careers and the micro-political situations in which teachers are located. Part of the reason for the absence of these issues may be attributed to the research access which researchers have obtained in the course of conducting their studies. For example, in my first study of Bishop McGregor School my focus of interest was upon school organization and departmental activities rather than management strategies and patterns of staffing (Burgess

1983).

In part, my choice of focus was determined by the key issues that confronted the teachers in Bishop McGregor School in the 1970s. However, in the 1980s it is a very different story. During the period 1983-85, I have been engaged in a restudy of Bishop McGregor School. As with many schools in the 1980s Bishop McGregor faces a declining school roll, and with it comes the real possibility of redeployment for teachers. However, the school has also been designated a community college so that contraction on the 'school side' is, to some extent, offset by expansion through adult education classes. Finally, the Authority in which the school is located offers secondment to a proportion of teachers as a way of avoiding redeployment and ultimately redundancy. As a consequence of these activities teachers are confronted with temporary periods of promotion and demotion consequent upon the secondment and redeployment of their colleagues and the expansion of the community college.

Such developments have resulted in a range of research questions about management, about staffing and about teachers' jobs and careers. In part, this has influenced the focus of my second study which has involved studying teachers and teacher careers in a comprehensive school. The areas to which I have needed to gain access have included governors' meetings, meetings of school staff and sections of the staff, and teachers' job interviews. All of these areas of study have been examined using observation and participant observation which has been complemented by unstructured or conversational interviews with teachers (Burgess, 1988) and the collection of a vast array of documentary evidence including job advertisements, sets of further particulars, teachers' letters of application for posts and planning documents prepared by the senior management in the school.

The study has therefore looked at a range of teacher appointments with temporary posts, and permanent posts at all points in the Burnham scale in a large number of departments. Job appointments whether temporary or permanent cannot be seen in isolation but need to be examined in context. Accordingly, this paper focusses on one job appointment in the Physical Education Department. It is presented as an extended case study (Van Velsen, 1967) which is intended to assist our analysis of school structure and sets of relationships among teachers at Bishop

McGregor School. The data about a job interview in the PE Department is therefore presented in the context of other activities in the school. We begin by examining the school, and the staff in the PE Department before turning to a sequence of events which have been subdivided into the pre-interview phase, the interview and the post-interview phase. Accordingly, the ethnographic data that are presented are related to features of school organization and sets of formal and informal relationships between teachers. Finally, some explanation is offered of the social mechanisms at work in the process of this staff appointment based on the ethnographic material presented in this case study.

## THE CASE STUDY SCHOOL

When Bishop McGregor School was first studied in the 1970s it was in a period of expansion for both staff and pupils but in the 1980s falling rolls have resulted in some contraction which has been offset to some extent by the development of adult education courses and classes. Many teachers are now evaluating their career options in the context of strategies that are being developed by the head and his senior management team. In Bishop McGregor School it is now common to find teachers considering the possibility of secondment, redeployment and promotion on a temporary or a permanent basis. Many of these options are presented alongside each other and therefore we need to consider how teachers perceive their career opportunities in this changing context. For the purpose of this analysis I want to examine the Physical Education Department at Bishop McGregor School which in the summer term 1985 was faced with the redeployment of one teacher and the secondment of another which both gave rise to temporary promotion prospects for other members of the Department. In presenting ethno-graphic data on this situation we focus on some of the social mechanisms and social processes involved which hold implications for our understanding of the structure and relationships within this secondary school and the way in which teacher appointments are conducted.

## THE PHYSICAL EDUCATION DEPARTMENT

At Bishop McGregor School the PE Department was subdivided in terms of boys' PE and girls' PE and given the way in which appointments had occurred there was no longer an equal number of points given to staff. At the start of the summer term the staff members were as shown in table 7.1.

**Table 7.1: Physical Education Staff at Bishop McGregor School**

| Name | Scale post | Responsibility (if any) | Years of teaching | Other information |
|------|------|------|------|------|
| Terry Dean | 4 | Head of boys' PE & community sport | 12 | |
| Kay Stokes | 3 | Head of girls' PE | 10 | |
| Paul Healey | 2 | Second in charge of boys' PE | 8 | Previously held scale 3 for pastoral & acting HOD |
| Roy Cooksley | 2 | Pastoral care | 8 | Seconded in 1985/86 |
| Pat Swift | 1 | | $7\frac{1}{2}$ | Returned from maternity leave |
| Colin Burden | 1 | | 5 | Previously temp. scale 2 |
| Jane Whaley | 1 | | 2 | |

In the previous academic year 1983-4, both heads of departments had been on secondment after which the head of boys' PE had successfully obtained a further scale post of responsibility to be head of community sport. Automatically this had implications for the points allocated to Paul Healey as he had held a temporary scale 3 post as the person temporarily in charge of the boys' PE Department and so he returned to a permanent scale 2 post. However, the Department was not required to shed staff in 1983-4 as it

125

was evident that the community involvement would support the staff complement. Indeed, this was the case as far as boys' PE was concerned at the end of 1985, but the same could not be said of girls' PE where the decline in pupil numbers meant fewer lessons and as a result someone would have to leave. Here, it was thought by senior management and for that matter several other staff that Tricia Swift who had been on maternity leave would either not return to school or return only on a part-time basis. As Tricia realised that assumptions were being made about her future plans she went to see the head but as she explained:

> I think he was very surprised. I felt sure that he'd expected me, when I said I was coming in to see him to say I wish to resign or I would like part-time. When I'd said that I decided I'm happy, I like working, suits me fine, I want to stay for a time, I thought I'd come and let you know my decision, he seemed taken aback, quite surprised and he suggested ... he said something like ... anybody man or woman who puts their career before their family was a rather dangerous person to have around.

She continued:

> He covered himself very cleverly by saying man or woman to which I questioned ... I said, 'man or woman do you really believe that?' And he said 'yes' which to me was quite a strong indication that he was suggesting I was doing the wrong thing in his eyes. Although he didn't say as much but, I mean, they [the senior management] word things rather cleverly to you. The intimation is there.

As we shall see later this decision not only had implications for staffing but also came into direct consideration when staff appointments were made in the department later in the term. Gender relations were, therefore, to play a significant role in staffing strategies in the Department during the term.

The result of Tricia's decision to stay as a permanent member of staff meant that someone would have to be redeployed from girls' PE before the end of term. Meanwhile, in the boys' PE Department Roy Cooksley discovered that he had obtained a place to study for a degree during a period of secondment. As a consequence a temporary scale post would be available but not just among the staff in the boys' department but among all PE staff. Redeployment and promotion were therefore a reality for all the women PE staff, while temporary promotion was available for two of the male PE staff (Paul Healey and Colin Burden). It is with this situation that we are concerned as an analysis can help us to understand the constraints in which teachers operate through a portrayal of an interview and the events that surround it. The post was widely regarded among staff as 'Colin's post' as it was known that he had done much work in the school, was liked by the head and considered by his peers to be worthy of promotion from scale 1 to scale 2. We shall, therefore, examine the pre-interview, interview and post-interview phases of Colin's post.

## THE CASE OF COLIN'S POST

### (a) The Pre-Interview Phase

When it was known by Terry Dean (the Head of Boys' PE) that Roy Cooksley was going on secondment he started to make suggestions to the head about the ways in which work could be reorganised in the Department. In particular he suggested that Paul Healey's scale 2 post should be extended to take in work on outdoor pursuits that would replace his pastoral responsibility as this would 'leave the [scale] 2 that would go hopefully to Colin to develop other areas, i.e. community'. It was this plan that Terry had worked out with Colin and with the head as he saw this as an opportunity for Colin to redevelop community sports teams. However, Terry had found that the head was:

> Well, cagey as usual. You see the post, because of the union business, has got to be advertised in such a way that it doesn't look as though it's sort of clear cut for somebody, stuff like that, so that opens it out really. I mean, even then having said that I think it'll be a post that four people in the PE department would be able to go for, so, well that will be Paul and Colin on the boys' side and Tricia and Jane on the girls' side. When I first spoke to the head I mean he intimated to me that

127

when I was pushing hard for Colin to get a permanent 2 he said, well, he would say to me he thought he would get Roy's 2, but only for one year. So if you want me to predict I think that Colin will get that point for the next year but if he doesn't I'll certainly have strong words I think because you know he more than anybody else deserves it.

At this stage in my discussion with Terry it was apparent that he wanted the post to be provided for community sport. However, he thought there was a danger that the head would advertise it as outdoor pursuits but this would then mean the post could go to Paul. Nevertheless Terry argued that 'Much as perhaps Paul deserves a 3, Colin deserves a 2 more. That's the situation.' On this basis, Terry was only considering male PE teachers so I asked: 'What about all the girls' PE staff?' to which Terry replied:

Well you've got Jane who's just ... this is only her second year teaching, so I mean even at the best of times you wouldn't expect to get a scale point in less than two years. I think you'd have to go back about fifteen years for that sort of thing to have happened to get a scale 2 after one year. That's eight or ten years to get it up to 2, unless you just happen to be in the right place at the right time. In Tricia's case well, yes she would fit the bill 'cause she's been teaching quite a long time. I suppose what the head would have to decide is how committed she is now that she's got a family.

With the introduction of Tricia's family into our discussion I decided to ask why he included this issue in his deliberations so I said:

Why don't we ask those questions of the men? I mean you've got a family so why shouldn't we be asking...

However, I was not allowed to finish as Terry, who had been reclining on his chair with a foot nonchalantly placed on the coffee table quickly sat up straight and said:

TD  Well, absolutely yes. Oh, no, I mean like I say, that's ... the only reason I say that is because I think that Tricia said that when she had the baby she would prefer to come back in a part-time capacity. She actually stated that. Now when it came to the reason that she's now elected to come back full-time is because there were problems over redeployment and things and it would ... or not so much redeployment as ... let me get it right ... if she came back part-time, she would offer less on the extra curricula.

RB  Oh, I see.

TD  Right?

RB  Yes.

TD  When you've got as much as we like to do and you've only got two point something that puts an awful lot of work on the two full-timers, so it was better from the girls' side if she came back full-time. It was also something to do with redeployment as well, I'm trying to work out what it was now. Oh, I know, yes, the action. The girls [by which he means women] on the girls' PE side because of the amount that they teach outside the department is less, they really can only have 2.7 teachers or something like that would be ideal from the timetabling point of view. So if she, if Tricia came back on a .7 that would have suited the timetable perfectly. There was ... I can't remember the exact details now, there was some business over ... it was the redeployment issue. I can't really remember what it was now in the finer details but the crux of the matter was at the end of the day was that in view of all this going on, Tricia herself didn't know, she, I mean the baby was only a matter of weeks old. She didn't know how she was going to be able to cope. If she finds that she can cope, adequately, without any problems, then obviously she would be a strong candidate. If she found that having a family was more stressful and that she couldn't manage to put in the commitment or whatever, then it might be a

129

different matter. But those are things I suppose that the head would have to make his mind up about. But in terms of the balance yes, I quite agree that the balance should be, there should be an equal balance, a more similar balance between girls and boys.

Clearly, in Terry's mind 'commitment' was a clear criterion involved in the post but where women were concerned this involved considering family commitments - a factor which he never raised in relation to the men. In addition, it appeared that not only Tricia but also Tricia's baby would have to be considered for the post if she decided to apply.

While the head was being seen by the head of boys' PE with a view to gaining Colin the post, the head of girls' PE and her staff were being seen about redeployment by the head and an adviser. In these circumstances the head of girls' PE advised her staff to apply for the scale post that was available and decided that she would opt for redeployment; a situation that resulted in a further point being available for girls' PE that could be used internally. As a consequence both the women candidates had an opportunity to obtain scale points or to obtain two points. However, as we shall see this was effectively blocked by Phil Barlow, a Deputy Head in the school who sat in on the interviews in place of the head.

## (b) The Interview

The interview for the additional scale point for an aspect of Physical Education that had become available through Roy's secondment took place in the head's office. Four candidates were to be called for interview (Paul, Colin, Tricia and Jane). Both heads of departments were asked to present their views of the candidates in writing to the head who circulated the information to the interview panel. Both heads of department submitted two handwritten pages of comments on the candidates. However, Kay Stokes evaluated all the candidates arguing the case for each of them being given an additional point but concluded that on the basis that Tricia's knowledge and commitment needed to be put to the test this one year temporary post would be suitable as she stated:

As the post is for one year only, I would like to see

Tricia given the opportunity to show us and herself what she can do.

Meanwhile, Terry Dean only compared the two men for the post and concluded:

Both members of staff deserve recognition for the work they have done and are prepared to do but on balance and after great consideration I feel Mr Burden deserves a scale 2 post more than Mr Healey a scale 3 in this particular situation.

It was this information together with a reference for Mr Healey that was circulated to the interview panel.

The interview panel consisted of three school governors, Phil Barlow (a Deputy Head who was replacing the head) and an adviser. However, it was only two minutes before the interviews were due to start that an adviser arrived. He had no expertise in Physical Education, had no idea what kind of post he was due to interview for and had yet to read the papers. The Deputy Head provided a set of papers and gave some background by saying:

We are interviewing for a PE post due to Roy Cooksley's secondment.

The adviser listened to the procedures that had been adopted in the school and said that he would try and sort things out as he went along. As the governors wished to see another teacher he had five minutes to sit and 'read' the papers. At this point Phil Barlow provided a summary from the heads of department by saying:

Kay Stokes says all the PE candidates are good. She thinks Jane Whaley is inexperienced, but would like to see Tricia Swift get something. She thinks Paul Healey and Colin Burden are good, and Terry Dean says that Colin Burden and Paul Healey will be good but that Colin Burden is better as Paul does not get on well with the staff.

Governor   Why?

PB   He is a very good Catholic and does not like some of the things that go on.

With these comments the interviews began with each candidate being given twenty minutes to face questions from each governor, from the adviser and the Deputy Head. Here, similar questions were asked of the candidates with the adviser asking an identical question on the teaching of physical education to mixed classes. At the end of the interviews the discussion began:

Governor    A point of responsibility for an area or activity. I would throw out the two girls [by which he means women] not because I'm a male chauvinist pig but because they are vague.

Adviser    I thought Mrs Swift performed best. I thought one of the men rambled and the other I had doubts about in terms of his relationships. The third person was far too general. Mrs Swift I thought was good.

Governor    I think that she was too vague.

Adviser    I thought Mrs Swift had a wide vision while the others were too narrow. Has she got a good reputation?

At this point, there was no reply. The Deputy Head said he was unimpressed by Jane Whaley and Colin Burden and then commented:

> Tricia - I thought there was little evidence of commitment. Nothing came out as an actual idea. The answers weren't her ideas. There was nothing coming from her.

Having demolished her case that was being advanced by the adviser, he turned to promote the case of Paul Healey who he argued had broad experience, enthusiasm and involved many pupils in outdoor activities. However, when the adviser promoted Tricia Swift's case again the Deputy Head remarked:

> The women will get a chance at another post. Jane Whaley is out so I think it's between the two men

but the boss thinks Paul Healey is good.

With this remark, Paul Healey was proposed for the appointment and given the post.

## THE POST-INTERVIEW PERIOD

During the course of that morning the group who had been involved in these interviews continued with similar tasks for other subject areas before they returned to consider staffing in physical education. The Deputy Head outlined how they now had two scale 1 teachers in girls' PE and a Head of Department was required on either a permanent or a temporary basis. However, when Tricia Swift's name was mentioned there was some division among the governors about whether she should be given the post. Here, it became essential for the adviser to indicate that the post should be advertised, whether it was to be permanent or temporary. At this point, the Deputy Head came in again with the view that the post should be advertised but he remarked:

> I would agree that we need a Head of Girls' PE but
> I do not agree that we need Tricia. She recently
> had a young baby boy and she wasn't thinking of
> carrying on but she has obviously changed her
> mind.

The comment met with no response from the group but was potentially damning having been made in front of the group who could be interviewing Tricia Swift in just under a week.

During this time post-interview discussions also occurred in the staff common room and in the local pub where I am told teachers who were meeting for a lunch time drink had greeted the news of Paul's appointment with some horror as they had always perceived this post as 'Colin's job'.

The following week, which was the final week of the summer term, resulted in continuing debate both formally and informally. Successful and unsuccessful alike made requests to see the Head to demand some explanation about what had occurred on the previous Friday. Staff expressed surprise to me about the result of the interview as many considered it to have been 'Colin's job'.

Even Paul Healey recognised that Colin was 'bitterly disappointed' - a point which was self-evident by mid-week as Colin had persuaded the Common Room Association to call a special meeting at which he and Tricia were particularly prominent. It was Colin who demanded that:

(a) the Head should in future be present at all interviews.
(b) heads of department should be present at all interviews in their subject area.
(c) whenever possible specialist advisers should be involved in the appointment of staff.

While these views were shared by the majority of staff for onward transmission to the Head they were not unanimously agreed upon. For example, Paul Healey considered that he had been in direct competition with other members of the department and had obtained the point on the basis of making the best case.

However, this was not a view shared by Colin who argued that he would not be doing as much work as he would only have a scale 1 post compared with Paul's temporary scale 3. It was this situation which he summed up by saying:

> I mean I look at it from the point of view, Paul's three times a better teacher than me so he can work three times as hard. I'm bitter, I really am. I'm not deriding him. I'm just, you know, I'm good enough to think I could do a reasonable job because when I am on form and things are going right I do get quite a buzz out of it. I'm not the world's most gifted teacher by a long chalk but I do get quite a buzz out of things. But you know my buzz, so to speak, isn't exactly kindled by the fact that I'm not getting on here.

Yet, while Colin was disappointed, Tricia expressed no surprise at what had happened despite the fact that she had had a good interview. She had previously seen the Head the day before the interviews who had told her that a scale 2 post would be available in girls' PE. She explained:

> I asked him 'well what about these interviews tomorrow?' because he hinted that Jane and I would be able to apply for Kay's scale point. So I said 'What am I going to do tomorrow for a point?' and he said that I was to interview as normal and to give it my best shot and that if I didn't get it, I would know that the other was in line.

134

RB    I see, what was your reaction to this?

TS    Well my reaction to this was that he was virtually
      telling me I'm not going to get it but at the same
      time he was telling me there was a fairly strong
      chance that I will get the 'in charge of girls' PE' so
      I went into the interview thinking it was a big
      waste of time.

For Tricia, the second interview resulted in success as she
was given a temporary scale 2 post - temporary for one
term so that the governors could review her progress later
in the year. However, Colin found that no points were found
in PE that he could apply for over a further eight months.
During this time, some senior staff persuaded him to chair
the Common Room Association as they saw this as a means
of diverting his energies. However, Colin used his position at
the Christmas Social to comment on what had occurred. In
his speech summing up the end of term he announced 'And
wait for it folks. Next term there is to be a scale 2 post for
getting people to queue up at the pool table. I've already
prepared my cv' as he threw a bundle of paper at the feet of
the visibly embarrassed Head.

## DISCUSSION AND CONCLUSION

As Connell (1985) has recently remarked teachers are aware
that there are inequalities between men and women
teachers; that women are underrepresented in positions of
power, have unequal access to posts, suffer discrimination
and are allocated to subordinate positions. Certainly, some
óf these themes have arisen in the presentation of this case
study of a staff appointment in the Physical Education
Department in Bishop McGregor School. In particular the
data draw attention to such issues as gender inequality,
staff/management relations and staffing strategies.
    While these data focus our attention on the Physical
Education Department it also illustrates the way in which
the apppointment brings together the staff as a collectivity
to challenge the governors, the advisory staff and the senior
management team. In turn, the data provide further
evidence of a rift in the management team between those
who gave support for the school and those who supported the
community (Burgess 1986b). Here, the school/community
distinction was expressed by the way in which one Deputy

supported the appointment that was made, while the Community Deputy would have supported Colin's appointment as a means of reinforcing his own position. Secondly, the manipulative strategies of the Deputy Head on the governors' appointments committee highlights elements of overt and indirect sex discrimination by raising doubts and making assumptions about a woman candidate (cf. Byrne, 1978; Kant, 1985; Davidson, 1985). Indeed, this Deputy highlighted and used gender divisions and reinforced patriarchal relationships when portraying an image of Tricia as a mother with a baby when the governors were deciding on this appointment. Here, the power and influence of Catholicism is also involved with women being cast in the role of wives and mothers. Furthermore, the way in which Paul was defined as 'a good Catholic' provided a positive image for the governors in considering him for a scale post. Indeed, one teacher cryptically referred to such teachers as 'scale Catholics' which was defined as someone who 'swings the rosary beads about and makes much of his or her Catholicism'.

Such evidence points to inequalities in the appointment of teachers; especially as far as gender is concerned. In a competitive job market women are able to leave teaching for a statutory period of maternity leave before returning to their protected job. But we need to explore how far maternity leave can be used against women (cf. Kant 1985); secondly, how domestic and family commitments are used when considering women's rather than men's appointments (Sikes, Measor and Woods 1985); finally, how women have to overcome overt and indirect forms of discrimination in the all too common situation where men control appointments ánd act as brokers and gatekeepers on behalf of other male teachers (Equal Opportunities Commission 1983).

Such evidence raises several implications for those engaged in staff appointments. First, they need to consider that all appointments are genuinely available to men and women candidates. Secondly, they need to look at the way in which equal opportunities policies are implemented, for this school was located in an authority with an equal opportunities policy. Thirdly, job descriptions should be defined without considering the domestic commitments of candidates. Fourthly, the balance of appointment committees needs to be considered in terms of gender and expertise. Finally, self-critical evaluation is required so that the members of appointments committees begin to understand their own use of 'power' and 'control' in allocating points and posts in comprehensive schools at a time of increased competition for posts, declining resources, low morale and increased control of teachers in the latter part of the twentieth century.

## ACKNOWLEDGEMENTS

Earlier versions of this paper were presented at the British Educational Research Association's conference entitled 'Comprehensive Education in the 1980s' held at the Centre for Educational Studies, Kings College, University of London in February 1986 and at a seminar in the Division of Education, University of Sheffield in November 1986. I am grateful to the seminar participants and to Stephen Ball, Hilary Burgess, Janet Finch, Tony Green, David Hamilton and Gaby Weiner for their comments that have been used in revising this material. I would also like to thank the Nuffield Foundation and the University of Warwick Research Innovations Fund Committee, who supported the restudy of Bishop McGregor School.

## REFERENCES

Acker, S. (1983) 'Women and teaching: a semi-detached sociology of a semi-profession', in Walker, S. and Barton, L. (eds) Gender, Class and Education, Lewes, Falmer Press, pp. 123-139.

Ball, S.J. and Goodson, I.F. (eds) (1985) Teacher Careers and Life Histories, Lewes, Falmer Press

Burgess, R.G. (1983) Experiencing Comprehensive Education: A Study of Bishop McGregor School, London, Methuen.

———— (1986a) Sociology, Education and Schools: An Introduction to the Sociology of Education, London, Batsford.

———— (1986b) 'School and community: it's so close together you can't see the join' in Journal of Community Education, vol. 5, no. 2, pp. 5-9.

———— (1988) 'Conversations with a purpose: the ethnographic interview in educational research' in Burgess, R.G. (ed.) Conducting Qualitative Research: Studies in Qualitative Methodology Volume I, New York, JAI Press.

Byrne, E. (1978) Women and Education, London, Tavistock.

Connell, R.W. (1985) Teachers' Work, London, Allen & Unwin.

Davidson, H. (1985) 'Unfriendly myths about women teachers' in Whyte, J. et al. Girl Friendly Schooling, London, Methuen, pp. 191-208.

Deem, R. (1978) Women and Schooling, London, Routledge and Kegan Paul.

Department of Education and Science (1983) Statistics of Teachers in Service in England and Wales, London, HMSO.

Equal Opportunities Commission (1983) Formal Investigation Report: Sidney Stringer School and Community College, Manchester, Equal Opportunities Commission.

Kant, L. (1985) 'A question of judgement' in Whyte, J. et al. (eds) Girl Friendly Schooling, London, Methuen, pp. 166-190.

Lacey, C. (1977) The Socialization of Teachers, London, Methuen.

Sikes, P., Measor, L. and Woods, P. (1985) Teacher Careers: Crises and Continuities, Lewes, Falmer Press.

Van Velsen, J. (1967) 'The extended case method and situational analysis', in Epstein, A.L. (ed.) The Craft of Social Anthropology, London, Tavistock, pp. 129-149.

# 8

## Home-School Relations

### Miriam David

## INTRODUCTION

Relations between families and schools obviously underpin any education system. Secondary state education in England is no exception. Although talk of parent-school relations dominates popular discourse, curiously the analysis of these relations for their implications for men and women's lives both separately and together has rarely been explored. In this paper, I want to tease out some aspects of the complexity from a feminist perspective. I take a feminist perspective to be to make sexual divisions visible and to analyse such from the 'standpoint of women', as well as men or apparently genderless people (Smith, 1979). I shall look at both the formal organisation of parent-school relations around the notion of 'parental participation' and at the development of courses in 'education for family life'. Both of these issues have been central to the debate about how to implement equality of educational opportunity, particularly through comprehensive, secondary education. However, the focus of the debate has not been on sexual equality but rather on socio-economic equality. The result has not been very different from the status quo, from a feminist point of view.

A lot of change has taken place over both parent participation and parent education over the last 20 years, but it has been within a particular and, I would argue, narrow, frame of reference. Although aimed at different objectives, the effect has tended to be to reinforce rather than modify sexual divisions both within the privacy of the family at home and in the public world of school and work. The unpaid work of women as mothers has been made more explicit and codified. Indeed, the elaboration of parent-school relations has begun to restrict mothers' activities in other spheres, particularly making the combination of paid and unpaid work more problematic to negotiate especially for working class women, confining them more to the home.

## PARENTAL INVOLVEMENT

The ideology that has informed the organisation of state secondary education, since it origins in the 1944 Education Act, has been that of equality of educational opportunity. Equality has been taken to mean social equality, that is providing educational opportunities to reduce the evident inequalities between children from different social class or home backgrounds. The aim of equalising educational opportunities has changed and not been merely social but also economic: to allow children of different social backgrounds access to forms of paid employment, on the basis of intellectual merit or ability, irrespective of social class, and parental income. During the period of implementing the goal of equality of educational opportunity there was a shift from equality of access to education, irrespective of social background, to equality of outcome or achievement; ensuring equal job opportunities. In its original specification, sexual inequalities in educational opportunities were ignored. In the last 15 years or so, sexual inequalities have given more cause for concern. But given the changing notion of equality of educational opportunity this has had some problematic effects on girls' opportunities. Ignoring sexual inequalities, or adopting a 'sex-blind' approach had the effect of opening up educational opportunities for some 'able' girls. But the objective of equal employment opportunities could never be realised in the same measure as for boys, given the different forms of 'occupation' expected of girls in adulthood. This dilemma remains for the pursuit of social and sexual equality of educational opportunity, as joint aims.

An even greater dilemma, from a feminist perspective, has been the changing notions of how to achieve social equality of educational opportunity. In its origins there was a wide party political consensus on the aim; signalled in the fact that a coalition government of Tories and Labour devised the 1944 Education Act, widely acclaimed as the legal and social framework for the post-war education system. The simplest notion was that compulsory education, for children from 5-15 years old, should be 'free', irrespective of parental income or means. But parents had no obligation to send children to school; they could 'choose' to educate them at home. As the aim was implemented, over the next twenty years, a divergence of views about actual strategy developed (Marsden, 1971; Benn and Simon, 1972). Nevertheless, the differences remained framed within certain assumptions about parent-school relations and the extent to which these could be modified (David, 1980). It was around the form of partnership between parents and schools that the debate developed. In that debate, as with the original specification, the term parent remained genderless. The family was a kind of black box, unopened and apparently unknown. In any event the original view of the parental role revolved around a 'political' and 'economic' theory of parents as citizens, around their rights and duties towards their own children. In practice, but not in theory, the activities of parents tended to be gendered, with fathers as 'authority-figures' and mothers as housewives and carers.

The changes to that role, proposed in the sixties, by the Labour party centred more on social and psychological, rather than political theories. Throughout the fifties, through official reports and research studies, evidence was accumulated of the nature and characteristics of child development and socialisation (CACE, 1954; 1959; 1963; CCCS, 1981). The theory of parents' crucial role in child socialisation began to gain ground (Craft et al., 1972). Applying this to the organisation of education around equality of opportunity, the notion of parental involvement and parental participation was applied to early childhood education and primary education (David, 1980). It reached its apotheosis in the Plowden Report entitled Children and Their Primary Schools (1967), and was translated into practice through both the Educational Priority Area (EPA) strategies and general prescriptions for early childhood education (Halsey, 1972).

It was accepted that young children's learning could be enhanced by their parents' involvement and interest in their schooling. Teachers were encouraged to involve parents in their own children's progress. More particularly, parents were to be used to achieve equality of educational opportunity (Craft et al., 1972). Dissonance between home and school rather than parental means or income, came to be seen as the major obstacle to reducing inequalities. 'Teaching' parents how to support their children's educational progress became a major objective. Parental involvement in the classroom was an easy and readily available solution, in addition to the creation of educational home visiting schemes in certain areas (Hasley et al., 1972). In this latter case, education social workers would visit parents in their home to help them 'learn' how to become more involved in their children's learning. In other words, a particular parental role at home was assumed to be a necessary prerequisite for adequate parental involvement at school. Bernstein's critique of the notion of 'compensatory education' as a solution to equality of educational opportunity is now a classic, although his emphasis was on the inadequacy of the concept of social class, defined through home background, rather than on the parental role per se (1970, pp. 344-7).

Despite these early criticisms that 'education cannot compensate for society', the notion of parental involvement was applied vigorously to all levels of compulsory education (Raynor & Harden, 1973). In secondary education, the concept was rather modifed and came to be understood not as daily involvement but as parental support of the school, through activities such as the PTA as well as interest in their own child's academic achievement.

Throughout these debates, the notion of parent remained genderless and derived from theories of child socialisation and political participation that themselves apparently were 'sex-blind'. The criticisms, too, ignored the question of gender. Nevertheless, in practice, the strategies relied more on maternal than paternal involvement. In particular, parental participation in classroom activities became mothers' 'work', but even in PTAs, organised outside of the regular hours of school or work, mothers predominated although not necessarily holding the key positions of influence. By the end of the sixties, parent-school relations in compulsory education were based not just on an assumption of a partnership between the family and education, but also on a prescribed set of activities for parents. These activities entailed a redefinition of mothers' 'work' with their children, from providing the physical and emotional 'care' necessary to sustain them at school to providing what amounted to educational 'work' in concert with the school (Smith, 1984). Indeed, with the increases in this 'work', women's role was slowly changed from that of housewife to 'first educator' (David, 1984). Both before the start of compulsory education and whilst children attended primary schools, mothers were increasingly expected to 'educate' their children and complement teachers' work in school. Indeed, there has been a massive growth in consumer goods to aid this (New and David, 1985). In other words, there has been a growing shift from 'care' to 'education' not only in institutional terms, but also in mothers' role. This is perhaps best illustrated by the change from mothers being at home to welcome the children back from school, to mothers handing their children over to the teacher or at the school playground and being at the school gate to receive the children back into their direct care (David, 1985).

This shift has not been so dramatic for secondary education but it has its parallels and implications, both in terms of the organisation and curriculum. In particular, mothers have been expected to ensure adequate standards of behaviour of their children even at secondary school (David, 1984). The curriculum, too, has focussed more directly on differential adult activities for men and women, particularly with respect to child care (a point to which we will return).

In any event, although the initial theory was aimed at using parents to achieve equality of educational opportunity, in fact that aim was blurred as parents began to recognise the possibilities for their active involvement. Middle class parents began to demand their own opportunities to 'help with the school'. They themselves were arguably an 'untapped pool of ability' (the language used to justify the initial developments in strategies to transform equality of opportunity). Teachers recognised this potential and began to 'choose' not just parents in need of advice and support but those with 'skills' that were commensurate with the needs of the classroom. Such parents quickly learnt about the character of educational politics through their intimate involvement and used this knowledge as a basis for developing further strategies to increase the part that they could play in the education system.

At the same time, the concept of parental choice was also being revised. This concept was seen as more directly related to secondary education and to the transition from primary to secondary education. Throughout the fifties, the concept was used narrowly and specifically in the context of a tripartite system of secondary education. The Education Act had proposed that local education authorities provide schools 'sufficient in number' to suit the 'ages, aptitudes and abilities' of their children and to ensure a measure of parental choice. Although the system of secondary education was not legally enjoined, the vast majority of LEAs developed systems of selective secondary education.

This provided grammar schools for the most 'able' twenty percent or so and either secondary technical schools for the next five percent and secondary moderns for the rest (making a tripartite system) or secondary moderns for the rest. (In fact, only 52 of the 308 LEAs went tripartite, not bipartite.) Parental choice came to mean being able to 'choose' a grammar school for one's child. This ignored the fact that the child had, as a prerequisite, to pass an examination of educational achievement at age 11 to enable her or him to be selected. The secondary modern schools became known as non-selective. But, nevertheless, parental choice came to be seen as virtually an 'inalienable right' of parents at the age of transition to secondary schools. In practice, this right was only fully exercised in the larger towns and cities where there was more than one grammar school. Even then, access to direct grant grammar schools was a function as much of a child's academic ability as parental choice.

Comprehensive secondary education developed by the Labour government was another attempt to achieve equality of educational opportunity, by means of delaying the point at which parents and children are chosen for particular kinds of education. This reduced the need for parental choice, although it was not vitiated altogether. Given the 6 different schemes of secondary reorganisation suggested by the newly elected Labour government the potentialities for parental choice seemed infinite (David, 1977). Yet it was no longer a 'choice' between selective and non-selective education. Apart from schemes of 'guided parental choice', such as in Kent, the choices were between schools based on different mixes of pupils - levels of ability, social class, proximity or ages, etc. Indeed, parental choice itself became a major reason for criticising the system of comprehensive education. An Enabling Act of 1968 was passed to redefine the whole notion. But in this, as in the previous ones, there was no exploration of gender. It remained a notion expressed entirely in terms of political rights. The Act merely suggested a procedural review for the process of ensuring that parental choice had been given expression. Most important, parental objections to reorganisation schemes could be considered in the planning process (David, 1977). No consideration was given, however, to the impact of such changes on the daily lives of mothers and fathers, or their daughters or sons. The administrative language remained that of parents and school as corporate entities or institutions. In practice, however, maternal duties were subtly and slowly being modified alongside of the development of parental rights.

In the early seventies, however, parental choice was used by the Conservative government as a subtle means of delaying the process of secondary reorganisation on comprehensive lines. A number of Conservative LEAs had not responded to the 'request' of successive Labour administrations to plan comprehensive education. Parental choice became the raison d'etre for this laggardliness, legitimated by a Conservative administration (David, 1980).

The new Labour administration of 1974 responded to this situation by pursuing a more determined policy of comprehensive education for those few 'recalcitrant' LEAs. But it was 'parental participation' rather than 'parental choice' as indicative of the relation between families and schools that was once again a cornerstone of policy development. This time, the language of citizens' rights and political participation as a form of democracy began to be reasserted. The debate centred not just on how to get parents to be more involved with their children's individual educational achievement, but with educational decision-making. A central plank of the Labour government's educational policy was how to reorganise school decision-making in the interests of greater local democracy. To this end, the Taylor Committee was set up, in 1975 to review the government and management of state schools. Their recommendations for a more streamlined system of school government focussed on the role of the parent governor (Department of Education and Science, 1977). The argument had been transformed from how to achieve individual equality of educational opportunity, by means of parental involvement, to achieving a more 'accountable' school system to the parents (Bacon, 1978). Parents had come to be seen as the key 'consumers' or 'clients' of the education system, entitled thereby to a 'greater say' in how their child's school was run and managed. The parent was no longer simply to be controlled by the teacher; rather teachers were to be controlled by the parent, in concert with other 'lay' political representatives (David, 1978a). The parent governor was to become the representative of the parental voice at the school level. The changes were argued for in part because of changing political theories of participation and in part as a result of the experiences of greater parental involvement. The argument of parental participation as a political right

145

drew its strength from the actual activities of parents. Again, although couched in gender-neutral language, the aim was to tap the resources of parents who had indeed learned the lessons of parental involvement, through their own efforts. A particularly stark instance of this could be found in the William Tyndale dispute at an inner London primary school (David, 1978). Here parental involvement led to a conflict between teachers and parents over the running and curricula offer of the school. It was indeed the middle class mothers of the children in the school that argued the case most vociferously.

Curiously, however, these arguments revolved chiefly around the questions of procedure and decision-making rather than the content of the curriculum. As a result, there was a broad political consensus on redefining a role for parents in education. Indeed, the Taylor committee's recommendations were incorporated into Labour's draft Education Bill. In that form, the bill never reached the statute books because Labour was defeated at the 1979 General Election. But the incoming Conservative administration did not question this or the refinement of 'parental choice' into a gentler notion of 'parental preference'. In this respect, parents' 'say' in schooling was to be confined to representative membership of a school governing body, rather than choice of school. Parental 'preference' for a school had to be acknowledged but not necessarily adhered to: and this was incorporated into the new Education Act, 1980. On the other hand, a system of appeal against these individual decisions was developed, legalising the process of educational decision making. The language of political rights had assumed a much greater place in the educational process (Bull, 1983).

On the other hand, the original aim of using parents differentially to ensure equality of educational opportunity had been completely lost sight of. In an unequal education system, if all parents, regardless of socio-economic background are given equal rights, social inequality remains untouched. A situation of what Stuart Hall has called 'an educational (super)market' has, in fact, been created, superimposed on a pre-existing unequal education system (Hall, 1984).

This scheme has similarly been pursued for special education as for compulsory education (Barton & Tomlinson, 1985). In the Education (No 2) Act of 1986, the role of parent governors has been further extended and given greater importance as the voice of the consumer. Parent governors will no longer be a small minority but a significant group on every school's governing body, in proportion to the size of the school.

At the same time as affording parents more rights over state education, the system itself has been severely eroded not only through policy change but through a reduction of resources to finance such education. Successive HMI reports have documented the extent to which the effect has been to increase, rather than decrease, inequality of opportunity (1984, 1985). The most recent proposals for a shift of resources in secondary education from the state-maintained system to that of the individual school, through the creation of 'city technology colleges' financed in part by industry and in part by grants from central government aims to restore a system that was abolished in the interests of greater equality of opportunity. Both the state maintained tripartite system and direct-grant grammar schools were abandoned to reduce parental privilege on the basis of parental choice. Reintroducing parental choice to the city secondary schools, in the form proposed, can only divert resources from the state system and again privilege those already privileged parents who are able to 'choose' such schools.

Similarly, the idea of parental participation has become incorporated into policy proposals and practices, but in such a way as to be far from the original aim of equality of educational opportunity. For instance, the Inner London Education Authority commissioned a series of studies of the state of their education. The Hargreaves Report, entitled Improving Secondary Schools (1984), is particularly committed to using parental involvement as a means of improving education. The terms of reference were to investigate specifically 'pupils who are underachieving' and, later, working class pupils (p. 1). The report acknowledges by way of introduction the difficulty of suggesting any improvement without consideration of the teacher/parent partnership (p. 14). It goes on, 'if we want children to achieve more, especially working class children, then improved home-school liaison and increased parental involvement must be a top priority. Cooperative home-school relations will enhance everything the school does ...' (loc. cit.). To achieve this they recommend not only increases in the number of representative parent governors, but also tutor group parents' associations and a home-school council (p. 20).

Although the report recognises the centrality of home-

147

school relations to the success of any system of secondary education, it does not grapple with the problems that this entails in terms of implementation within the present context. Indeed, it dismisses this with the disclaimer that:

> there is very little the school can do towards removing poverty or improving the adverse social conditions in which many such parents live.

In other words, the original hopes that equality of educational opportunity could and would reduce social and economic inequalities have now been shifted off the agenda, even of Labour-controlled LEAs. The most that can be hoped for is to bring working class children up to a level of educational achievement that might be generally considered adequate, in some ill-defined way. In this respect, the solution to the problem is entirely educational, rather than a wider social solution. Nevertheless, parents are implicated in that it is assumed that they are a necessary prerequisite. Yet again it is an ungendered parent that is the subject. But the Hargreaves Report pointed to the fact that there had been a massive demographic change in the composition of its school population. 'Over a quarter of ILEA pupils come from single-parent families, which is far higher than the national average' (p. 7). What it does not acknowledge is that the vast majority of lone-parent families are, in fact, lone mothers: in the ratio of approximately 9 to 1 on a national average (David, 1986). Solutions to the 'educational' problems that rely on uncritical acceptance of past axioms, given the dramatic change to lone mother families, inevitably increase the expectations of motherhood rather than parenthood per se. Although these changes are more stark in inner London than the rest of England and Wales, parental involvement has now a totally different resonance than it had in its initial conception.

A further indication of this is to be found in the massive Swann Report, entitled Education for All Cmnd 9453 (1985). This report, commissioned by the Department of Education and Science, under a Labour administration, initially as a study of the 'under-achievement of children of West Indian origin' and subsequently of all ethnic minority children, was over six years in the making. In recommending a system of education for all children it too relies on an uncritical notion of home-school relations as necessary to the success of an education system. Although it acknowledges disparities in the cultural, social or home backgrounds of schoolchildren, these are not reflected in the assertion of a traditional liberal form of family-school relations. Indeed, the particular notions of gendered parental roles underpin not only the administrative and decision-making structure recommended, but also curricular proposals.

Two particular recommendations illustrate the traditional, 'liberal' view of parents. First, it argues against 'mother-tongue teaching' in primary schools, and favours instead bilingual education or mother-tongue maintenance in secondary schools, as a minority language along with others. Several arguments are proferred against mother-tongue teaching, all implying that ethnic minority families and their languages are in some ways deficient and, more important, should not be afforded the same respect in home-school relations as 'home-grown', Christian families. It claims that mother-tongue teaching would lead to 'semi-lingualism', would just delay problems with adjustment to school in Britain, would lead to social divisions. Instead, it is argued that mother-tongue teaching should be part of the child's cultural heritage and taught in 'the community' not school. In other words the Plowden premiss of the necessity of good home-school or community-school relations for educational success is not accepted for non-British families. Yet it argues for a 'bilingual resource' in place of mother-tongue teaching, as a general 'parent-figure' for all young children. To quote:

> Such a role may be undertaken by a bilingual teacher, non-teaching assistant or nursery nurse already on the staff of the school, or even by a parent, or possibly by a fifth or sixth former from a local secondary school as part of their child care courses or community service experience. It should not be assumed, however, that the bilingual 'resource' will as a matter of course relate to pupils from the same linguistic, cultural or ethnic groups when their backgrounds may be entirely different: nor should they be seen as 'catering' just for the ethnic minority pupils but rather as an enrichment of the education of all pupils. (p. 508) (my emphasis)

The assumption appears to be that, in the case of ethnic minority children, 'proper' home-school relations can be learnt from mothers or girls from any background, rather than from their own parents' involvement.

Second, it argues against 'separate schools' for ethnic minority secondary children, seeing them as 'interchangeable' with 'single-sex, girls secondary schools' (p. 505). The argument is advanced on apparently non-sexist, or sexual equality grounds. The presumption must be that state-maintained, secondary, co-educational schools have achieved sexual equality. The grounds for rejection are that Islamic schools teach girls 'a way of life' which affects the 'ethos of the school', covering not only subjects but meals, uniform, PE and religious instruction (p. 503). In that respect they 'exacerbate' girls' feelings of rejection (p. 509). Secondly, careers education is seen as irrelevant for the point of Islamic education is marriage and motherhood for girls. In other words, separate schools provide an 'education for motherhood' (p. 501). No evidence is provided to show that comprehensive schools provide anything other than 'education for motherhood' for girls, or adequate 'careers education' except for 'male-type' jobs. The Swann report argues, nevertheless, that 'parents' fears are allayed' if education is provided for all and if ethnic minority parents are able to influence policy developments. No specific recommendations are made. The model remains a genderless, co-educational comprehensive school.

Clearly, over the last twenty years there has been a growing acceptance of the centrality of home-school relations to the success of secondary education. But these have been specified in such a way as not to enhance equality of educational opportunity through reducing disparities in home background and particularly 'parental means'. Indeed, most recently such differences have been used to exacerbate rather than erode the influence of home-school relations on educational achievement and success.

## EDUCATION FOR FAMILY LIFE

Parallel changes within the secondary school curriculum have also taken place over the same period of time. The effect has been to replicate the particular notion of home-school relations, within the various curricula that have developed. Although the notion has been implicit in existing courses especially those which are now seen as the core curriculum or part of the common core, it is now explicit in the courses introduced in the post-war period. The main innovation has been around the development of home economics or domestic science courses. Such courses had formed part of the curriculum of both elementary schools and secondary schools in the first half of the twentieth century (David, 1980). They had, in their origins, attracted special grant aid. They had also been directed chiefly at girls in adolescence, both middle and working class. In some cases such courses were taught to instill what has been referred to as 'dutiful womanhood' (Kamm, 1965).

In the post-war period, the aims and direction of the courses have appeared to be rather more complex and ambiguous. The changes have occurred under the broad rubric of providing 'education for family life' (Whitfield, 1980). In this respect, the emphasis has shifted from a concern with housewifery and household management to one of parenthood and, in particular, motherhood. The titles of the new courses have been instructive - preparation for parenthood, child care and development, parental skills and education, etc. They have all embraced the notion that the work of the home is more than merely domestic (Pugh and De'Ath, 1984). It entails the idea of caring for members of the household.

Many of the changes to the secondary school curriculum have been argued for, in the last twenty years, on the grounds of changes in family life and demography. The rationale has been to fit the next generation for such changed family circumstances. There are two key developments that have stimulated such changes. One is the growth of lone-parent families through several complex social changes - widowhood, divorce, separation, and out-of-wedlock teenage parenthood. The other change that has provoked the debate has been the changing social and economic climate and the increasing opportunities for women's paid employment, especially for mothers of dependent children (David, 1986).

It has also been argued that all children of secondary school age need to learn about family life as such, and to develop particular social and personal skills to help them cope with adulthood rather than the world of employment itself (Pugh and De'Ath, 1984). So the curriculum of state secondary schools has witnessed the inclusion of not only specific courses but a whole range of skill-based forms of education; often under the rubric of social education or personal and social development (Hargreaves report, 1985).

A major study of these developments was undertaken by the National Children's Bureau, given the commitment of the late director.

> Mia Kellmer Pringle argued that parenthood, and particularly motherhood, has been undervalued for far too long ... She was one of the first to argue for a compulsory 'core' element in the school curriculum of all young people which would include human psychology, child development and preparation for parenthood. (Pugh & De'Ath, 1984, p. 2)

Pugh and De'Ath look not only at changes in secondary schools but also primary and post-school education.

> In brief the extent of family life education in schools shows that whilst this is still not a part of every school's curriculum, some schools are beginning to adopt a more coherent approach to the social and emotional development of their pupils. Courses whose primary aim is family life education tend to fall within the ambit of childcare and development, and as optional subject (offered at CSE or O level) are taken almost entirely by girls and often less-able girls. (Ibid., p. 199)

The effect of such innovations has been to reinforce a gendered notion of parenthood, particularly for working class girls. Indeed Pugh and De'Ath point to the paucity of courses for boys or mixed groups.

> There are as yet few courses which offer boys and girls alike an opportunity to develop self-confidence and self-knowledge, to build up satisfactory relationships, to consider whether or not they wish to become parents, to discuss values and attitudes towards parenting, to develop some insight into child development, and to gain some first-hand experience of life with young children. (loc. cit.)

The effect of the innovation appears, then, to be that girls who are unlikely to develop academic interest are channelled towards these types of courses. The courses themselves appear to accentuate a sexual division of labour in the home, and the differential roles of mothers and fathers. They also emphasise mothers' crucial role in child development and socialisation.

More recent developments to the secondary school curriculum have included the Technical and Vocational Education Initiative (TVEI), launched in 1983. Initially it was to be a pilot scheme of education for pupils aged 14 to 18 years old based partly in schools, partly in further education and funded partly by the Manpower Services Commission (MSC). Although the original statement of principle specified equal opportunities for boys and girls, the Women's National Commission (WNC) reviewing the first year, state:

> Because of the short time available it was not easy for LEAs to make preparation to meet the very considerable challenge of equal opportunity before the projects began. It was therefore probably inevitable that, if the design of the projects involved immediate choice between courses on sex stereotyped lines, boys and girls reacted predictably. Sex stereotyping has therefore emerged to a very marked degree ... (WNC, 1984, p. 52, para. 32)

The other development has been the Youth Training Scheme (YTS) for school leavers at age 16 or 17 years old, who cannot find employment. The WNC, who also reviewed this scheme found that it did not work equally well for girls as for boys. They found that the problem lay with the restrictive age of entry.

> Some girls have difficulty in relation to the restricted YTS age group. It is common for girl school leavers to be expected to help at home for a period before finally going into the employment market. We were told of three categories of girls:
> - Asian girls whose families seek to keep them at home;
> - West Indian girls with working mothers;
> - girls in rural areas where jobs for women were often scarce
> ... who might at the more mature age of 18 to 20 decide they want a YTS placement, but will by then have lost their opportunity. The Group would like a study to be made of the prevalance of these cases and, if a significant number of girls

> experience such difficulties, a policy of deferral to
> be considered (Ibid, p. 60-61, para 43)

They argue for a deferral policy on the assumption that the
present system of home-school relations is perfectly
acceptable, with only mothers doing the 'work' of caring for
children. This seems to be the case not only for traditional
working class girls but also for those from racial minorities
whether of Afro-Caribbean or Asian home background.

The Swann Report on the education of ethnic minority
children confirmed this type of approach. They also aimed
to reinforce it not only through these various post-school
schemes but also through the involvement of ethnic minority
girls at secondary school in early childhood education. They
see this involvement as an important 'bilingual' or 'mother-
tongue' resource to enhance the primary education of ethnic
minority children (op. cit., p. 508). In this way, home-school
relations do not remain confined to the playground and the
individual child's educational achievement. They begin
thereby to form a crucial part of the curriculum itself.

The YTS scheme was, in July 1986 through the White
Paper entitled Working Together - Education and Training,
Cmnd 9823, extended to all school leavers at 16 years old on
a two-year basis.

> High quality vocational education and training is
> therefore becoming widely available to school and
> college leavers under 18. The systematic, work-
> related training which was available in the past
> only to a minority of young people (mainly men)
> through apprenticeships will in future be available
> more widely. And the old approach of training to
> perform only an immediate and limited job will be
> replaced by training for competence suited to
> whatever sector or occupational group the young
> trainee may enter. (p. 15, para 4.8)

The deferral policy, for girls, was not accepted and the
scheme remains relatively gender-blind. Yet a pious plea
was made at the end of the White Paper:

> But if all those concerned in education and training
> work together to achieve the objectives set out in
> this White Paper we shall begin to earn the
> dividend which investment in learning will bring.

There are few areas of national life more important to the future of our economy, our people and our families. (p. 28, para 7.7)

The government remains here committed to a genderless notion of families. Yet in the debates about a 'core' curriculum in secondary schools and in introducing 'sex education' into schools, such a notion of family is not genderless, but linked to a traditional sexual division of labour and morality. The relevant section of the Education (No. 2) Act 1986 states:

The local education authority by whom any county, voluntary or special school is maintained, and the governing body and head teacher of the school, shall take such steps as are reasonably practicable to secure that where sex education is given to any registered pupils at the school it is given in such a manner as to encourage those pupils to have due regard to moral considerations and the value of family life. (my emphasis, p. 48, para 46)

## CONCLUSIONS

The range of developments within home-school relations, in the last 20 to 30 years, has not changed the particular emphasis on gendered relationships. On the contrary, the effect of both schemes for parental involvement and participation, as well as education for family life and sex education courses, has been to reinforce the differences between motherhood and fatherhood. Motherhood has increasingly been defined as the emotional and educational 'work' entailed in being complementary to the school, for rearing children. Fatherhood has increasingly come to be seen as responsibility for parental income and decisions over school choice. All of these developments have occurred despite dramatic changes in the nature and characteristics of family life over the same period of time. For those women rearing children alone either by choice or force of circumstances the conditions of this have become much more clearly circumscribed. Even at the level of secondary education, the negotiations over paid and unpaid work, in the context of home-school relations become commensurately more problematic.

The shift that has taken place has been to make the sexual division of labour for child care and children's education much clearer and an integral part of the education system. Various schemes have signalled these developments. The most important effect has been to increase sexual inequalities in educational and job opportunities for all social classes and minority ethnic groups. Despite the rhetoric of educational equality of opportunity, the reverse has become the pattern of family life.

## REFERENCES

Acker, S. et al. (eds) (1984) World Yearbook of Education Women and Education, Kogan Page.

Bacon, W. (1978) Public Accountability and the Schooling System: a sociology of School Board Democracy, Harper & Row, London.

Benn, C. and Simon, B. (1972) Half Way There, Penguin, Harmondsworth.

Bernstein, B. (1970) 'Education cannot compensate for society' New Society, 26 February, pp. 344-7.

Bull, D. (1983) 'Privatisation of Exportation', Where, 1983.

Central Advisory Council for Education (CACE) (1954) Early Learning, HMSO, London.

_____ (1959) 15 to 18 (Crowther Report), HMSO, London.

_____ (1963) Half our Future (Newson Report), HMSO, London.

_____ (1967) Children and their Primary Schools (Plowden Report), HMSO, London.

Centre for Contemporary Cultural Studies (CCCS) (1981) Unpopular Education, Hutchinson, London.

Craft, M. (ed.) (1970) Family, Class and Education: a reader, Longman, London.

Craft, M. et al. (eds) (1972) Linking Home and School, Longman, London (2nd edition first published 1967).

David, M.E. (1977) Reform, Reaction and Resources: The 3Rs of Educational Planning, NFER, Windsor, Berks.

David, M.E. (1978a) 'Parents and Educational Politics in 1977' in M. Brown and S. Baldwin (eds) Yearbook of Social Policy in Britain 1977, Routledge and Kegan Paul, London.

David, M.E. (1978b) 'The Family-Education Couple -Towards an Analysis of the William Tyndale Dispute' in G. Littlejohn et al. (eds) Power and the State, Croom Helm, London.

David, M.E. (1980) The State, the Family and Education, Routledge and Kegan Paul, London.

David, M.E. (1984) 'Women, Family and Education' in S. Acker et al. (eds) World Yearbook of Education 1984: Women and Education, Kogan Page, London.

David, M.E. (1985) 'Motherhood and Social Policy: A matter of education?' Critical Social Policy, 12, Spring pp. 28-43.

David, M.E. (1986) 'Teaching Family Matters' British Journal of Sociology of Education, vol 7 no. 1 pp. 35-57.

Department of Education and Science (1977) A New Partnership for our Schools, London.

Hall, S. (1984) 'Education in Crisis', in A.M. Wolpe & J. Donald (eds), Is There Anyone Here from Education? Pluto Press.

Halsey Report (1972) Educational Priority: vol 1 Problems and Policies, HMSO, London.

Hargreaves Report (1984) Improving Secondary Schools, ILEA, London.

Kamm, J. (1965) Hope Deferred: Girls' Education in English History, Methuen, London.

Marsden, D. (1971) 'Politicians, Equality and Comprehensive Schools' in P. Townsend & N. Bosanquet (eds) Labour and Inequality Fabian Society, London.

New, C. and David, M.E. (1985) For The Children's Sake, Penguin, Harmondsworth.

Pugh, G. and De'Ath, E. (1984) The Needs of Parents: Practice and Policy in Parent Education, Macmillan, London.

Raynor, J. and Harden, J. (eds) (1973) Equality and City Schools: Readings in Urban Education vol. 2, Routledge and Kegan Paul, London.

Smith, D. (1979) 'A Sociology for Women' in J.A. Sherman and E.T. Beck (eds), The Prism of Sex, University of Wisconsin Press, Madison.

Smith, D. (1984) 'Women's Work as Mothers' in R. Millband (ed.) The Socialist Register, Merlin Press, London.

Swann Report (1985) Education for All, Cmnd 9453, HMSO, London.

Whitfield, R. (1980) Education for Family Life, Hodder and Stoughton, London.

Women's National Commission (1984) The Other Half of Our Future, Cabinet Office, London.

Working Together - Education and Training, Cmnd 9823, HMSO, London.

# 9

The Career of an Antiracist Education School Policy:
Some Observations on the Mismanagement of Change

Barry Troyna

## INTRODUCTION[1]

One of the most significant developments in contemporary
educational thinking and planning has been the growing
support for whole school policies. The basic premiss of this
innovation is that schools should endeavour to ensure that
there is coherence and consistency in the student's learning
experiences within the institution. It is believed that this
goal would be expedited by the setting up of a framework
within which a consensus could be reached regarding the
ethos and pedagogical, administrative and general orientation of the school. This is an attractive argument which has
been in the ascendancy especially since the publication of
the Bullock Report, A Language for Life, in 1975. There, it
will be recalled, the committee proposed a general policy
for the promotion of language development in the school:
'language across the curriculum' constituted one of the
important organising principles of the report. Since then,
recommendations for whole school policies have figured
prominently in a number of influential educational documents. Amongst these, the Cockcroft committee's inquiry
into the teaching of mathematics (1982), David Hargreaves'
report for the Inner London Education Authority (ILEA),
Improving Secondary Schools (1984) and the DES White
Paper, Better Schools (1985b) immediately spring to mind. In
the first of these, for instance, Cockcroft and his colleagues
were keen to ensure that consistency and some degree of
uniformity underpinned the way in which mathematics was
taught in schools. To facilitate this aim they recommended
the formulation of general strategies within the school for
the teaching of mathematics. This would comprise, amongst
other things, 'liaison between teachers so that those who

make use of mathematics in the teaching of their subjects do not use an approach or a language which conflicts with that which is used in mathematics lessons' (1982, p. 148).

On the face of it, it is difficult to envisage many educationists dissenting from the principles on which whole school policies are based. After all, few teachers would want to see their efforts in the classroom challenged or negated by their colleagues, however unwittingly this might occur. Nevertheless, in the absence of a broad consensus, facilitated by greater dialogue between colleagues and enshrined in a whole school policy, there remains the potential for contradictory messages to be conveyed by individual teachers to their students. The following incident described by Kate Myers, demonstrates vividly the truth of this argument:

> A nursery teacher reported how she changed the 'Wendy house' to the 'home corner' and painstakingly encouraged the boys to use this area of the classroom. She was subsequently horrified to hear a classroom assistant tell two little boys who were playing with the dressing-up clothes that boys didn't do that sort of thing and wouldn't they prefer to play with the lego. (1985, p. 30)

For Myers, one way of obviating such a situation is through the formulation of an equal opportunities policy in which teaching and support staff are all implicated in its formulation and implementation.

It is important to recognise the influence of this broad trend in contemporary educational policy on the development of initiatives and strategies for multicultural and antiracist education. In an area of debate characterised by dissent and conflict there is, as James Banks points out, at least one issue on which consensus has been reached. Namely, 'that total school reform is needed' and that this embraces, minimally, a concern with: 'the learning styles favoured by the school, the languages and dialects that are sanctioned, the teaching materials and the norms toward ethnic diversity that permeate the school environment' (1986, p. 226). The evidence suggests that this holistic conception of school reform is currently being advanced in the United States, Canada and Australia, as well as in the U.K. (see Banks and Lynch, 1986). In the U.K., local education authorities (LEA) have assumed an increasingly significant role in their attempts to ensure that local schools and colleges reappraise their normal practices and procedures along multicultural and antiracist lines. To begin with, the years following the 1981 urban disturbances have seen a growing number of LEAs formulate policies which declare a commitment to multicultural (and to a lesser extent, antiracist) education. These policies are intended to have implications for all educational institutions within the Authority. On the whole these policies reflect a permissive or <u>laissez-faire</u> style of intervention; that is to say, they provide a lead rather than direction in the move towards multicultural and antiracist education. In contrast, there is a smaller group of LEAs which is more prescriptive in its advice to schools. These Authorities have eschewed the permissive style of intervention and have insisted that local education institutions provide explicit and formal evidence of a response to the LEA's policy on multicultural and/or antiracist education. In some authorities, such as the ILEA, individual schools have been required to produce a policy and a timetable and programme for action within a specified period (ILEA, 1983, p. 4).

Putting to one side for the moment my reservations about this strategy in the development of antiracist education in schools (see Troyna and Ball, 1985) these recent initiatives at LEA level support my earlier claim that the general trend towards the formulation of whole school policies has impacted directly on current thinking in multicultural and antiracist education. Further encouragement for this development can be found in <u>Education for All</u>, the final report of the Swann Committee. As part of its overall strategy, the committee suggested that all LEAs should:

> expect their schools to review the curriculum, both taught and 'hidden', in the light of the principles we have put forward, to prepare appropriate policy statements and monitor their practical implementation. (DES, 1985a, p. 352)

The Swann committee also recognised that individual schools needed to reappraise their curriculum in the light of recent DES publications and called on schools to include 'some reference in their policy statements to the need to reflect today's multiracial society throughout their work' (1985, pp. 352-353).

It seems to me that the development of whole school

policies as one element in the general move towards the institutionalisation of multicultural, antiracist education in schools should be applauded. Such policies formalise and enshrine particular approaches and practices and provide the framework within which teachers might operate collaboratively in their attempts to mitigate racism in their schools. At the same time it is important to acknowledge that these policies are likely to make only a partial and limited impact on the general ethos and habitual practices of the school unless those involved in their implementation also participate in the formulation. This is a point stressed by Kate Myers (1985) and others. Following on from this, I share the concerns of Brian Boyd (1985) about the managerial and organisational implications of the process of whole school policy making. Boyd suggests that advocates of this trend have not confronted these issues, which are particularly salient in secondary schools. As Boyd notes, the problem centres on

> how one achieves the aim of persuading a school staff, made up of subject specialists with boundary maintenance a high priority, of 'restricted' and 'extended' professionals, of people with fundamentally different values, and indeed different ideas of the aim of education, to work together to produce effective whole-school policies. (1985, p. 80)

For some involved in the antiracist struggle in education, Boyd's cautionary comments would seem irrelevant, at best, and at worst a diversionary tactic designed to impede the progress of reforms along antiracist lines. Resistance to a whole school policy on multicultural, antiracist education which rested on the managerial and organisational grounds which Boyd mentions would be seen as an exemplar of institutional racism. Such critics would contend that those who invoke 'explanations' such as these are providing reasons for not challenging directly and explicitly a system which reproduces racial inequality. Consequently, they are complying with and supporting that racist system; ergo, institutional racism.

Those few studies which have documented the formulation of whole school policies on multicultural and antiracist education have, with the conspicuous exception of Peter Mitchell's account (1982), followed the analytical approach which I have paraphrased above. That is to say

161

they focus exclusively on what Jennifer Hochschild (1984) terms 'racially relevant variables' (see for instance, Lax, 1984; Straker-Welds, 1984 and Willey, 1984). Now I would not wish to underestimate or deflect attention away from the powerful role assumed by teacher racism in the process of race-related policy formulation and implementation. The recent research of Cecile Wright (1985a; 1985b; 1987) along with the studies of Peter Green (1982) and Peter Figueroa (1984) demonstrates the pervasiveness and effects of teachers' racist attitudes on the educational experiences and outcomes of black students in U.K. schools. Wright's research in two Midlands secondary schools was especially alarming in that it showed how racism informed the judgements of teachers in the allocation of students to examination and non-examination classes. What determined the destination of these students had more to do with the teachers' subjective assessment of the students and less to do with their actual performance in a range of tests (Wright, 1985a and 1985b).

What I want to do in this article should not, therefore, be misunderstood. I am emphatically not underestimating or discarding 'racially relevant variables' in considering factors which might inhibit the development of antiracist whole-school policies. On the other hand, I have grave reservations about the use of 'institutional racism' as the only explanatory framework within which such an analysis must be situated. It seems to me deterministic and reductionist to incorporate the array of themes and issues related to this complex matter within this single formulation. The processes of change are far too complex and varied to be accommodated neatly within one interpretive model unless that model is expanded to such an extent that it loses precision and explanatory power. Indeed, as Jenny Williams and her colleagues have argued this is the problem with the concept, institutional racism; it has been used in a taken-for-granted, cavalier manner to the extent that its conceptual precision has been lost (Williams, 1985; Williams and Carter, 1984; Troyna and Williams, 1986). Williams points out that institutional racism is 'a bridging concept, linking and blurring the distinction between the material and the ideological' (1985, p. 335). Thus while the existence of racial inequalities alerts us to the existence of institutional racism, the relationship between the various mechanisms said to exemplify this concept in operation and the causation of racial inequalities is rarely specified or demonstrated empirically. As Williams notes:

> ... differential catchment areas, stereotyping by teachers, monocultural curricula, narrow and particular standards of assessment, white monopoly of positions of authority, differential expectations by teachers of achievement, racist textbooks and the undervaluation of black experience and history, have all been used to illustrate normal institutional procedures which explain differential educational achievement ... They are all examples of injustices and clearly should be removed from educational practices; but their exact relationship to racial inequality can only be theorised, not demonstrated at the moment. (1985, p. 335)

The conflation of these various practices, and their ideological underpinnings within the unitary formulation of institutional racism has meant that its existence has tended to be defined by its consequences. This impoverished approach to analysis therefore absolves the researcher from the responsibility of testing empirically the relationships between ideologies and practices, on the one hand, and the existence of inequalities in, say, educational outcomes on the other. But more than this, the pinpointing of institutional racism as an explanatory concept - a 'catch-all' phrase for the generation and reproduction of racial inequalities - has led to the growth and legitimation of Racism Awareness Training (RAT) courses, predicated on individual conversion and attitude change as the main strategy for combatting racism. This is not the place to present a detailed critique of RAT courses (see Sivanandan, 1985 and Gurnah, 1984 however). Suffice it to say at this point that the impact of RAT courses, as they are presently constituted, is likely to be minimal in anti-racist campaigns.

In the rest of this paper I want to try and demonstrate empirically some of the arguments I have proposed so far by drawing on research carried out in a school where a group of staff was involved in the move towards a whole school policy on antiracism. In the role of 'researcher-consultant' I was in a privileged position to observe and document the process of policy formulation, the tensions this generated and the compromises and settlements which were negotiated. The experience also supported my view, expressed in an earlier article, that it is misconceived to presume that 'the non-institutionalisation of multicultural education derives entirely from the ('unwitting') racist attitudes of teachers' (Troyna, 1985, p. 209). My subsequent collaboration with Jenny Williams has prompted reservations also about institutional racism as an all-embracing explanatory model (Troyna and Williams, 1986). In all, these experiences have strengthened my conviction that those involved in multicultural and antiracist education have to liberate themselves from the restrictions imposed by the exclusive use of 'racially relevant variables' if their efforts are to contribute to substantive and meaningful gains in the struggle for equality in education.

## THE CAREER OF AN ANTIRACIST EDUCATION POLICY IN 'OUTSKIRTS' COMMUNITY COLLEGE

### i) The Background

'Outskirts' community college is a co-educational comprehensive upper school in 'Eastshire' LEA.[2] Formerly an old-established grammar school, it became fully comprehensive in 1968 four years after it moved into new buildings in a rapidly growing middle-class suburb about 5 miles south of the main urban centre of 'Eastshire'. It is a Community College and caters for approximately 1,500 part-time students. Its 1,200 full-time students are aged between 14 - 19 who are included in a catchment area which extends to villages up to 8 miles away from the college. The Principal estimated that approximately 90 students (i.e. 7.5 percent) are Black and these comprise mainly students of Afro-Asian origin whose parents were expelled from Kenya and Uganda in the late 1960's, early '70s.

The pastoral side of college life is based on mixed ability tutor groups whilst the academic structure of the college is organised on a faculty basis, of which there are six: Design; English; Mathematics; Humanities; Sciences; and, Languages. It seems reasonable to label the college as a 'pressured academic environment', to use Colin Lacey's term (1974, p. 150). The size of the sixth form (around 400 students) and the relatively high number of students who proceed to Higher Education are matters which are emphasized in the College publicity/information sheets. Similarly, the college handbook makes it clear to prospective parents and students that: 'the college is not mixed ability. Students are put into sets by Heads of

Faculty according to grades supplied to us by High School staff' (1984, p. 20. Original emphasis). As the Principal put it, one of the possible sources of staff resistance to change is that 'they're good at their jobs'. Thus in the Humanities faculty, the notion of a common-core curriculum has been rejected by staff in favour of retaining single subject teaching. In the words of the Principal the reason for this decision was simple: these subjects 'show good performances'.

The college handbook provided an accurate indication of the importance attributed to credentialism within the institution. The same document provided clues regarding the commitment of the college to antiracist, antisexist values and modes of practice. After all as Alan Weeks has remarked, if an educational institution 'feels a strong duty to its ethnic minority pupils one would imagine that this would be expressed in a document going out to these parents' (1982, p. 23). The college handbook for 1983-4 drew to the attention of its prospective and current students that the following was one of its rules:

> Behaviour of all members of the College Community is based on the fundamental principle of showing respect; that is respect for others, respect for the environment, respect for the law of the land, and last, but by no means least, respect for self. Respect for others involves rejection of all forms of prejudice whether it concerns a person's sex, class or race. (1983, p. 17)

This rule was reaffirmed in the 1984-5 handbook and although there is little evidence to suggest that it was enforced vigorously, or even adhered to as a procedural value of the college, nonetheless it suggests some element of sensitivity and awareness. It is also important to point out that this rule was not formulated simply in response to the LEA's request for action along multicultural lines. On the contrary, along with the formation of the college working party on antiracism it was written before the LEA published its formal policy on this issue.

So why was a working party formed in the College? Undoubtedly the initiative stemmed from the Principal. To start with, her previous experience had been in a multicultural community college in a nearby LEA and she considered that the college's well-publicised initiatives on

165

multicultural matters had relevance to 'Outskirts'. She also considered such initiatives in terms of pre-emptory action; that is to say, she conceived of them generally as one way in which a recurrence of the 1980/1981 disorders in Bristol, Brixton, Liverpool and elsewhere might be averted. 'I believe in it [multicultural education]', she told me. 'Our future as a society, as a U.K. citizen depends on antiracism. The alternative is horrible; dissension and more of the Brixton riots.' Against this background, however, more immediate concerns impinged on the college. During the academic year, 1983-4, the Principal was approached by some fifth year students of Afro-Asian origin who complained of discrimination at 'Outskirts' and wished, therefore, to transfer to another school to complete their studies. The Principal was sceptical of their accusations and suggested that the real reason for their request was that they wanted to 'be with more of their own folk'. Despite these reservations, the Principal brought the matter to the attention of the Staff Association which comprised all full-time teachers and which met once a month as a consultative and decision-making body. Having previously declared its opposition to 'any form of discrimination in terms of race, class or gender' the Association agreed to the setting up of a working party on multicultural education to which members would volunteer.

The working party met formally for the first of what was to be seven meetings in March 1984. Its membership, coincidentally, comprised staff from each of the College faculties and divisions and included both senior and junior members of the teaching force. One of the defining characteristics of its membership, however, was that it contained recently appointed staff. In the absence of formal terms of reference it was agreed at the first meeting that the group should be known as the antiracist working party, that it should extend its constituency to include representatives of the students, parents and governors as well as 'outside speakers who had experience of multicultural education and of dealing with racism in schools' and that it should aim to: 'i) raise awareness within both the staff and the student body; ii) combat racism' (Minutes, 1 March 1984). Subsequent meetings saw the working party extended to include representatives from the students and governors (who attended intermittently) and 'outside speakers', including the LEA adviser for multicultural education, some local specialist workers in the Authority and myself. During its meetings the working party studied relevant policy documents from other LEAs and educational institutions, discussed articles on antiracist and multicultural education, and watched videos used by the local Industrial Language Unit in its RAT courses. By its seventh meeting, in April 1984, the working party had agreed on a policy to be submitted for ratification by the Staff Association on 21 May and for subsequent inclusion in the 1984-5 college handbook.

### The Proposed Policy Statement of 'Outskirts' College

The Principal and teachers of 'Outskirts' College have adopted the following statement:

We aim to develop education at 'Outskirts' College in assemblies, lessons and tutorials and to take all available opportunities to:

i)   impress upon all members of the college community that racism and the discrimination it leads to are offensive and unjust;
ii)  explain the historical, political, economic and social backgrounds to racism in this and other societies;
iii) prevent wherever possible any abuse of a racist nature within the college community.

The community college should be a place that brings people together, increases understanding and promotes justice. We shall do all we can to protect this principle.

### ii) The Discussions

The momentum and enthusiasm generated by the working party during its short but productive life was seriously undermined by the onset of industrial action in the final term of 1983-4. This prevented any further discussions amongst the working party about how the policy might be implemented and monitored. It also ensured that the Staff Association would not meet until the beginning of the new academic year. In the light of these events, the working party abandoned reluctantly the hope that the policy would feature in the new college handbook.

## An Antiracist Education Policy

By the beginning of the new academic year industrial action had receded and the policy was presented for ratification at the Staff Association meeting on 10 September 1984. It was introduced formally by a member of the working party who reminded the Association that it had provided a brief for the working party, that the group had representation from all faculties and departments and that 'the aim of today's meeting was to obtain ratification for the policy'. Clearly, however, members of the Staff Association did not share this view of their role. Overwhelmingly, the position taken was that the policy should be scrutinised by faculties, divisional and departmental members, its implications for pedagogy and curriculum content discussed and formulated and that, with any revisions that may then be necessary, adopted formally by the staff and included in the next handbook. The stance of most working party members was entirely different, however. For them adoption of the policy constituted the basis for discussion. In other words, the priority should be ratification after which the minutiae of the policy, including its operationalisation should be discussed by members of individual faculties and departments. The debate, then, crystallized primarily around the <u>style</u> of adoption, rather than the content of the policy.[3] This was reflected in the formal proposal offered by one member of the Staff Association: 'The policy should be discussed at departmental and faculty meetings and the results fed back to the next Staff Association meeting.' This was accepted by the meeting. However, it proved to be an optimistic appraisal of future events. Although each faculty, department and pastoral division of the school discussed the policy and its implications for practice in their meetings, other matters intruded on the agenda of the Staff Association. The result: by the end of the winter term of 1984-5 the issue had still not appeared before the Staff Association and the entire enterprise was in danger of collapse. Indeed, scrutiny of the minutes of departmental, faculty and division minutes where the policy was discussed suggested that there was little support for its adoption. The criticisms voiced by staff throughout 'Outskirts' covered a range of issues and themes. At the risk of oversimplification, however, it could be said that they focussed on two predominant concerns. First, a reluctance to concentrate exclusively on racism as a matter for action. A number of staff insisted that there were other forms of discrimination in the college which also needed to be tackled, perhaps more urgently. Thus one divisional meeting concluded that a more broadly conceived equal opportunities policy should be formulated: 'A more general statement that made reference to <u>any</u> discrimination (race, religion, sex, etc.), might be preferable' (minutes, 24 September 1986). This was also the argument put forward in the science faculty: 'Racism as a particular discriminating attitude should not be singled out from other forms of prejudice such as against fat people or others who did not conform to a norm' (minutes, n.d.). Simply put, staff in different areas of the college believed that the policy was too narrow in its concern and focus. Their conclusion does, of course, ignore the history of the policy initiative and the original brief provided by Staff Association to the working party.

The other major bone of contention crystallized around the professionalism of staff and their perceived role as mere operatives in the acceptance and implementation of the policy. This argument featured prominently in the English faculty. There the minutes revealed that: 'the policy implies ignorance and failure on the part of the staff in their current, existing attitudes and practices. It is therefore insulting.' These members of staff also felt that, 'the policy is prescriptive and intends to "force" staff into practices in the classroom as teacher and/or tutor which they may not want to be involved in' (minutes, 1 October 1984). Precisely the same criticisms were voiced during the meetings of the various Divisions of the college. In one of these it was claimed that the policy 'implied a lack of awareness on the part of the staff and as such could be interpreted as criticism of their professionalism' (minutes, 24 September 1984). In another, 'the purpose of the statement was questioned: is it merely to be approved?' (minutes, 24 September 1984). A related issue concerns the protective attitude displayed by some staff towards their subject area. The minutes revealed how some staff were reluctant to engage in cross-faculty collaboration or dialogue. For instance, maths staff insisted that the policy had little relevance to their work and they would resent the intrusion of other staff from different faculty areas into their deliberations and curriculum planning. Amongst other points raised in their meeting, maths staff claimed that they had 'checked through syllabus and textbooks etc. for problems with course content but these are not really applicable to Maths(!)' (minutes, n.d.).

## iii) The Outcome

For the latter part of the 1984-5 Autumn term the debate about the policy was moribund and was destined to be consigned to the annals of the college's history. Events at the beginning of the new term altered that, however, and precipitated a more immediate commitment to the policy.

Early in that term, some students of Afro-Asian origin at 'Outskirts' called on their friends from the city to join them at 'Outskirts' in combatting racist abuse from a group of white fifth form students. What resulted can best be described as 'ritual violence' in the playground and the groups soon dispersed. Nonetheless, the event alerted the Vice-Principal of the college to the need for 'Outskirts' to resurrect the policy on antiracism. He insisted that the policy be placed on the agenda of the next Staff Association meeting which was to be held on 21 January 1985. In his words, the imperative was 'to demonstrate the college's rejection of racism' and he believed the policy could play an important part in declaring publicly that stance.

The meeting on 21 January was poorly attended with less than half of the full-time teaching staff present. In this context it was agreed that any decision on the policy could not be said to be democratically representative of the staff's views; an agreement which helps to clarify the otherwise obscure phrasing of the recorded minutes:

> It was proposed that the policy statement developed by the Anti-Racist Working Party be adopted by the meeting with the exception of the apparently contentious second aim. The essential nature of democratic action was called into question. The meeting adopted the policy statement with 20 votes for, 0 against and 8 abstentions. (minutes, 21 January 1985. Emphasis added)

What emerged then, as the official policy of 'Outskirts', was an emaciated statement of principle which absolved staff from a commitment to 'explain the historical, political, economic and social backgrounds to racism in this and other societies'. Along with the LEA's recently published policy and guidelines on multicultural education, the college statement provides the framework in which the member of staff now designated with responsibility for this issue currently operates.

## DISCUSSION

This reconstruction of events leading to the adoption of a whole school policy on antiracism reveals some of the complexities inherently associated with policy innovation in schools. In this particular instance, those complexities were exacerbated by the politically contentious nature of the proposed innovation; namely, a policy against racism. It is clear from the transcripts of meetings that some staff at 'Outskirts' were unwilling to engage explicitly with strategies designed to mitigate the effects of racism in the school. Whether or not this reluctance derived directly from the racist attitudes of these teachers is impossible to say. After all, these same members of staff had already endorsed a Staff Association decision to oppose all forms of discrimination at the school. Against this, however, there were at least two recent occasions when students of Afro-Asian origin had felt that they were discriminated against in the school. Clearly then, whatever the root cause of this resistance, its manifestation cannot and must not be under-played in the analysis. Nor should it be ignored in the development of future strategies to institutionalise changes in schools along antiracist lines.

However, the narrative also alerted us to other forms of resistance to change which, for reasons I have already suggested, should not be dismissed simply as evidence of institutional racism. On the one hand, the narrative points to the part played by the established ethos or modus operandi of the school in facilitating or limiting the potential for change. On the other, it highlighted the role of the professional culture of teachers in this scenario. In the extant literature on the formulation and adoption of whole school policies on antiracism these matters have generally been ignored. But they exert enormous power in determining the outcome of the innovation. Let me elaborate on this point.

In one of the few attempts to link the debate about whole school policies on antiracism to general theories of curriculum change and educational innovation, Peter Mitchell has observed that: 'The sine qua non of successful whole school policies is dialogue between staff across departments' (1984, p. 32). It is clear that some schools have neither the tradition nor the organisational structure to support the type of relationship to which Mitchell refers. This may be particularly true of secondary schools which have become increasingly larger and more complex institutions. There, as David Hargreaves indicates, 'Strong subject identities and weak pedagogical perspectives' prevail (1980, p. 142); precisely the context which is anathema to the developmental approach on which the theory and practice of whole school policy is based. Quite simply, there are some schools which are not in the habit of organising discussions about anything and have little experience of establishing or making public the procedural values which inform the way in which the institution and its constituent members operate. Thus the insistence of some LEAs that their local schools and colleges provide evidence of anti-racist, antisexist policies might go some way towards ensuring that forms of dialogue and collaboration are present throughout the Authority. For this reason the initiative should be welcomed. But to impose a deadline by which all schools and colleges must submit a policy is to defeat the object and to ignore the different stages already reached by schools in this process (see Troyna and Ball, 1985).

On the face of it, 'Outskirts' might have appeared the ideal school for the successful introduction of a whole school policy. The Staff Association, for example, had been established with the aim of facilitating dialogue between staff and increasing general participation in decision-making processes. However, as I have already suggested, attendance at Staff Association meetings was voluntary and often poor. Furthermore, the school had little tradition of making its procedural values explicit; that is, with the exception of promoting its record as a 'high-achieving' school. Indeed, the 'pressured academic environment' of the school was based on the maintenance of strict subject differentiation rather than cross-subject or inter-Faculty exchange and collaboration. Hardly then the most conducive context within which a whole school policy would be expected to attract support and flourish. In fact against this background the innovation was almost bound to fail.

A closely related issue concerns the ways in which the professional culture of teachers can militate against the whole school policy approach, as Geoff Whitty has noted:

professional culture at the chalk face retains a certain capacity to be resistant to change initiated elsewhere, even if its role is essentially defensive. This poses a problem not only for governmental and

> industrial attempts to give schools a more utilitarian bias, it also poses problems for those who wish to see schools as a context within which critical insights into the nature of the wider society can be developed. (1985, p. 148)

In his discussion of this issue, Hargreaves conceives of the occupational culture of teachers being ordered around three themes: status, competence and relational (1980, pp. 125-148). It is the relational theme which is of particular interest here. Hargreaves draws attention to the 'cult of individualism' in teaching where the 'live and let live' maxim is often axiomatic in schools. As he puts it: 'like sexual activity, teaching is seen as an intimate act which is most effectively and properly conducted when shrouded in privacy' (1980, p. 141). Naturally, the tenacity of a commitment to the cult of individualism within the professional culture of teaching is influenced strongly by the school's ethos and internal organisation. In 'Outskirts' it was not challenged systematically or firmly. Rather, in the interests of the school's academic reputation it was allowed to persist. It is partly for this reason then, that a sizeable handful of 'Outskirts' teachers resented the intrusion into their routine practices and arrangements which the policy implied. It also helps to explain why they perceived the policy as a critique of their current work.

But this is not the complete story. In recalling the experiences of the Girls into Science and Technology (GIST) project, Alison Kelly has made the important point that: 'All innovation in schools includes, at least implicitly, a critique of teachers' previous practice, and is thus potentially threatening' (1985, p. 140). These fears are likely to be hightened in the present climate where moves towards centralisation in the education system involve gradual erosion of teachers' relative freedoms in the classroom over the content, organisation and thrust of their teaching. Kelly goes on to suggest, however, that teachers' defensiveness about their current practices is exacerbated further in discussion about equal opportunities and antiracist initiatives. The reason: because 'However we [the GIST project team] tried to disguise it, the message to teachers was that they had been disadvantaging half their pupils all their professional lives' (1985, p. 139). Again, there are close parallels with the experiences in 'Outskirts'. This helps to explain why some teachers refused to see racism in the school as the priority for ameliorative action and why, also, members of the Maths department were reluctant to view the matter as relevant to their subject area. Simply put, both constitute strategies of resistance to the perceived challenge to these teachers' competence in ensuring equality of treatment for all their students. As I have argued before:

> one of the covert messages conveyed to practitioners by the multicultural education movement is: you have failed demonstrably to ensure that black students enjoy equality of opportunity in education; therefore you need 'expert' assistance (from specialist advisors and inspectors, support staff and consultants) and pre-packaged materials to facilitate the realisation of this goal. (Troyna, 1985, p. 221)

In their efforts to minimise this threat the GIST team focussed primarily on the professional concerns of teachers (i.e. the concept of equality of opportunity) and avoided 'the personal ramifications of sex stereotyping' (Kelly, 1985, p. 139). Similarly, the working party at 'Outskirts' drew attention in the policy to the integral role of antiracism in the principle of community education to which the school as a community college was geared. In both cases, this strategy met with limited success.

## CONCLUSION

Tuku Mukherjee has made the important point to white people that: 'Your racism has been your silence ... Inaction or silence to me, means action. To me inaction means collusion' (1984, p. 6). His criticism clearly applies to the experiences at 'Outskirts'. There, the staff prevaricated over the adoption of an antiracist school policy for almost a year. They rejected what was, arguably, the most important of the proposals for action in the policy: and they accepted, reluctantly, only a diluted version of the original, for purely expedient reasons; that is, to pre-empt the possible recurrence of racial tension within the institution. Despite the fact that these minor, even hesitant initiatives go beyond what is happening in the majority of U.K. schools it is difficult to dispute the claim that the staff colluded with a system in which many of the rules, regulations and procedures ensure the reproduction of racial, gender and class inequalities. Nonetheless, to conflate the actions and attitudes of these teachers with practices and actions which are racist in intent (such as the introduction of 'colour bars') and label them as 'institutional racism' seems an unproductive basis on which to develop change. To reaffirm an earlier argument: 'the relationship between racist intent, racialist practices and racist effects (in the form of inequality) is not as clear-cut as many would have us believe. The imperative must be to clarify empirically these relationships if realistic and productive antiracist policies are to be formulated' (Troyna and Williams, 1986, p. 56).

In the context of the antiracist/multicultural strategies adopted by a number of LEAs the interpretation of events at 'Outskirts' in terms of institutional racism might well precipitate the claim that the teachers should attend RAT courses. This seems to me a misguided and complacent policy response. Such courses focus on individual conversion and fail to grasp the tenuous relationship either between attitudes and behaviour or individual conversion and institutional change. Even if RAT courses succeeded in converting these teachers to an antiracist philosophy (and there is no evidence to support this presumption) this would do little to change either the internal organisation and ethos of 'Outskirts' or the 'cult of individualism' which currently presides amongst staff in the school. What I have suggested here is that these constitute some of the other variables which militate against the development of whole school policies on antiracism. Unfortunately, however, they are matters which are rarely debated in antiracist education. The object has not been to deny the existence of racism amongst staff. Rather it has been to suggest that the struggle to achieve racial inequality in education is more complex than some antiracists might assume.

## NOTES

1.  A version of this chapter was originally prepared for the conference, The Swann Report: Its Challenge for a Monocultural Region and appears in the conference report, Multicultural Education for All (University of Exeter, 1985). It has been revised considerably since then. Wendy Ball, Stephen Ball and Tony Green made important criticisms of the original paper. Above all, however, I am grateful to my 'adversary' at the BERA

seminar on Progressive Education in the Secondary School (London University Institute of Education, February 1986) who drew attention to a number of weaknesses in the original. I'd also like to thank the Principal and staff at 'Outskirts' for their support and co-operation during the period of the research.

2. Both 'Outskirts' and 'Eastshire' are pseudonyms. For more detail on the development of 'Eastshire's' policy on multicultural education see Ball (1986).

3. During the meeting only one member of staff attacked the content of the policy. In her view it was 'moving into the area of indoctrination and propaganda'.

4. See also Foster and Troyna (forthcoming) for evidence of this in other schools.

## REFERENCES

Ball, W. (1986) Policy Innovation on Multicultural Education in 'Eastshire' Local Education Authority (Policy Paper in Ethnic Relations, No. 4), Warwick, Centre for Research in Ethnic Relations, University of Warwick

Banks, J. (1986) 'Multicultural education and its critics: Britain and the United States', in S. Modgil et al. (eds) Multicultural Education: The Interminable Debate, Lewes, The Falmer Press, pp. 221-231

Banks, J. and Lynch, J. (eds) (1986) Multicultural Education in Western Societies, Eastbourne, Holt, Rinehart and Winston

Boyd, B. (1985) 'Whole School Policies', Forum, Vol. 27, No. 3, pp. 79-81

Cockcroft, W.H. (1982) Mathematics Counts, London, HMSO

Dept. of Education and Science (1975) A Language for Life, London, HMSO.

Dept. of Education and Science (1985a) Education for All, London, HMSO.

Dept. of Education and Science (1985b) Better Schools, London, HMSO.

Figueroa, P. (1984) 'Race relations and cultural differences: some ideas on a racial frame of reference', in G.K. Verma and C. Bagley (eds) Race Relations and Cultural Differences, London, Croom Helm, pp. 15-28.

Foster, P. and Troyna, B. (forthcoming) 'Conceptual and ethical dilemmas of collaborative research', Educational Review.

Green, P. (1982) 'Tolerance, teaching and the self-concept in the multi-ethnic classroom', Multi-ethnic Education, Vol. 1, No. 1, pp. 8-11.

Gurnah, A. (1984) 'The politics of racism awareness training', Critical Social Policy, 11, pp. 6-20.

Hargreaves, D.H. (1980) 'The occupational culture of teachers', in P. Woods (ed.) Teacher Strategies, London, Croom Helm, pp. 125-148.

Hargreaves, D.H. (1984) Improving Secondary Schools, London, Inner London Education Authority.

Hochschild, J. (1984) The New American Dilemma: Liberal Democracy and School Desegregation, London, Yale University Press.

Inner London Education Authority (1983) Race, Sex and Class, London, I.L.E.A.

Kelly, A. (1985) 'Changing Schools and Changing Society: Some Reflections on the Girls into Science and Technology Project', in M. Arnot, (ed.) Race and Gender: Equal Opportunities Policies in Education, Oxford, Pergamon Press, pp. 137-146.

Lacey, C. (1974) 'Destreaming in a "pressured" academic environment', in J. Eggleston (ed.) Contemporary Research in the Sociology of Education, London, Methuen, pp. 148-166.

Lax, L. (1984) 'Anti-racist policies' in ALTARF Challenging Racism London, ALTARF, pp. 207-18.

Mitchell, P. (1982) 'Developing an anti-racist policy: the secondary experience', Multi-ethnic Education Review, Vol. 1, No. 1, pp. 16-17.

Mitchell, P. (1984) 'The headteacher's role as curriculum manager', in J. Maw et al., Education Plc? Headteachers and the New Training Initiative, Bedford Way Papers No. 20, London, Institute of Education, pp. 25-34.

Mukherjee, T. (1984) 'I'm not blaming you - an antiracist analysis', Multicultural Teaching, Vol. 2, No. 3, pp. 5-8.

Myers, K. (1985) 'Beware of the backlash', School Organisation, Vol. 5, No. 1, pp. 27-40.

Sivanandan, A. (1985) 'RAT and the degradation of black struggle', Race and Class, Vol. 26, No. 4, pp. 1-33.

Straker-Welds, M. (ed.) (1984) Education for a Multicultural Society, London, Bell and Hyman.

Troyna, B. (1985) 'The great divide: policies and practices in multicultural education', British Journal of Sociology of Education Vol. 6, No. 2, pp. 209-223.

Troyna, B. and Ball, W. (1985) 'Styles of L.E.A. policy

intervention in multicultural/antiracist education', Educational Review, Vol. 37, No. 2, pp. 165-173.

Troyna, B. and Williams, J. (1986) Racism, Education and the State, London, Croom Helm.

Weeks, A. (1982) 'The conservative curriculum', Times Educational Supplement, 21st May, p. 23.

Whitty, G. (1985) Sociology and School Knowledge, London, Methuen.

Willey, R. (1984) Race, Equality and Schools, London, Methuen.

Williams, J. (1985) 'Redefining institutional racism', Ethnic and Racial Studies, Vol. 8, No. 3, pp. 323-348.

Williams, J. and Carter, B. (1984) 'Institutional racism: new orthodoxy, old ideas', Multiracial Education, Vol. 13, No. 1, pp. 3-8.

Wright, C. (1985a) 'Learning environment or battleground?' Multicultural Teaching, Vol. 4, No. 1, pp. 11-16.

Wright, C. (1985b) 'Who succeeds at school - and who decides?' Multicultural Teaching, Vol. 4, No. 1, pp. 17-22.

Wright, C. (1987) 'Black students - white teachers', in B. Troyna, (ed.) Racial Inequality in Education, London, Tavistock, pp. 109-126.

# 10

## Social Class and the Process of Schooling
## - A Case Study of a Comprehensive
## School in a Mining Community

### William Dubberley

The purpose of this chapter is to re-introduce the fact of social class as a major variable in the process of schooling. Since the 1960's traditional social class divisions have largely been neglected in assessing the quality of statutory education children receive. The vogue is now to focus upon gender and race as, rightly, pressing problems to be addressed in our schools, but my contention is that unless the problem of social class discrimination be properly addressed the process of schooling as an agent of social and cultural reproduction will not be fully understood.[1]

Comprehensive education in this country was introduced piecemeal and with no coherent guiding philosophy. As Ball (1981) points out, this lack of a guiding principle has led to a situation whereby three models of comprehensive education, the Meritocratic, the Integrative and the Egalitarian, can be identified. This is not the place to consider the issue in detail but it is important to recognise that different LEAs and indeed different schools offer quite different provision to pupils. For instance the typical meritocratic school draws heavily on the traditional Grammar School model and as such, in my view, continues to maintain social division. At the opposite end of the continuum, the egalitarian model is aimed at achieving equality through educational innovations designed to remove discrimination arising from social structures such as class or ethnicity.

The failure of educationalists to even debate, let alone resolve the issues arising from the above situation means that in spite of the liberal rhetoric associated with the comprehensive principle, schools have failed and continue to fail working class kids. Indeed with mass unemployment especially and particularly amongst working class youth, and the Y.T.S. initiative in response to this, it would seem that the liberal rhetoric of the comprehensive principle is to be abandoned altogether. Paul Willis (1986) in a searching treatment of this issue argues that 'mass youth unemployment finally blows the whistle on certain social democratic (welfare development and individualistic development compatible with future occupational and industrial roles) conceits and illusions in the educational field'. It is therefore high time that social class be placed at the top of the agenda in the debate over education.

The study on which this chapter is based is of a mining village in the Yorkshire coalfield. The research was begun in January 1985 and coincided with the final three months of the NUM strike against pit closures. The method used was that of participant observation, and my intention, eventually, is to produce an ethnographic account of the school.

Coalton School is a moderately sized mixed comprehensive comprising of 690 pupils, age range 11-16, and 46 staff, set in the centre of the mining village of Coalton. The towns and villages in this area are built on coal, literally and metaphorically, and the local culture cannot be even remotely understood unless this obvious fact is recognised.

As to myself, I have had a Northern working class background and I was born and brought up in South Lancashire. The experiences of Grammar School and particularly University created emotional and intellectual divisions in myself that sought resolution in an interest in politics and the theory of education. As a result of my experiences as a student and later as a teacher in a number of sectors of education, I believe one of the main effects of education is to perpetuate social class divisions.[2]

Before I turn to the subject of the paper proper I must issue one more caveat. I focused my attention during the research on two groups of 16 year old working class pupils, the 'lads' and 'lasses', all of whom were in bottom sets throughout the school. I interviewed these groups on a weekly basis, observed their behaviour in the classroom situation and contrasted the data by observing the behaviour of pupils in the other sets, particularly the top sets, throughout the school. I also closely monitored the teachers both in the classroom and outside of it. I have not set any of the groups of 'lads', 'lasses', 'snobs' and the various groupings of the teachers in the broader context of the community in any detail, allowing the terms used by the actors to stand without comment. However I do acknowledge that not all working class pupils, for instance, are to be found in bottom sets and consequently not all 'snobs' will be middle-class.

Turning now to my research, I found the working class pupils of the community were very strongly aware of marked cultural differences between themselves and the majority of the staff. The way that pupils and staff respectively used language was readily commented upon by the pupils. However this awareness often included a shrewd analysis, as is the case with this 4th year lad from the bottom sets.

Carl       Teachers sometimes contradict yer - like if you say summat, they say 'no this is the proper way to say it' and they tell you the proper way.

Me         How do you feel?

Carl       You feel sometimes shown up and then, you know, you realise that if you are from a certain place that's how you speak - you can't help it.

The analysis contained in the above is clear and perceptive. There is the notion that there is a universal, correct code and that teachers are the arbiters of it. Further, shame and disadvantage are associated with alternative codes yet they argue all this is surely unjust because the code reflects your culture over which you have no control. He continues:-

When we were in Maths, we were like talking and she just came out with summat - 'even people in Africa can speak in better English than you.' We just looked at her and laughed. Yer know, she knows a lot more how to speak proper cos she probably comes from a different place.

The comparison here is clearly racist as well as a social class sneer; Africans are un-cultured (<u>even</u> people in Africa) yet even they manage to use English better than these pupils. Sadly, however, the acceptance of the idea, that the local culture is deficient and parochial is suggested by the acknowledgement that the teacher's code was superior and that this had been learnt in an entirely different community.

The theme of social discrimination by language is continued in a conversation with a group of pupils in a 5th year English group.

Girl 1     If you say summat, reight, they say '<u>pardon</u>' [emphasised]. Like I said in cookin, I goes, 'ev

| | |
|---|---|
| | yer got a te-ar towel' [strong local accent] and she goes '<u>pardon</u>' [ultra posh]. She made me say it reight. |
| Girl 2 | They just talk posh like - they 'aven't got an accent - they don't come from no wheer, like if yer say 'ta' - they say [plummy] 'what?' |
| Lad | They don't understand what we're like. |
| Girl 2 | Yeh, they just don't understand what we're like. |
| Lad | Cos they come from a different area with their views and are [our] views are totally different, just abaht, and they don't know what to do. |
| Girl 1 | They expect yer to talk posh when yer from round 'ere and yer can't - cos yer talk like people from round 'ere, don't yer? |

Such an eloquent analysis of the arbitrary imposition of linguistic and cultural norms needs no further comment!

However, the pupils are aware that it is not simply a question of cultural discrimination per se. Its implications are more serious than that as is shown by the following conversation by a group of 5th year lasses concerning a teacher whose effusiveness they found irritating.

| | |
|---|---|
| Carly | If you ask him the meaning of a word, he's explaining it, where it comes from, whether it's an adjective or noun ... We don't want to know about all that - we only wanted to know what the silly word meant. |
| Me | What do you think of that? |
| Diedre | Ignorant! - the way he does it. He does it as though yer <u>thick</u> [accentuated]. You only asked him what a word wor - yer didn't want to know where it came from and how it originated -yer just want ter know what it means - and he talks as though you were thick. |
| Me | ... what do you think he's trying to do? |
| Carly | Show us he's brainy. |
| Diedre | Just show yer that he knows all about this word and we don't ... I don't think he tries to learn yer by doing it ... he just tries to prove that he knows what it means. |

(I ask does he do this to everybody - they claim he

doesn't do it to everyone but -)

| | |
|---|---|
| Carly | He does it to duggies - like me. |
| Me | He does it to who? |
| Carly | Folk who are thick like me. |
| Me | And who doesn't he do it to? |
| Elaine | Snobs! |
| Me | Who are the snobs? |
| Elaine | All them that get high marks. |
| Me | And who are they? |
| Elaine | Posh |
| Carly | Stuck up |
| Elaine | Them wi money and like their parents have got good jobs. |
| Me | ... Why do you think you are talked down to? |
| Diedre | Because they think we're thick. |
| Me | And who are you? |
| Diedre | Oh, we're nobodies - inferior - we're just working class people! |

(The dialogue continues)

| | |
|---|---|
| Diedre | They [teachers] give more attention to posh people - cos they think because we come from a working class background we haven't got as good a background - we're not as capable of achieving what posh people can. |
| | Cos our parents have only got rubbish jobs - they think we're only going to get rubbish jobs, so why bother wi us. They work them as got good jobs and secure jobs - we've got to be them as work in factories. |

Their irritation begins with his display of erudition and the fact that it is completely unnecessary in their view. One could argue that this shows a lack of intellectual curiosity on the part of the pupils, but apart from the fact that he has quite a reputation for this behaviour, Diedre also complains about 'the way he does it', 'as though yer <u>thick</u>'. Consequently associated with the erudition is the notion of a 'put down', of knowledge (largely sterile at that) as power. Significantly, this exercise does not take place with all students, but with the 'duggies'; he does not do this to the 'snobs', 'wi money', 'whose parents have got a good job'. The analysis is quite clear. Certain cultural norms are arbitrarily imposed by teachers in a discriminatory manner. Pupils whose parents have money and a good job benefit whereas the duggies do not. This is because they are regarded as 'thick', as 'inferior', as 'just working class'. They receive a second rate form of education and are expected to do 'rubbish jobs' like their parents.

The lasses are arguing that working class culture is regarded as deficient. Therefore unless working class children can adopt the cultural characteristics of the dominant social class they will be disadvantaged at school either by self-selection, in rejecting the norms, or by rejection by the institution as 'we're not as capable of achieving what posh people can'. They will not be allowed to take exams, or will not receive the same encouragement or will simply reject the whole idea. Whatever the reasons the results will be the same. No exam results will mean no cultural capital in the form of certificates; no certificates will mean leaving school early whilst their counterparts go on to acquire even more cultural capital in further and higher education. In the labour market they will suffer adversely.

In case I am accused of over interpretation I include here a number of remarks by pupils concerning exam-inations, setting and the kind of education they receive.

Adele    We 'ave Mr. Caborn and when he teaches an higher set he's reight strict. Wi' us we don't do any work and sit theer every lesson just playin' cards and tellin' jokes and messin' abaht, but when he teaches higher sets he makes sure they get on wi' the work all t' time. I find in this school, if you are in a lower set, they just don't want ter know yer.

Certainly I found this to be very much the case, that the style of teaching, the content and the commitment varied markedly between 'top sets' and 'bottom sets'.[3] There was also a peculiar situation whereby people who were not doing exams in the particular subject being taught, could carry on with work on another subject on their own. Certainly the following situation described by a fifth year girl, was often the case.

She's er, well - before we decide who are takin' em she

ses if yer not tekin' t'exam I can get on wi' those who is and I can help them to do their work better, she ses, cos er, if yer not willing to do yer work I'm not bothered abaht yer - stuff like this ... so yer just don't ... an all t'brainy boxes sits in middle o't' classroom next ter t' teacher's desk an t'others sit round t' class - all over - don't they? [Hopeless tone].

Of course, this is not a personal attack on teachers. It is the system they operate that discriminates against working class cultural norms (and those of ethnic minorities) and validates in the form of exam success, middle class cultural norms. However, I would argue that they are the instruments of such a process, wittingly or unwittingly, and if such a perspective is correct, it adds insult to injury when the teacher blames the discriminated pupil for her situation. Cultural discrimination is explained away in this particular case by the teacher's argument that pupils fail through lack of ability, or in this case, effort.

if yer not willing ter work I'm not bothered abaht yer.

Different cultural perspectives regarding school are revealed in the whole orientation of working class pupils and of the working class community generally to education. Working class pupils' attitudes often appeared, on the surface, to be contradictory. Many, if not most of them, resisted the school uniform, often in very subtle ways, but complained that the school should make them wear it. They were most withering about teachers who were 'scruffy' (particularly the women) because they should be dressed 'reight'. Even though they were critical of posh talk from teachers, they should 'talk proper'. They objected to teachers being too 'hard' but preferred hard teachers and thought the school badly disciplined. In fact this last feature was one which preoccupied teachers, the working class community and the pupils alike. The Head, a genuinely caring and liberal man, could not win. Many pupils and their parents thought the cane, which the Head had banned, should be re-introduced and that the Head was too soft.

The reasons for these contradictions are complex and multi-factorial, but one broad explanation lies in the notion of 'partial penetration' I wish to borrow from Willis (1977). Pupils and their parents are aware that they are disadvantaged, but blame the individual school, not the national system that it has to operate. One stereotypical model of the successful, academic school is that of the Grammar school looked on particularly favourably in northern working class areas as a route of escape for a few 'bright' and therefore 'deserving' pupils. The reality of cultural reproduction, I would argue, is hidden by a view that underpinned the Grammar/Secondary Modern system, i.e. the bright and the hard working succeeded in the Grammar schools while the lazy or 'slow' pupils deservedly went to Secondary Moderns.

Grammar schools were typified by a rigidly applied hidden curriculum; a meticulously observed uniform, elaborate formal ceremonies, harsh corporal punishment, begowned staff, etc. The traditional Grammar school did provide working class people with token successes, albeit wholly disproportionate to the successes of those of middle class pupils. Nonetheless these few working class successes were identifiable - they could be named and seen. Success is equated with the cultural aspects of the Grammar school - formal, disciplined, ceremonial, etc. Consequently attempts to liberalise the regime of the school were met with hostility as it was regarded as synonymous with reducing the quality of education the young people received. It is a partial penetration in that the understanding that they are disadvantaged in the educational system leads them to insist on those very processes of education which are most clearly hostile to their culture and consequently to their educational performance.

One example of many such complaints was:

Sheila     I wouldn't want my kids to come to a school like this. I don't want my kids to be mucked up like I have been. ... When me dad came up to this school he said, 'if yer want 'em to behave, what yer need ist' cane' and the Head said 'oh no Mr. Thompson we don't believe in that here'.

Most of the staff seemed deeply frustrated, sometimes hostile, and even fearful of the inability of 'the school', reified, to control large groups of young people. I am not saying that the school was a 'black-board' jungle but that there was a major culture clash between most working class pupils and most of the middle class staff. The staff seemed unable to see this process except in deficit terms. They saw themselves as having to work within a culture which, by its nature, was hostile, aggressive and coarse. Except in a minority of cases, the staff saw this culture clash as an expression of unilateral truculence on the parts of working class kids. They did not see the situation resulting in part at least as an expression of resistance to the cultural hegemony of the dominant group in society and also as an expression of a culture they did not understand.

One process that the working class pupils adopted which reflected the divisions which lay between middle class staff and working class pupils, was of staff categorisation. The pupils tested each teacher and categorised them on the basis of being 'soft', 'hard' or 'all right', though some extreme cases did not even fit into these categories!

| | |
|---|---|
| Carly | With all new teachers we start off mekin a noise [makes humming noise]. |
| Me | And what then? |
| Carly | If they tell us to do summat we'll say no and start an argument. We'd start cheekin' em. Like if they'd say 'get on wi' yer work' we'd say 'no'! |
| Elaine | When we wor wi' Mr. Horbury ... we started cheekin' 'im and he couldn't do owt abaht it. |
| Sheila | If we do this and we find out that they're soft, they're like that for t'rest o' t' time we've got 'em. But say somebody new comes along and they're O.K. wi' us, we're O.K. wi' them. |
| Carly | You can hum and that and they can just start cryin' and go out and they can say [in mincing voice] 'Oh, I don't like you' [laughter]. |
| Me | What happens after you've set them up? |
| Sheila | They send yer to another teacher or they send us down to Mr. Clayton or they just leave - leave t' school altogether. |
| Me | If they ignore you or send you down to Mr. Clayton what decision do you make? |
| Elaine | That they're soft. |
| Sheila | Yer do it all the more. |
| Diedre | Yer can do what yer like wi' em. |
| Me | If they're soft what can you do to 'em? |
| Sheila | Start takin' urine out of 'em. |
| Carly | Spit at 'em. |
| Diedre | Chuck stuff at 'em. |

| | |
|---|---|
| Jane | Anythin' |
| Elaine | Swear at 'em. |
| Carly | On ice skatin' we covered Mr. Jones' coat wi' spit, didn't we? |
| Janet | Like Mrs. Jackson, she's got ginger 'air and they all call 'er ginger minge and all sorts [shocked laughter]. |
| Me | Right, so those people that are soft you can do what you like to them and you don't feel sorry for them. |
| All | Yeah. |
| Sheiia | But they want yer to feel sorry for them when they turn watter works on though. They think 'oh, If I roar they'll give up. |
| Carly | But we don't - we do it all t' more. |
| Me | What other kind of teachers are there? |
| Elaine | Then there are those who are hard and go round and crack yer. |
| Jane | They're better teachers cos yer get more work done. |

However, there are teachers who are approved of.

| | |
|---|---|
| Me | What about those teachers that you like? Do they fit into any of the categories or are they in a different category? You mention Mr. Earle, Dave, how would you describe him? Is he hard? |
| Dave | No. |
| Me | Is he soft? |
| Dave | Yeah - but like yer don't say owt to him 'cos he's reight wi yer. |
| Janet | If they are reight wi you, you're gonna be reight wi them, aren't yer? |
| Me | So people who are 'right' with yer don't fit into any of these categories? |
| Elaine | No - they're all reight. |

The criteria that the working class pupils applied to teachers who were 'all reight' were 'not talkin' down to yer', 'A sense of humour', 'good discipline', and 'being kind and helpful and not bossy' - As one girl said RE-SPECT-FUL!

The qualities that the pupils identified seemed to indicate an insistence on egalitarian warm human behaviour from the staff. However, it was interesting that of the few individuals who were variously identified as 'all right', the majority had some understanding if not experience of the local working class culture; some of them actually originated from that area of the Yorkshire coalfield. However, some staff, even though from clearly a different social class and region, were accepted as all right because they did not 'talk down to yer', they 'talked reight soft to yer' 'asked yer to do things' and 'talked to yer as yer talk to yerselves'. Is it not reasonable to assume that the respect of staff for pupils must contain a respect for their culture. Certainly when 'soft' teachers were identified, their weakness was parodied by mincing weak protestations in a 'posh' accent, 'Oh, girls, I don't like you'.

What was also interesting was the ruthlessness with which manifestations of 'soft' behaviour were received. Pupils were contemptuous of 'watter works', and insisted that staff should be able to 'stand up for themselves'. They were angry because they couldn't teach you anything and if asked whether they shouldn't feel sorry for such teachers, the retort was they should have thought about that when they came into teaching - that they should be able to 'control yer'. The hard teachers, though often not liked, were to be preferred because they could teach you something.

There seems to be a number of processes, many contradictory, that are occurring here. The testing of the teachers and the form it takes and the nature of the abuse to teachers reflects a rather neat way of resolving a contradiction. The 'deviant behaviour' represents an aggressive expression of their own culture which resists the imposition of an alien culture and also tests the teacher's familiarity with and/or respect for that of their own. It represents a gesture of resistance and also of cultural identification. It also neatly explains why pupils are failed, or conversely, why teachers, on the whole, are doomed to failure with working class pupils. The imposition of an alien culture is rejected as, amongst other things disrespectful. Teachers who cannot respect working class culture are rejected and their efforts at teaching ruthlessly and contemptuously thwarted. The punishment that the teachers receive in the form of pupil hostility is deserved because they can't teach.

That's what they're paid for - to teach us summat - to control us.

The following conversation between two teachers about social class illustrates some of the above points.

Mrs. Jackson  I don't think about these things.

Mr. Stonehouse  Acceptable behaviour - language etc. that's a bad word - behaviour we recognise as normal. I think that we're regarded as foreigners - we don't belong. We don't come from a mining background ...

Mrs. Jackson  [Heavily ironic] Their attitude to us is <u>wonderful</u> you know - <u>we</u> don't work with our hands.

Mr. Stonehouse  We are paid to teach them. That's our job.

Mrs. Jackson  When we say 'you can't have any paper', they come out with a whole spiel of 'we pay our taxes!'

Mr. Stonehouse  It's not often you get children telling you that (i.e. that you're paid to teach them) [but] If they're failing, it's <u>our</u> fault. Kids come to lessons with no pen - they say 'lend us a pen'. It's my responsibility to provide them with a pen and above all a brain with which to do it. <u>They</u> have not to do anything.

Mrs. Jackson  We're paid to do the whole thing, including the learning. I think our kids think they're finished when they've actually attended.

There are other cultural elements here as well. Mining is a harsh, demanding and dangerous job based on a clear division of labour. Men must be tough to withstand its physical demands and their womenfolk loyal and supporting to enable them to continue. Fierce loyalty and co-operation is needed to survive down the pit and in the village generally, particularly in times of economic hardship. This has led to a close co-operative culture, used to hard work and danger and these qualities find expression most clearly when under attack, as has been admirably demonstrated in the N.U.M. strike of 1984-85.

People in this community have no time for people being soft, or not standing up 'for themsens'. This is not simply a matter of taste - an inability or refusal to support others when in danger, threatens everyone. Further, there is the question of division of labour and with that, demarcation lines and the notion of what is expected of you and what is not. Teachers are paid to teach as miners are paid to hew coal. If they can't teach, and they can't if the class are running amok, then they shouldn't be there.

This notion was reflected in the pupils' indignation at not getting 'the proper teacher' at times. On one occasion a chemistry teacher took a class for P.E. in the absence of another teacher. The pupils felt angry because he was a chemistry teacher and should not have been teaching another subject to them. Similarly in one French class I observed, a lass, Diedre was told to get on with some English as she wasn't doing the exam in French. Out of deference to my presence the teacher took it upon herself to check on her work. Diedre was scathing.

> I don't know what she's doing coming over here pretending she's t'English teacher ... she usually ignores us or puts us in detention.

Again, I think there are a number of factors here. The idea of 'the proper teacher' owes something, perhaps to the model of 'good' schooling and the Grammar School, as mentioned above. It also has something to do with the working class division of labour and that you are what you are paid to do. This idea is also reinforced by the mystification of professional skills in order to maintain the status and privilege of the professional worker. The indignation suggests the idea of being 'short-changed'. We are as good as anybody else - our money is as good as yours. We should therefore get what we pay for - a proper teacher.

Certainly there were very strict rules concerning the general social and moral behaviour of teachers which reinforces the above arguments. However, the moral code is very much working class not middle class.

| Jane | Mrs. Vades - she were dead scruffy. |
| Diedre | She were filthy, weren't she? Greasy hair - nobbut Oxfam clothes. |

Great indignation was expressed by both groups of lads and lasses over the story that one female teacher had had a relationship with a boy pupil in the school.

| Fred | She's a reight stuck up cow - she chases yer. She used ter go wi one o't lads in the 5th year here. |

| Me | What do you think of that? |
|---|---|
| Bill | Disgusting. |
| Fred | Yeah. |
| Bill | Going out wi a teacher shouldn't be allowed ... |

It seems here that the suggestion is that teachers should not fraternise with the pupils as in demeaning their status (as teachers) they are insulting the pupils by not being a 'proper teacher' i.e. as not living up to the class stereotype contained in the professional one. Yet they can still accuse her of being stuck up!

The rejection of the middle class teacher was often expressed in sexually abusive terms. Female teachers who annoyed either the lads or lasses, were described as 'a bitch' or 'a slag'. This was not confined to the pupils, however, as staff often described the lasses, as sluts or bitches.

| Jane | Yeah, Mrs. Shea, she called mi a tart cos I were brushin' me hair. |
|---|---|
| Sheila | Who? |
| Diedre | Mrs. Shea. |
| Sheila | Slap head |
| Janet | We'ad Mr. Jackson, reight? |
| Tricia | Ee, 'e's dopey 'im! |
| Janet | He were teaching our Maureen and she were talking to 'er mates and he called er a set of sluts, just for talkin. |

When the staff used such language to the girls, they and their male peers were incensed as the pupils argued that when <u>they</u> used the word, they didn't mean it literally. When the staff did, they felt they meant it as impugning their morality, their sexual integrity. The lasses did explain to me at one time exactly what the various terms of abuse meant. Slag, bitch, etc. ... meant

| Elaine | Sleeping around an that. |
|---|---|
| Sheila | Sleeping around |
| Carly | Opening your legs ... [embarrassed laughter] Going wi all different fellas. |
| Sheila | A bitch is where they flaunt their body but they don't want it when it comes round to it. |
| Carly | A prick teaser [laughter]. |

The lads claimed

Fred    I don't think that's reight. I don't think they should be called names.

Bill    No - cos they get upset when they get called names.

Fred    I don't think they should be called names at all, like slut and things like that - most of t'lads are just t'same [as regards behaviour in class] and they don't get called names - sexually like - they act same as girls but don't get called names like that.

Me    Do you lads call the girls names like that?

Fred    Sometimes. Only for the fun of it. We don't mean it. <u>Teachers do.</u>

It seems that when lads or lasses call teachers such names it is because it is one of the most shocking things they can do. The resistance is sexual in terminology but is meant as a general term of abuse. Staff, on the other hand, seem to use it in a social class sense, as it was used particularly when girls wore make-up etc.

What the staff are highlighting is their view that the girls are not so much sexually promiscuous as to be so low in the social order that they are on a level with the lowest, the common prostitute. The insult is social. The lasses, however, take this as a deep insult in another sense as they feel it is impugning their moral standing.

A girl's reputation is still something to be protected zealously, as the boys also supported. Further one girl, who was teased by the lads for wearing suspenders, was terrified that her reputation would be damaged.

Are they saying I'm a slag or things like that?

Perhaps the differences between the staff and the pupils and the working class community generally were best seen in their attitudes to work, or, more particularly, in the form of industrial action they took. The school is on a campus at the very centre of the village. On the same site are the baths, the County Council Offices and the Civic Hall. The local people can walk freely past the school in going to any of the other buildings. On the day the N.U.M. returned to work, the miners from the local pit assembled on the car park by the baths. Accompanied by their families and behind their banner they formally marched back to work together. Two days later the older pupils, angered by the fact that they were kept out of school at dinner times because of the teachers' action, staged their own 'strike', refusing to return to afternoon school and giving an impressive and a little frightening demonstration in the process. Chants of 'Scab! Scab! Scab! One-two - one-two-three - and Maggie Thatcher's got V.D.' mingled with 'The school kids, united will never be defeated.'

Clearly the events in the village generally and in the school on that afternoon are complex and deeply significant and demand more than a few lines of exploration. However, I simply wish to comment on a few details which reveal clear and significant differences in cultural attitudes and values. After the pupils' strike the staff, generally were hurt and angry:-

| | |
|---|---|
| Mrs. Thompson | I was within an inch of giving up [trying] this morning. Now I'm 1/16" away from becoming a 9.00 till 3.30 teacher. |
| Mrs. Jackson | Yes - I'm giving up, when they [miners and families] went past us on the march yesterday some of them were going like that [makes a 'V' sign]. |

Before I comment any further, I must stress that approximately 8 of the 46 staff were contributing to the N.U.M. strike fund, though the N.U.M strike as a whole was not often openly discussed. However, there were critical remarks made by the staff, albeit obliquely, if not about the strike then about the culture generally which indicates the gulf that exists between attitudes to work and union politics and explains the 'V' sign. One young member of staff, whose husband was also employed by the local authority in a different capacity, appearing on the surface to lead relatively comfortable lives, casually volunteered the following remark during a conversation regarding a T.V. programme on the N.U.M. strike and the treatment of scabs.

If one of them [i.e. coal mining community] say one thing, they all think the same. They haven't the ability to recognise that it's probably more courageous to go to work than to stay on strike.

Further, the Head claimed that the community were 'very angry' about the way the staff had used the Civic Hall, 50 yards away from the school, during the summer. Because of their own industrial action, the teachers left the school at dinner time and went to have their dinner in the Civic Hall. In the same building the striking miners and their families were queueing to use a soup kitchen that had been set up. As the Head reported, on one side of the Hall were the miners getting soup and on the other side the teachers taking industrial action and reading newspapers.

To be fair, the Head was loyal to his staff when negotiating with the striking pupils after their ½ day action.

Head        But you must respect the right of teachers to say, work to rule or go on strike. I'm sure that no-one, particularly in Coalton having been through what you've been through, would deny them that right.

However, one 5th year pupil, to spontaneous applause, said

Yer know, when the miners went on strike, they were doing it to save jobs. All't teachers are doing it for is more money. They're being greedy.

Perhaps more revealing however, was the feeling that the teachers were not proper trade unionists, "why couldn't they do it [strike] properly?"

What is worth noting is that none of the teachers expressed any sense of mutual interest or commonality between themselves and the striking miners. In the light of subsequent events the parallels between the miners' dispute and the teachers' are clear. In both cases a strong centralised government has attempted to curtail the power of the union so that it may impose its own will on the industry to the detriment of the work force. It was left to one of the striking pupils to make this observation after he had discussed the above events with his dad, a striking miner.

We ought to support teachers. We're supporting Thatcher, otherwise ...

It is not the purpose of this paper to detail all the differences in culture that expressed themselves during my research; the above will suffice if it establishes the fact that they do exist and that they do indeed constitute a major variable affecting the education of working class people. 'But we've heard it all before' is the cry. Exactly - and if this is so why has it not influenced our educational policies and most of all, the consciousness of the teachers? It is to the latter that I wish to turn.

Many teachers did not bother to hide their contempt of many of the lower groups in the school. Classes were variously referred to as 'grots', or 'thickies' and it was not unusual to hear the following question asked by a Head of Department in the staffroom: 'Who's got Helen's rubbish group?' Even one teacher who was genuinely sympathetic to one 'lower ability' group, a rural studies group who had named themselves the 'Duggie Diggers', implicitly accepted the notion of I.Q. and culture deficiency when describing the kind of curriculum the students should be following.

Mr. Marshall  I'd like to teach fishin' next year if the boss O.K.'s it.
Me  With everybody?
Mr. Marshall  No - with the 'Duggie Diggers' - have you heard of them?
Me  I've heard of them but who are they?
Mr. Marshall  They're of very low ability. There t'hardest group I have. ... I take em for rural studies and duggie is a local term - it means 'thickie'. They call themselves that - 'Duggie Diggers'.
Me  Why not fishing across with the 'O' level group?
Mr. Marshall  Well you try to give kids what they need. They need this.

Similarly, one member of staff praised another with the following remarks.

Tom Ferguson is an intellectual - a traditional academic - who now has a comfortable background - yet when teaching he is saying to the kids 'I value you'. If he is elitist at all, it is in terms of getting kids to University. Yet he's fair. Some academics like Tom would encourage some kids to read Wuthering Heights, say, but not bother about other kids - saying 'oh they lack ability', whereas Tom would pull down a fish and chip novel and say 'here, you should read this'.
The other thing is that when the kid comes back -

and he's [Tom] read such a lot of books - and I include bad books - that he's likely to ask the kid about the book and know what it's about.

All but a few of the staff seemed either not to be able to comprehend the community or to fear it. One prevalent notion, however, was the culture was 'parochial'.

Mr. Lawler  Kids in this school are generally quite parochial ... I'm very careful now about the words I use. This is where they get the thing about snob. If you listen to Shakespeare and Chopin you're a snob ... they're naive. It's the community ... so many people in Coalton are obsessed by the pub and club and that's as far as it goes...

Mrs. Tilly  We shouldn't go down to their level. We should get them to change ... they don't know any other way. Who else is going to tell them if teachers at this school don't? They'll do the same as their parents.

Mr. Lawler  They're not willing to adapt. The community is not prepared to look outwards - they're too introspective ... it's the club and pub syndrome.

When confronted by the question of social class and whether they felt it influenced teaching, many teachers were remarkably coy.

Mrs. Dunn  I find that very difficult. I would categorise children's behaviour towards me without it being consciously class. But I am aware of children coming from better homes. I'm also more lenient towards kids from poorer homes. They are not terribly clean and tidy and I am more lenient as far as standards of work - I have less expectations.

Mr. Ferguson  When you get the top groups they come from better families. I don't know anything about the background - but I'll bet it conforms to social/economic divisions. The problem we have is the lumpen proletariat. The poorer kids come from the poorer families.

Me  Do you mean economically poor?

Mr. Ferguson Well no - culturally poor ... I don't think it is social class that causes the problem ... it is their behaviour.

The same person went on to attack streaming because it exacerbates the problem of deviance in that 'all the bad uns are in one group'.

The two broad explanations for 'deviant' behaviour and lack of success were 1) cultural deficiency in the form of the parochial community or of poor families 2) poor ability in terms of I.Q. capital, although the following remark offers a biological perspective(!)

Kids, particularly lads when their balls drop, need to know exactly where they are in the pecking order - like the animal kingdom. They need to know that if they go one way they'll get hurt, another and they're the boss. They think 'oh, I'm No. 2 - I'm happy'. The best thing that happened to me was playing rugby in an all boys grammar school. It did me a world of good to have spots knocked off me.

Teachers who did see the process of schooling in social class terms were very much in the minority. The following teacher felt that as many as 80% of the staff were unsympathetic to working class culture because of their own social class background.

| Mr. Thompson | Most of the staff will see certain pupils' behaviour as good - you know, the traditional school values - showing interest in the work, the way they express themselves, the way they communicate. |
| --- | --- |
| Me | You mean as first order categories these qualities are seen in terms of the school - but in second order categories, they really represent social class, in that schools are middle class or bourgeois institutions? |
| Mr. Thompson | Yes, but not everybody. |
| Me | How many? |
| Mr. Thompson | About 50% - but it varies. At some times it's 100%. I know that when I'm under pressure I fall back on the school criteria - pressure. Perhaps they do see it but believe it's right [i.e. that middle class values are right]. |

| Me | Why? |
|---|---|
| Mr. Thompson | Their social class plus the socialisation of teachers as teachers when they're training for the job. |

Another teacher argued that the majority of his colleagues are unaware that they do discriminate on the basis of social class.

| Mr. Salt | They would probably deny it. They would say they are only recognising kids' ability but they are divorcing kids' backgrounds and their performance in schools. When pressed they do see the correlation of working class kids and poor ability - but they won't see the link between ability and talking down to them. Also their background [middle class] will lead to them talking down to them. They've never had the experience [i.e. of working class culture]. |
|---|---|

However, the following teacher himself asked the question to which this chapter is also addressed, namely why do the majority of teachers fail to consider social class as an issue central to the process of education. As a caveat, whilst I share his curiosity, I do not necessarily support all his views or the way that he expresses them!

| Mr. Black | Do you think we have a lot of problems in secondary schools because we [teachers] are not very bright? I realise my own limitations yet I really do recognise other people's limitations. |
|---|---|
| Me | In what way - intellectually? |
| Mr. Black | Yes, and I mean that - but not subject-bound. I mean we have quite a lot of people who in their subjects are extremely knowledgeable - but they are not people who I would regard as specialists in education.<br>They are limited because one, they haven't studied education, or two, that they haven't studied education because of their intellectual limitation. I hope I am critical enough myself to criticise what I am doing. I have been very critical of the boss - but through encouraging |

| | people to go on courses - in setting up study groups - he has raised the intellectual level of debate ... and that is praising a man I think a pillock. |
|---|---|
| Me | Isn't there a group who are genuinely critical and concerned about what is going on? |
| Mr. Black | Yes, there is such a group and I would like to include myself in that. I think there are 7 or 8. |
| Me | 7 or 8? |
| Mr. Black | 7 or 8 possibles, yeah. |

Clearly I have lumped the teachers together into two groups, as far as their perspectives on social class are concerned. Of course this is a gross simplification as there were mainly different shades of opinions and variations of ideology within both groups. However it cannot be within the scope of this paper to highlight all these. What I do claim is that the majority of teachers had a deficit model of the working class culture within the community and that their explanations as to the failure of working class pupils was pathological. By this I mean that the teachers regarded the cause of failure to lie within the weaknesses of the pupils themselves and the inadequacy of their home backgrounds and culture generally. Even those few teachers who saw the problem in terms of a culture clash had a confused analysis, falling back onto the deficit culture model in claiming that working class kids were not given the chance to overcome their initial disadvantages.

Overall I thought the level of analysis poor when teachers were encouraged to explain why some pupils fail and were a problem. The majority of staff had some grasp of psychologistic explanations and an implicit, though crude, understanding of the structural functionalist perspective. With one exception, and that in the management team, I do not think that I came across anyone who was totally familiar with a conflict analysis of school processes.

This leads me to conclude the paper by asking how can this be? Working class pupils fair as badly as ever in our schools if not worse. There are no policies designed to remedy this state of affairs, in fact the reverse if we look at the massive influence of M.S.C. schemes in our schools. Most worrying of all, if my research is typical, then most teachers seem reluctant to appreciate or understand working class culture with consequent disastrous results for the pupils. Cultural hegemony does not even seem to feature on the agenda of the education debate as far as social class is concerned so what is the status of professional training in our Universities and Polytechnics? How the attitudes of professional educators and policy makers can be genuinely influenced by academic research is a matter of pressing concern <u>for</u> academic research.

## NOTES

1. Bourdieu, P. and Passeron, T. (1977).
2. At this stage a brief word about the kind of document I am producing here; I do not believe it is possible to produce an objective 'scientific' account of such a project. Bias in the social sciences is inevitable, and most obviously in phenomenological accounts. At best, therefore, I must confess my perspective and make claim to produce a problematic text, although confessing interest I do not relinquish the necessity for consistency and rigour.
3. See Woods (1979) and Burgess (1983) on this.

## REFERENCES

Ball, S.J. (1981) <u>Beachside Comprehensive: A Case-study of Secondary Schooling</u>, Cambridge, C.U.P.

Bourdieu, P. and Passeron, J. (1977) <u>Reproduction in Education, Society and Culture</u>, Sage Publications, London.

Burgess, R.G. (1983) <u>Experiencing Comprehensive Education: A Study of Bishop McGregor School</u>, London, Methuen.

Willis, P. (1977) <u>Learning to Labour</u>, Farnborough, Saxon House.

———— (1986) 'Unemployment: the final inequality', <u>British Journal of Sociology of Education</u>, vol. 7, no. 2.

Woods, P. (1979) <u>The Divided School</u>, London, Routledge and Kegan Paul.

# 11

## Class, Culture and Schooling among the New Middle Classes

### Peter Aggleton

## INTRODUCTION

How young people respond to the process of schooling is a topic that has been of perennial interest to educational researchers. Early small-scale interpretative studies of school experience such as those carried out by Werthman (1963), D.H. Hargreaves (1967) and Lacey (1970) helped establish a tradition of educational enquiry in which students' experience of schools and schooling became a central focus. They also laid the foundations for many of the more broadly based enquiries carried out in the 1970s and 1980s.

In recent years, interactionist and social phenomenological studies by Woods (1979), Ball (1981), and Turner (1983) have extended these earlier analyses of students' experience of schooling. They have also led to the development of a number of typologies of student responses to education. Concurrent with this work, other studies have explored more specifically the role that schooling plays in reproducing class and gender relations. Researchers such as Willis (1977), McRobbie (1978), Connell, Ashenden, Kessler and Dowsett (1982), Anyon (1983), Davies (1984) and Furlong (1985) have, with varying degrees of success, explored how student responses contribute, via processes of cultural production and cultural reproduction, to the social reproduction and transformation of class and gender relations. Many of these studies have seen radical potential in the challenging and 'resistant' behaviours of pupils, a claim which has led critics such as Walker (1986) to argue that some may run the risk of romanticising the actions they describe.

The research described in this paper arises from a number of concerns highlighted by investigations such as these. In particular, it has its origins in debates stimulated by recent work concerning the radical significance, or otherwise, of student 'resistance' to schooling. Much of this takes as its starting point Willis's (1977) study of 'resistance' among a group of working-class 'lads' in an English secondary school, <u>Learning to Labour</u>. Although Willis's work has often been regarded as a celebration of working-class 'resistance' to capitalist schooling from a socialist stand-point, it has also been seen as deeply pessimistic in that, as its subtitle (How Working Class Kids get Working Class Jobs) implies, it demonstrates how this 'resistance' serves to reproduce rather than transform existing social relations. Subsequently of course, Willis (1981) has argued that neither of these interpretations is entirely in line with his theoretical argument, which suggests that the significance of 'resistances' to schooling can never be given, but depends on how they are worked with, and how they articulate with other practices within the social formation. A similar picture emerges from Anyon's work in American elementary schools (Anyon, 1981a, 1981b), though she has been criticised by A. Hargreaves (1982) for regarding almost all negative responses to schooling as potential challenges to capitalist social relations, thus devaluing any utility that the concept of 'resistance' might otherwise have. Echoing the projects of earlier interactionist studies of students' responses to schooling, Hargreaves calls once more for the development of a <u>typology</u> of student responses to schooling, though if the significance of responses is dependent upon their articulation with other practices within the same site and elsewhere, a more dynamic and empirical analysis of particular cases would clearly be necessary.

Because of its focus on a group of working-class students, Willis's work cannot shed much light on the significance of negative responses to schooling among students from other class backgrounds: responses that are also sometimes, somewhat naively, characterized as 'resist-ances'. The question therefore arises whether these can properly be described as resistances in the sense that, if they become articulated with other practices in appropriate ways, they too share the potential to become <u>transformative</u> rather than <u>reproductive</u> in their effects. The extent to which the potential to transform society lies not merely (or even mainly) with the traditional working-class but rather with (among others) disaffected professional and middle-class groups has, of course, been a matter of considerable debate among social theorists ever since the emergence of the countercultures of the 1960s (Roszak, 1968; Marcuse, 1969; Gintis, 1972). In addition, writers on both the political right and the political left have identified teachers and social workers as potential vanguards of revolutionary activity. Claims like these are all the more pertinent at a time when there is much debate about the strategies that should be worked with by educators committed to a socially transformative politics (Giroux, 1983; Aronowitz & Giroux, 1985; Whitty, 1985; Aggleton & Whitty, 1986).

## THE STUDY

In this chapter, efforts will be made to examine some of these issues by analyzing data from an empirical investigation carried out among a group of 'new middle class' students attending a college of further education in a small English city called Spatown (Aggleton, 1984; Aggleton & Whitty, 1985; Aggleton, 1987). In many ways, therefore, this study seeks to complement others in this book by exploring post-16 responses to schooling in a specifically college-based context.

Spatown as a city has relatively little traditional industry, the bulk of its residents being employed in administrative, educational and other professional occupations. It is also a major centre of tourism, being a city which has long-standing associations with the arts. It has therefore attracted as residents many members of the new middle class and, in particular, that fraction of the class that Bernstein (1977) has called <u>agents of symbolic control</u>. The students in the study were aged between 16 and 20. Most of their parents were engaged in teaching, lecturing, social work, or various artistic or creative pursuits. In terms of their class background, therefore, the young people in this study differed considerably from those studied by Willis (1977).

This particular group of students was selected because their tutors at Spatown College regarded them as somewhat anomalous in that, despite coming from homes rich in <u>cultural capital</u> (Bourdieu and Passeron, 1977), they lacked motivation towards academic study and seemed likely to attain and be content with relatively low grades in the GCE Advanced Level examinations for which they were studying. From an initial core of respondents thus identified, a final group of thirteen male and fourteen female students was selected by creating a snowball sample based on mutual association and friendship. Because of sibling relationships within the group, the respondents came from a total of twenty households.

Of particular interest within the analysis of data from this study was the extent to which the responses of this group of students to schooling could be regarded as potentially transformative in their outcome. However, because studies earlier referred to, argue that determinate effects are likely to be the outcome of an articulation between students' responses to schooling and other social practices across different sites of experience, it was felt necessary to enquire into the practices of the group not only at school and college, but also in domestic and subcultural contexts as well.

Before reporting on findings arising from the study itself, and in the light of issues raised earlier to do with how best to conceptualise students' responses to schooling, a brief outline will be offered of the ways in which practices within and across sites articulate with each other to produce hegemonic and counter-hegemonic effects. A more extended analysis of these issues can be found in Aggleton (1987).

## CLARIFYING WHAT IS MEANT BY STUDENT 'RESISTANCE'

With regard to the variety of practices referred to within the literature as student 'resistance', it is clearly necessary to differentiate first of all between 'resistant' intentions and 'resistant' effects. The former may, on some occasions, be forerunners to the latter, but all too often they may lead instead to essentially hegemonic outcomes. We can find illustrations of such processes in operation in the work of Willis (1977), McRobbie (1978), and Anyon (1981a, 1983).

Second, in analyses of the role played by responses to schooling in processes of social reproduction and transformation, care should be taken to specify the focus of acts of 'resistance'. In particular, we should distinguish between actions directed against power relations that operate pervasively throughout society and those directed against localised principles of control (Bernstein, 1977, 1982). For the sake of conceptual clarity, I intend to call only the first of these types of acts resistances. The latter I will refer to instead as contestations.

Third, any analysis of students' responses to schooling should remain sensitive to the possibility that there may

205

exist some tension between 'resistant' subjectivity and 'resistant' behaviour (Giroux, 1983). Within the former of these two stages in the working up of oppositional practice, there are likely to be two separate moments. During the first of these, understandings of the nature of power and control relations are likely to be transitory, sporadic, and personally held. At the second, such culturally penetrative insights are likely to become more collectively shared and systematically organized so as to prefigure counter-hegemonic practice.

Fourth, Gintis and Bowles's (1980) work suggests that on many occasions, 'resistant' behaviours at one site of practice (say, the school or college) may be the result of 'resistant' intentions <u>transported</u> or displaced from another site of experience (say the home). In the light of this, care should be taken to guard against too direct a reading of the nature of student subjectivity and practice within any one particular context.

Finally, we need to remember that it is the net effect of articulations between practices across sites of experience and within different, but inter-related, sets of power and control relations that establishes the overall balance between socially reproductive and socially transformatory tendencies. A necessary, though not sufficient, basis for the analysis of 'resistances' must therefore involve an exploration of the <u>articulation</u> between hegemonic and counter-hegemonic practices <u>across different sites of experience</u>.

In this chapter, these distinctions will be worked with in an analysis of the data generated from the empirical study of the practices of this particular group of students across three main sites of experience.

## HOME

Gaining access to the homes of the students involved in this study proved to be a relatively simple matter because of some of their distinguishing cultural qualities. Compared with traditional working-class or managerial middle-class households, there was little sense that respondents' homes were an essentially private domain to be protected from outsiders. It therefore proved possible to visit each of them on at least three occasions during the two years over which fieldwork took place.

Drawing on conceptual frameworks provided by Bernstein's (1971, 1977) analysis of new middle class cultural practices, it was possible to identify as one of the most prominent features of students' homes a selective blurring of <u>classificatory relationships</u> both within them, and between them and the outside world. In most of the households visited, day to day activities took place within a large living area on the ground floor - a kitchen or breakfast room, perhaps - into which were introduced (in an apparently chaotic fashion) objects and practices conventionally associated with other settings.

> In ten of the homes visited there was a large open-plan kitchen living area in which most of the social visiting took place. ... Such kitchen/living areas were frequently decorated with postcards, children's art and books of various types. Magazines would lie stacked on shelves or would spill out of cupboards. ... At first sight the appearance of many such settings gave the impression that almost any object could have been expected to be visibly present as toilet rolls, the complete works of Shakespeare, half-eaten apple pies, aerosol deodorants and recent airmail letters lay jumbled together. (Aggleton, 1984)

Through these common living areas would pass a near-constant stream of visitors who dropped in, stopping for short periods to talk over cups of tea or coffee.

> There were always people coming in and out of the house. We always had the backdoor open. We never locked it. We had nothing really valuable so people just dropped in and out of the door. It was just like Paddington station. (<u>Stuart</u> in Aggleton, 1987)

A more detailed analysis of such settings, however, revealed that within them, this blurring of categories and practices was informed by certain underlying principles. Thus, only certain sorts of objects and practices were imported into the home from outside it. Artefacts indicating acquaintance with the worlds of fine and creative art were particularly in evidence in the form of art posters or theatre or art gallery programmes. Similarly, postcards, apparently carelessly left lying about or pinned to cork notice-boards, the backs of doors, or sides of shelves, all seemed to originate from overseas. The most frequent visitors to these homes also revealed a concern with the arts and the media and with the foreign and the exotic. Authors, artists, and film directors were particularly in evidence. Members of the local artistic and literary community, especially men who were known to be gay, were frequently present. Conversation seemed to be used to reveal acquaintance with the latest forms of literary or artistic practice or to display personal commitments to socialism, feminism, peace, or ecology. Stickers indicating the family commitment to these causes were also displayed outside windows.

As we shall see later, this selective blurring of distinctions between public and private modes of experience within the home had important implications for students themselves. At one level, parents' importing into the home of people, artefacts and practices associated with culturally exotic forms of experience helped establish criteria enabling students to differentiate between 'culturally acceptable' and 'culturally non-acceptable' spheres of practice. At another, it helped imbue the former of these two realms with an authenticity seen as lacking in the latter.

Within students' homes, there was also a blurring of distinctions between work and leisure; in particular, between paid employment outside the home and more family-oriented pursuits within it. The nature of parental occupations meant that work associated with paid employment was often carried out in the home, and time was not neatly divided between a nine-to-five working day and home-centred evening and weekend activity. Some parents held tutorials for their students in their homes, others held 'academic soirées' or undertook counselling work at home. Involvement in drama and other artistic pursuits was often organised using the households as a base. Thus, some of the more usual distinctions that exist in modern industrial societies between paid employment, the home and leisure activities were less easy to discern in these particular settings (Rojek, 1985).

However, this blurring of the distinction between work and leisure also had consequences for students, in that it enabled their activities to be more carefully monitored by parents themselves. For example, the open living spaces through which visitors passed, and in which the members of the family spent much of their time talking, arguing, and reading afforded those present the opportunity to observe the behaviour of others with some intensity. Parents were thus able to acquire considerable insight into the motives, projects, and subjectivities of their offspring - something further consolidated by the process of elaborate verbal justification required from students when absence from the household was being negotiated. While respondents had been free to visit friends and stay out late from an early age, the granting of parental permission to do this was conditional upon detailed information first being provided about the precise intentions of those involved. Similarly, while many respondents had been encouraged by their parents to drink alcohol or smoke marijuana, this too had been conditional upon them using such substances under parental surveillance within the home.

> Well, first I had wine with water. I suppose that was when I was about seven or eight. Then I used to get a glass to myself. Then there would always be cider when Mum had one of her parties. It's just that it's always been there. (Ric in Aggleton, 1987)

> I don't know, I smoked my first joint when I was about eight with my parents. I mean, I think I could do things which they agreed with really, things which they thought were all right. (Jane in Aggleton, 1987)

Similarly, permission to sleep with a friend of the opposite sex was also willingly given, provided parents received information in advance about the intentions and commitments of both parties involved. Successful negotiations of a wide variety of situations therefore required respondents to use communicative strategies by which their personal motives and intentions were made apparent. As we shall see later, such processes had important implications for the way in which the respondents negotiated the educational sites of practice.

However, parental surveillance operated differently for female and male respondents. In particular, parents' concern for the development of industrious and committed heterosexual involvements among their offspring led them to encourage different modalities of practice among their daughters and sons. In particular, there were rather different limits to the degree of liberalism involved in the encouragement of heterosexual liaisons. Female respondents

209

were more insistently interrogated about the nature of their present and proposed heterosexual relationships, while males were more readily granted permission, and even encouraged, to absent themselves overnight for liaisons, which were perceived to be important for their personal development but did not seem to involve the degree of commitment required of female respondents.

> I couldn't bring ... I couldn't come home with a boy she (Mum) didn't know, and spend the night together and then never see him again. She'd let ... It would happen but she would get funny about it. There's no rules, but you wouldn't upset Mum. (Jill in Aggleton, 1984)

> I can remember when I started bringing girls back. No one really said anything about it but I got the feeling that they were really rather proud. (Phil in Aggleton, 1984)

Parents also displayed a profound ambivalence in their attitudes towards homosexual practices. While they openly welcomed gay men into their homes as friends, they viewed with considerable disquiet the possibility of homosexual activity among members of their own family. In one case, this went as far as a threat to invoke therapeutic counselling. These limitations to parental liberalism also had important implications for the way in which students negotiated educational and subcultural contexts.

## SCHOOL AND COLLEGE

The parents of students in the present study showed a great deal of interest in the education that their daughters and sons obtained. Many of them had taken deliberate steps to ensure that the latter attended either primary schools with a 'progressive' ethos or private 'Free Schools'. In both of these contexts, integrated day and child-centred curricula were likely to be the norm.

> I used to go to this Free School in Broadville ... to a Free School right? You pay fees and do what you want. The idea is that each stage you go through, if you learn something, you will learn it better

because you want to. Yeah? (<u>Norma</u> in Aggleton, 1984)

Did they choose this Free School for you? (PA)
Yeah, and we were going to move back to London because there was a better one there, but there was nowhere to live. (<u>Jill</u> in Aggleton, 1984)

For many respondents, transfer to secondary school had been yet another occasion for parental intervention in students' educational careers. At the time of the fieldwork, secondary education in all but one of Spatown's schools was organised on the basis of single-sex provision. It was therefore significant that less than one-third of the respondents attended such single-sex schools.

However, once at secondary school, students displayed a great deal of antipathy towards certain aspects of the schooling process. These included compulsory attendance at religious assemblies, the need to wear uniform, the requirement to attend school between certain hours, and the reluctance of teachers to accept the strategies of verbal self-justification that respondents used to negotiate how they spent their time. Reactions towards these elements of perceived oppression varied in intensity from minor arguments with teachers and the refusal to wear a school uniform to persistent absence from school and head-on confrontations with head teachers and senior staff.

You know, I used to argue with the Headmistress over points. OK, the majority of the points were totally trivial. But you know, just points of school uniform. And I did that once and had a very large argument with her and made her cry and got pulled up before the Deputy Head and got told I wasn't allowed to speak to the Headmistress like that. (<u>Patsie</u> in Aggleton, 1984)

In a number of instances, such was the intensity of students' non-conformity that, had it not been for parental intervention, they would have been required to transfer school.

At the same time as they pose a threat to the dominant ordering of the school, challenges against aspects of the process of secondary schooling concerned with the management of spatial and temporal arrangements and against

211

teachers' use of positional control techniques (Bernstein 1977) affirm the importance of personalised control over the use of time and space (a prevalent practice in respondents' homes). Students' refusal to accept an externally imposed timetable by arriving late for class, their use of self-justification as a tactic in arguments with teachers, and their adoption of styles of self-presentation articulating with personal ideological and political commitments can best be understood as effects arising from the transport-ation of practices from the family site to the school (Gintis & Bowles, 1980).

However, since such challenges were directed primarily against principles of control within the localised context of the school (and not, in Bernstein's (1982) terms, against relations of power), and since such strategies of challenge help consolidate modes of habitus[1] associated with personal-ised control over systems of meaning, there are reasons to be less than optimistic about the outcomes of such struggles for social transformation. Indeed, while such challenges were instrumental in ensuring that students left school at age 16 to attend college of further education, their continued existence after transition had further conse-quences for students' educational experience in this latter context.

Two such effects are worthy of special attention. The first of these relates to the curricular choices that took place at Spatown College itself. Students responded to the curriculum at Spatown College in a highly selective manner. Subjects likely to fall within criteria of 'cultural accept-ability' as defined within the home were those most likely to be studied. Hence, History of Art, Fine Art, English Literature, Theatre, and Communication Studies were by far the most commonly preferred options. The pure sciences and Mathematics were much less frequently chosen. Further-more, attendance at classes was highly sporadic, and the completion of assignments was similarly uncommitted. When questioned about this, respondents frequently referred to the limited possibilities for personal expression existing even within chosen curricular options. As a result, students involved themselves only in those activities that allowed the greatest amount of personal expression. Hence, visits to theatres and art galleries were well attended, as were film and theatre production classes. On the other hand, classes requiring the committed production of written work or acquaintance with the opinions and writings of others were far from popular. As they had done at secondary school, students also showed an unwillingness to attend classes at predefined times and places. It is therefore possible to find elements of both affirmation and challenge in their behaviour at this site as practices transported from the home articulate with those in educational settings.

It is important to recognise as well, that students' opposition to aspects of the schooling process was <u>non-collective</u> in form. Indeed, many of them actively eschewed involvement in collective struggle organized concurrently by Spatown College's Students' Union, preferring to challenge <u>personally</u> principles of control within the college. In view of this, it is best to regard such challenges not as resistances but as <u>contestations</u> which affirm the value of <u>personal control</u> over the management of space, time, and systems of meaning. As such, they contribute towards hegemonic tendencies within processes of cultural reproduction. At the same time, however, they may also have rather special consequences for the individuals concerned, since irregular class attendance and limited involvement in academic study are modes of practice likely to militate against success in examinations. Such was clearly to be seen in the lack of success students displayed in public examinations.

## SUBCULTURE

Beyond home and college, students spent much of their time in the <u>Roundhouse,</u> a large bar in the centre of Spatown; the <u>Tube Club,</u> a discotheque popular with members of the local gay community; and the <u>Dugout Club,</u> a late-night bar. During the day, popular meeting places included an open-plan coffee area in the local arts centre and respondents' own homes. Non-preferred subcultural sites included discotheques owned by commercial chains and bars where 'straights' (those of comparable age to respondents, but in full-time paid employment) were likely to go. Towards the end of the fieldwork, when a number of respondents had obtained casual work in restaurants and fast-food outlets, these too became significant sites of subcultural activity.

When asked about the importance of these contexts, students frequently commented on the fact that within them, they might meet 'interesting people' with 'interesting ideas':

> You know, you would go down to the pub and you
> would think that you were going to have a really
> fantastic time, and you were going to meet all
> these new and interesting people ... An interesting
> person for me would be someone who could
> actually talk about what they had been reading
> recently, and would talk about it, films and things
> like that. (Carol in Aggleton, 1984)

A number of female respondents also mentioned that these
contexts had been those in which they had first developed an
appreciation of feminism and sexual politics and feminism.

> What did you used to do in the Roundhouse?    (PA)
> We used to chat about politics and things. They
> weren't intelligible conversations ... We were
> trying to get our political ideas together and the
> things we believed in. And then we moved on from
> that to talk about Women's Liberation and had
> vicious fights with men across the room. (Wendy in
> Aggleton, 1986)

In part, such discussions seemed to have been triggered
by male students' attempts to dominate the use of space in
these settings. The latter frequently monopolised physical
space by spreading their clothes over several adjacent seats
and by throwing beer, peanuts, and crisp packets at each
other. They also attempted to exert control over conversational space by talking and laughing at high volume,
telling denigratory jokes about others present and making
comments with sexist implications. Such behaviours caused
female respondents on many occasions to physically
separate themselves from their male counterparts, thereafter developing an incipient critique of these aspects of
patriarchal practice.

Talk about others was a dominant practice in settings
such as the Wheel Inn, and a great deal of time was spent
making fun of others who were around. Such social
strategies exhibited a definite structure, involving first a
critique of another person's apparent identity, followed by
the substitution of a more 'authentic' understanding. For
example, someone's way of standing might be analyzed as
'posey' or 'pretentious', and the individual exhibiting it might
thereafter be interpreted as someone behaving that way out

of an inherent 'insecurity' or 'snobbishness'. Another person's hair or preferred clothing might be seen as 'trendy' (a term of denigration) - a sure sign of the person's real 'need to be accepted'.

> And as for Steve who plucks his eyebrows by all accounts. He's an arrogant bastard. ... I mean, know it's only because he feels so fucking inadequate in himself, but I don't see why he has to put that act on with me. (Dave in Aggleton, 1987)

Social strategies involving the deconstruction and reconstruction of personal identity in a process of personal authentication, were part of a more general concern to display privileged insight into other people's motives. However, the use of these strategies created conditions in which a problematization of interpersonal intimacy occurred. In particular, since status among students was closely linked to an ability to successfully authenticate the identity of others, there existed both a desire for involvement in such a process (in order to achieve status) and a more general apprehension that this might lay the self open to being authenticated by others as a 'bitch' (a term applied to both female and male respondents) or a 'gossip'. This pressing concern to display personal insight into the motives of others is yet further evidence for the transportation of practices across sites of experience: this time, from the home to the subcultural context.

A further significant dimension of subcultural practice concerned the types of paid employment undertaken by students. Throughout the fieldwork, two fast-food restaurants, specializing in the sale of beefburgers, kebabs, and chili dishes, were well frequented by respondents, both as staff and consumers. In each of these settings, personal acquaintance with management enabled employees to negotiate when and how they worked. Standards of appearance, timekeeping, and style of service were some of the more obvious aspects of employment amenable to personal control. Moreover, both restaurants were environments in which it was possible for staff to engage in sustained conversations with visiting friends. Within such contexts, therefore, there was a significant weakening of distinctions between work and leisure, allowing significant opportunities for personal autonomy with respect to the negotiation of employment conditions.

215

Finally, comment should be made about dominant modes of sexual practice among students. Here, significant differences existed between females and males. For the latter, clear distinctions were drawn between heterosexual relationships that were perceived as offering opportunities for long-term personal development and those that were not. Both types of relationship were engaged in, often simultaneously.

> I don't think it matters at all if you have relationships with other people (outside of a steady relationship) as long as you are sure about the other person. I mean, if you know that you mean a lot to them, then you're only going to let things go so far with someone else. I think problems stem from insecurity in the main relationship. (Doug in Aggleton, 1987)

Females, on the other hand, perceived as inappropriate, heterosexual involvements other than those that implied personal commitment on the part of both parties. Indeed, a number of them criticised girls outside college with whom males were casually involved, seeing them (and not the males concerned) as cheap or common. For females, therefore, heterosexual relationships had to be perceived as committed before they were entered into.

> I think it's important to have a relationship with just one man at a time. I don't think you can give very much to a number of people at the same time. Besides, what they (the men) would say is that you weren't giving them much attention if you were having a relationship with more than one at the same time. (Susan in Aggleton, 1987)

Differences also existed in the extent to which homosexual relationships took place. For males, these tended to be relatively infrequent, taking place only on the occasional drunken evening during holiday. For females, personal commitment towards modes of feminist practice impelled a number of them to deliberately participate in homosexual relationships in addition to committed heterosexual relationships.

## CONTINUITY, TRANSFORMATION AND THE REPRODUCTION OF CLASS RELATIONS

By examining students' responses within the home, at college and subculturally, it is possible to identify continuities and transformations between these and those of their parents. For both groups, high levels of personal control over systems of meaning was important.

In the case of parents, such concerns were witnessed both by the paid employment they undertook as agents of symbolic control and by dominant patterns of social practice at home. Their efforts to selectively import into the home elements of experience connoting degrees of 'cultural acceptability', and to insistently monitor the social practices of their children are related to such general tendencies.

For students, a desire to exert personal control over systems of meaning could be seen both in their use of specific communicative strategies to negotiate personal freedom over the use of space and time inside and outside the home, and in their responses to formal educational contexts. Their concern to explore to the limit personalising opportunities within the secondary school curriculum created confrontations with teachers and administrators, which, in many cases, were instrumental in securing their transition to college of further education at the age of 16. This desire was also responsible for their selective appropriation of the range of curricular options available at college and for their partial commitment to the pursuit of academic study once there.

These responses to formal educational provision are discontinuous with those of their parents. For the latter, post-school education had been a desirable goal. Twenty-two out of forty of them had gone on to further or higher education immediately after leaving school. Others had undertaken similar study subsequently, and thirty-two had first degrees or teaching diplomas at the time of the fieldwork. Thus, in a clear majority of cases, parents placed high value upon further and higher education. This did not seem to be true of students. On the whole, their academic grades were poor, and six years after fieldwork commenced, only three had become involved in committed academic higher eduation.

Such generational discontinuities require explanation. The beginnings of this may be found in parents' encouragement of acquaintance with artefacts and experiences ensuring familiarity with the creators of the fine arts, theatre, and media art forms. For students, these aspects of artistic production thereby come to be taken for granted and accepted as everyday elements of experience (something which was not the case for parents themselves). Moreover, the specificity of the manner by which these modes of acquaintance were encouraged was such that respondents came to perceive these artefacts and practices as intimately associated with the intrinsic qualities of individual creators and not with more general processes of cultural production, of which individual creators are but a part. Authorial ideologies such as these, emphasizing the immanent talents of individuals as creators of fine art, contrast sharply with those which instead emphasise the importance of training, diligence, and industrious commitment in the pursuit of creative and expressive goals. Hence, we can better understand why respondents displayed apathy towards elements of self-denial, ritualised training, and prior effort in the attainment of qualifications in these same areas of practice. Instead, they acted as if their own innate talents and cultural capital would, of themselves, provide sufficient basis for entry into, and success within, fields of practice associated with creative art forms.

The pursuit of personalising goals within education had additional consequences for respondents' academic attainment. Fifteen out of twenty-seven students in the present study left Spatown College with no qualifications other than those they had when they arrived. Six years later, however, at a time of high national youth unemployment, such underachievement was found to have had relatively insignificant consequences for students' employment. All were in paid employment at this time - working in cocktail bars and chic restaurants, as theatre staff, video and film technicians, or as personal assistants to those in the worlds of fine and media arts.

Such trajectories seem to suggest that the challenges directed against aspects of the schooling process within secondary education and at college of further education are far from structural in their effects. Rather, they are concerned with the winning of personal autonomy within social relations. Respondents' affirmation of communicative strategies attempting personal control over systems of meaning in these contexts may thereby serve to consolidate a mode of habitus by which students are later able to secure paid employment associated with institutionalized processes of symbolic control. Their <u>contestations</u> thereby serve what are essentially hegemonic moments in processes of cultural and social reproduction. They have an important role to play in generationally reproducing the cultural basis of class divisions.

## CONTINUITY, TRANSFORMATION, AND THE REPRODUCTION OF GENDER RELATIONS

Parental surveillance of respondents' practice was one of a number of factors contributing to a problematisation of interpersonal intimacy for students in the present study. Other factors included those associated with tendencies towards the subcultural <u>personal authentication</u> of others. Such processes, which de-privatise the desires of others, demonstrate clearly some of the tensions existing between personalization and socialization as cultural possibilities (Wexler, 1983). Indeed, insistent surveillance, the deconstruction of other people's intentions, and the trading of commodified indentities are all practices that serve to fragment our experience of others.

Yet this problematisation had different effects for female and male students. It was earlier suggested that patriarchally constituted messages within families ensured that females acquired degrees of competence within heterosexual relationships and a respect for the value of personalizing monogamous commitment. Such tendencies, it was argued, relate at least in part to parental concern for personal development through industrious and committed heterosexual practice. However, their existence also betrays a concern that female respondents acquire a competent heterosexual femininity. As such, they may be motivated by ideologies toward what Brunt (1982) has called a <u>hidden essentialism</u> informing middle-class female practice. In writing of recent tendencies encouraging middle-class women to become experts in sensuality and heterosexual practice, she has argued that 'as models of feminine conduct, both the "new" sensuous woman and the heroines of romance have a vocational attitude to their sexuality. Their aim is to build a sexual career with the ultimate purpose of trapping those men whose superior economic status and resources go with a barely controllable sex appetite' (Brunt, 1982: 158).

We can therefore begin to understand why potential

boyfriends were so carefully screened by the parents of female students in this study and why their friendship with openly homosexual men was encouraged (since the latter were perceived by parents as likely to pose little threat to the attainment of such competences).

Strategies like these, however, can also have unintended consequences. For some females at least, their interest in establishing personalising sexual relationships encouraged an active participation in homosexual activity. Such motivations may take their origins, at least in part, from the influence of new feminist ideologies within respondents' homes: ideologies which emphasise the expansion of boundaries relating to permissable sexual relations and which challenge the patriarchal nature of sexual commitment as practiced within the nuclear family. As such, these practices may be seen as affirmations of the political and ideological commitments operated with by both generations of women in the present study.

However, it is equally important to identify such explorations as cultural challenges, actions which win ideological space from male subcultural surveillance. As intentioned resistances sharing some degree of systematic insight into the nature of heterosexual gender oppression, they may well be forms of practice potentially prefigurative of emancipatory struggle. Nevertheless, there were also factors militating against these modes of critical insight and practice developing into effective resistances. Some of these related to attempts by male students to stigmatise the homosexual activity of females; others to the extent to which females themselves remained concurrently committed to the value of personalizing monogamous heterosexual relationships. Thus, for example, when questioned, a majority of female students continued to articulate a belief in the value of such relationships in addition to their commitment to feminist struggle. It would seem therefore that there are a number of disorienting factors militating against the development of effective resistances from such forms of cultural challenge.

If articulations between affirmation and challenge within the gendered practice of female students held the potential for socially transformative effects, this was not so obviously true for males. They, it will be recalled, drew clear distinctions between heterosexual liaisons that were perceived as offering opportunities for personal development and those that were not. Indeed, male students professed to finding it difficult to meet female partners offering possibilities for personal development. Involvement in casual relationships, however, took a serial form. Relationships varied in their intensity and degree but were essentially commodified in their nature, since involvement other than that minimally necessary to establish and consummate sexual relations must, of necessity, result in an objectification of the partner.

Such patterns of practice share considerable similarity with those of their fathers. They too publicly professed to believe in the value of committed, industriously pursued, and perceptibly personalising heterosexual involvements at the same time as they participated in more casual serial heterosexual liaisons. Similarly, both generations of males showed few signs of involvement in homosexual practice. Furthermore, they showed little willingness to critically analyse their sexual involvements. While females used both public and private opportunities to develop modes of critical appreciation and practice, males showed little interest in questioning the basis around which their own sexual practices and involvements came to be constituted. It therefore seems that the gendered practice of males in the present study displayed even fewer tendencies towards potentially transformative effects than that of the females.

## CONCLUSIONS

From the evidence in this study, it would seem that on the whole, the practices of this particular group of new middle class students are essentially hegemonic and thus repro-ductive in their effects. Any suggestion that their apparent rejection of the dominant ethos of schooling is anything more than a contestation needs to be viewed with considerable scepticism. There is little evidence from this study that challenges directed against the principles of control operative in particular sites, or carried across from one site to another, are effective resistances to prevailing patterns of power relations in English society. Even the limited examples of discontinuity between this group's practices and their parents' culture seem ultimately to be reproductive in their effects. At most, they are attempts to win a limited degree of personal autonomy within a broader acceptance of existing sets of relations. Any concern that their teachers at Spatown College may have had that their response to schooling poses a threat either to their personal futures or to the fabric of Western society would seem premature, to say the least.

Of course, this does not, of itself, imply that in other circumstances, the practices of this group lack the potential to become effectively resistant. The possibility that they could become articulated with other practices to produce such effects always remains open. However, there are important dimensions to their practice, especially those that seem to have developed out of their parents' culture, that would seem to militate against this. In particular, the emphasis on the personalised and personalising nature of authentic commitment makes it difficult for these students to develop their critique of prevailing power and control relations into more collectively and systematically organized counter-hegemonic practices. In this, the form of parental culture seems to have been more powerful in the socialization process than its content, for the students seem more suspicious of displaying commitment to causes as represented by unions or political parties than did their parents. This poses considerable problems for any educational programme that aims to work with the contestations of such students to produce a sense of solidarity with broader oppositional struggles in society (Anyon, 1981b; Giroux, 1983).

Overall, there is little in this study to suggest that the contestations of this group towards localized principles of control can be easily developed into resistance to broader patterns of class relations. With regard to gender relations, the position is somewhat less clear. Though the critique of patriarchal relations offered by the female respondents showed some signs of developing into an alternative mode of collective practice, it did not become actively oppositional to the continuance of patriarchal relations in general. However, it might have developed differently in different circumstances, and it certainly displayed more potential for becoming an effective resistance than did any of the other contestations identified. On the other hand, the emphasis on personalised modes of practice elsewhere within the culture of the group gives even this challenge a form that isolates it from other transformative movements in society at large, so that the practices of this relatively privileged group may not be as readily won to the broader feminist movement as it might at first sight appear.

In reflecting on the significance of the study as a whole, it can only be concluded that the role of new middle class students such as these in social transformation remains to be demonstrated. On the evidence of this study, there may be considerably greater difficulties confronting those who would wish to politicise the contestations of this group than those who wish to do so with those of working class youth.

## ACKNOWLEDGEMENTS

I would like to thank the following for their helpful comments on earlier drafts of all or parts of this paper - Basil Bernstein, John Fitz, Leslie Rothaus, Marilyn Toft, Geoff Whitty, Philip Wexler.

## NOTE

1.  Social perceptions, habits of thought and modes of practice common to a class or class fraction.

## REFERENCES

Aggleton, P.J. (1984) 'Reproductive "resistance": A study of the origins and effects of youth subcultural style amongst a group of new middle class students in a college of further education', Unpublished PhD thesis, University of London.
——— (1987) Rebels Without a Cause? Lewes, Falmer Press.
——— and Whitty, G.J. (1985) 'Rebels without a cause? Socialization and Subcultural Style among the Children of the New Middle Classes', Sociology of Education, 58, 60-72.
——— and Whitty, G.J. (1986) 'Components of a Radical Health Education Practice', Radical Health Promotion, 4, 24-8.
Anyon, J. (1981a) 'Social Class and School Knowledge', Curriculum Inquiry, 11, 3-42.
——— (1981b) 'Elementary schooling and disinctions of social class', Interchange, 12, 118-132.
——— (1983) 'Intersections of Gender and Class: Accommodation and Resistance by Working Class and Affluent Females to Contradictory Sex-Roles Ideologies', in S. Walker and L. Barton (eds) Gender, Class and Education, Lewes, Falmer Press.
Aronowitz, S and Giroux, H. (1985) Education under Siege,

London, Routledge & Kegan Paul.

Ball, S. (1981) Beachside Comprehensive, Cambridge, Cambridge University Press.

Bernstein, B. (1971) Class, Codes and Control, vol. 1, London, Routledge & Kegan Paul.

—— (1977) Class, Codes and Control, vol. 3 (revised edition), London, Routledge & Kegan Paul.

—— (1982) 'Class, modalities and the process of cultural reproduction: a model', in M. Apple (ed.) Cultural and Economic Reproduction in Education, London, Routledge & Kegan Paul.

Bourdieu, P. and Passeron, J.C. (1977) Reproduction in Education, Society and Culture, Beverly Hills, Sage.

Bowles, S. and Gintis, H. (1976) Schooling in Capitalist America, London, Routledge & Kegan Paul.

Brunt, R. (1982) 'An immense verbosity: Permissive sexual advice in the 1970s', in R. Brunt and C. Cowan (eds) Feminism, Culture and Politics, London, Lawrence & Wishart.

Connell, R.W., Ashenden, D.J., Kessler, S. and Dowsett, G.W. (1982) Making the Difference, Sydney, George Allen & Unwin.

Davies, L. (1983) Pupil Power, Barcombe, Falmer Press.

Furlong, V. (1985) The Deviant Pupil, Milton Keynes, Open University Press.

Gintis, H. (1972) 'Activism and counter-culture: The dialectics of consciousness in the corporate state', Telos, 12, 42-62.

—— and Bowles, S. (1980) 'Contradiction and reproduction in educational theory', in L. Barton, R. Meighan and S. Walker (eds) Schooling, Ideology and the Curriculum, Barcombe, Falmer Press.

Giroux, H.A. (1983) Theory and Resistance in Education, London, Heinemann.

Hargreaves, A. (1982) 'Resistance and relative autonomy theories: Problems of distortion and incoherence in recent Marxist analyses of education', British Journal of Sociology of Education, 3, 107-126.

Hargreaves, D. (1967) Social Relations in a Secondary School, London, Routledge & Kegan Paul.

Lacey, C. (1970) Hightown Grammar, Manchester, Manchester University Press.

McRobbie, A. (1978) 'Working Class Girls and the Culture of Femininity in Women's Studies Group', Centre for Contemporary Cultural Studies, Women Take Issue,

London, Hutchinson.

Marcuse, H. (1969) An Essay on Liberation, Harmondsworth, Penguin Books.

Rojek, C. (1985) Capitalism and Leisure Theory, London, Tavistock.

Roszak, T. (1968) The Making of a Counter-Culture, London, Faber & Faber.

Turner, G. (1983) The Social World of the Comprehensive School, London, Croom Helm.

Walker, J. (1986) 'Romanticising Resistance, Romanticising Culture: Problems in Willis's theory of cultural production', British Journal of Sociology of Education, 7, 59–80.

Werthman, C. (1963) 'Delinquents in School: A test for the legitimacy of authority', Berkeley Journal of Sociology, 8, 39–60.

Wexler, P. (1983) Critical Social Psychology, London, Routledge & Kegan Paul.

Willis, P. (1977) Learning to Labour, Farnborough, Saxon House.

———— (1981) 'Cultural Production is Different from Cultural Reproduction is Different from Social Production is Different from Social Reproduction', Interchange, 12, pp. 48-67.

Whitty, G.J. (1985) Sociology and School Knowledge - Curriculum Theory, Research and Politics, London, Methuen.

Woods, P. (1979) The Divided School, London, Routledge & Kegan Paul.

# 12

# On the Margins of Education:
# Finding a Dimension for Belief

## Bernadette O'Keeffe

The comprehensive system is variously described in terms of its educational goals and social aspirations. Reflecting the contemporary environment, values of an anti-racist stance, a drive for equality, 'parity of prestige' between schools and an end to selection at the age of eleven are all features which impart meaning and social purpose. It will be seen that either as a result of an exclusive focus on a single objective or conversely of merging various hopes and aspirations into an all-embracing social goal the comprehensive ideal has translated into a uniformity of structure and practice unable to admit plurality in values and priorities. An educational monolith has emerged defensive in the presence of other beliefs and cultures. Paradoxically the system of maintained education, which at both primary and secondary levels accepts responsibility for educating 7,043,164 children, draws upon a legal base which gives support and legitimacy to diverse approaches to education (DES 1986). In England and Wales the 1944 Education Act created a legal framework for a partnership between State and the Churches. The Act gave legal support to the already existing diversity of schools - namely provided and non-provided schools. The former were established and controlled by local education authorities, the latter by voluntary societies, which in the main were associated with the Church of England and the Roman Catholic Church. Under the Act non-provided schools could opt for a voluntary 'aided' or 'controlled' status.

Voluntary aided schools required the financial support of the Churches, who were required to meet 50% of the capital costs, external maintenance and the provision of new school buildings. The remaining 50% would be covered by central government grants. (This 50% grant was subsequently increased to 75% in 1959, 80% in 1967 and is at present 85%). The local education authority became responsible for all other running costs of aided schools. Two-thirds of Governors would be appointed by the Foundation (Church). The balance of responsibility for staff appointments, pupil admissions, and curriculum (in secondary schools) would rest with the Churches and Governors rather than the local education authorities. The Act also enabled aided schools to provide denominational religious instruction and denominational worship.

A controlled school, on the other hand, would be maintained by the local educational authority which became responsible for finance, pupil admissions and staff appointments, except in the case of 'reserved teachers' to be appointed by governors or managers of Church schools for the purposes of giving religious instruction. Denominational religious instruction was to be given not more than twice a week to those children whose parents requested it. One-third of the governors would be appointed by the Foundation (Church) and the remaining two-thirds by the local education authority.

The 1944 Act was passed in the face of strong opposition from political groups and some mainly non-conformist religious groups. Objections were raised to the State financially supporting 'religious' as well as secular schools. Since the 1944 Act, the dual system, as it became known, has not been without its critics. Never far from controversy, political and secular groups have, from time to time, sought to abolish the dual system, and to replace it with a unified secular one. For example, the British Humanist Society (1967) has been campaigning for the abolition of Church schools in the maintained sector for a number of years. They make clear their views in the following way:

> Aided schools giving religious and moral education in accordance with the doctrines of a particular church or religious body should no longer continue as part of the system of schools maintained by rates and taxes. They should be taken over as County schools or left to the Church to finance without State aid.

The overall purpose of the 1944 Education Act was to establish a viable maintained system of education by formulating a broad context for all foreseeable future developments. Both the State and the Churches as partners assented to one publicly-funded system of education - the 'dual system' of County and voluntary schools. The legal basis recognised a principle of differentiation, a principle which allowed for differing responses to be made by the State and Churches in meeting the needs of children and of society.

Legitimacy was given to contrasting approaches to education - differences which at base reflected the conflicting demands of 'this wordly' and 'other wordly' concerns. The County schools had a national unifying role with attendant contemporary social and educational responsibilities. The National Society speaking for the Church of England described the two-fold role of the Church of England school. The domestic role catered for the needs of the Christian community. The general role reflected an educational responsibility to all the children of the nation (The National Society, 1812/1813).

Differentiation was more marked in the case of Roman Catholic schools. These schools were 'separatist' in character and their role was to provide Catholic education for Catholic children in a Catholic environment (Catholic Bishop's Report, 1981). It is not uncommon to hear educationalists challenge the legitimate rights of the Churches to operate distinctive Christian schools. On philosophical grounds, Hirst (1972) argues that a concept of 'Christian education' is 'a contradiction in terms', and a 'misleading anachronism'. He asserts that, if Church schools are to retain a legitimate place in education, they must abide by the same rules as a secular school. From this premiss he argues that it is inappropriate for Church schools to undertake Christian nurture or catechesis where the 'aim is from a stance of faith, the development of faith'.

Today the social and secular priorities of much educational thought illustrate a refusal to accept those different priorities which are manifested in Church schools but whose legitimacy in terms of the 1944 Act is not in doubt. By extension, any educational expression of the wider differentiated society is also successfully repressed. That part of the educational system, accounting today for 67.7% of all maintained schools is thus endowed with a facade which alone is acceptable in maintained education. The endeavours of that section which lie 'outside' are called into question and various interest groups continue to deny the

Churches a role in education and other historic faith communities the right to determine the education of their young. 'Good education' becomes the prerogative of the County school sector.

The tendency towards marginalisation which had become evident in attitudes towards the Church sector, has since the 1950s become a pressing reality within the 'mainstream' sector itself. I will argue that the history, the development and the implementation of a wide variety of multicultural initiatives in education and programmes for action since the 1950s reflect at best an unwillingness to accept the reality of differentiation which is presented by a multifaith, multiracial and multicultural society or at worst, a willingness to marginalise large sections of the school population deriving from minority communities.

In the 1950s the increased number of immigrants from new Commonwealth countries led to an awareness that schools would have a crucial role to play in the resettlement of immigrant children. The initial response of the government was an overall policy of assimilation whereby the newly arrived population was required to conform with existing structures. The view adopted was that differences would not be so apparent if they were not emphasised, and that the language, culture, religion and identity of immigrant children would soon be assimilated into the British way of life without any undue disruption to the majority indigenous culture. Characteristic of this approach was the view that Britain was a unified society and schools had a unifying role into which other cultures and races could be absorbed and it was, therefore, legitimate to suppress other cultures and beliefs to achieve this end.

For their part, schools responded with the provision of English as a second language (ESL). Thus the major educational response consisted of teaching English to immigrant children. As far as policy makers were concerned, these children had two 'problems': the 'problem' of language and the 'problem' of culture shock. The accompanying official policy of dispersal which set out to avoid undue concentrations of immigrant children in schools, imposed a limit of 30% of immigrants in any one school.

Schools in areas with few or no ethnic minority groups were not required or encouraged to respond to the changing composition of society. It followed that all adaptation should come from ethnic minority children and those children who could not or would not adapt were provided with education on the margins (Hassan & Beese 1985).

A move to an integrationist model in the 1960s, emphasising mutual respect, co-existence and understanding between different cultures, suggested positive recognition of the multicultural and multiracial nature of society. Nevertheless, the emphasis was still on integrating the ethnic minority groups within the majority culture. Hence a policy of unity was continued, the diversity of religion, customs and values being recognised in name only. It was at this time that some schools expressed a social response with the addition of 'black studies' to the school curriculum. Multicultural education had become a means whereby limited diversity was to be tolerated providing it did not radically alter or challenge established educational theory and practice. Changes as such in the curriculum were confined to schools with a diverse pupil population, while the content of the curriculum remained unchanged in 'all white' schools. Black studies were introduced and piloted by the London Borough of Lambeth. They were offered to sixth form pupils as an optional subject.

> School authorities latched onto the concept of Black Studies like a drowning man clutching at straws. They saw immediately that here was a not-to-be-missed opportunity to channel the chaos being created daily by black children in the classrooms. (Hassan & Beese p.26)

These initiatives employed concepts where the main emphasis was on conformity and homogeneity.

A contrary viewpoint emerged which saw multicultural education as a means of redressing existing imbalances whereby the needs, interests and perspectives of ethnic and faith community groups would be better catered for and preserved. This alternative view looked to a way forward which accommodated pluralism and heterogeneity. Rejecting existing assimilationist and integrationist avenues initiatives emerged which positively embraced a stance of cultural pluralism. At the centre were the rights of religious and cultural groups to maintain their own identity and the recognition of the positive and enriching aspects of cultural diversity. What was not widely recognised was that the contrasting perspectives of homogeneity and heterogeneity in multicultural education had emerged from a common philosophy of education. A dominant feature of this

230

philosophy, one that prevails to the present time, is an exclusive definition of what constitutes good education together with a refusal to open structures to differentiation. Cultural pluralism approaches encountered criticism because interpretations varied considerably, from policies of sophisticated integration and cultural understanding to a policy of cultural separation requiring changes in the economic and political structures (Mullard 1982).

The pursuit of equality and justice combined with a growing awareness of racism in schools led to an anti-racist model. There followed on a commitment to challenge racism in schools and society, which accepts that multicultural education must go beyond tolerance, respect, and enrichment to tackling racism and acknowledging that the phenomenon of multicultural education has itself contributed to racial discrimination. For as Nixon (1985, p.16) notes:

> a recognition of racism ought to be one of the inevitable outcomes of multi-cultural education. From any study of the pattern of relationships existing between cultural groups within Britain [one] must sooner or later pick out racism as a recurring strand in that pattern. Moreover, those with a specific interest in multi-cultural education must face the fact that certain patterns associated with it have themselves contributed to the history of racial discrimination in postwar Britain.

Anti-racist practice purports to encourage pride in ethnicity, to actively challenge prejudice and the perpetuation of racism and, hence, implicitly to counteract the undesirable features of other earlier models. And so today anti-racist strategies as a central principle in developing multicultural initiatives have moved centre-stage. It is no longer regarded as sufficient merely to arrive at an awareness of diversity. As Ashrif (1985) observes, 'The Victorian intellectuals were well enough versed in other cultures, but this did not dispel their ignorance.'

In no small way Victorian intellectuals and present day educationalists share a common patrimony. From the earliest beginnings multicultural education approaches have been confined by a straitjacket of pragmatism. The parallel failure of educational theorists to accept as legitimate goals and practices derived directly from minority cultures and religions and which lie outside their own main domain must be addressed as a matter of urgency.

Institutional racism as a key contributory factor in under-achievement is recognised by Eggleston, Rampton/ Swann and others. In his research into the causes of under-achievement of West Indian pupils, Gibson (1986, p. 26) notes that 'West Indians born in this country; have fared, are still faring, even worse than the migrants did - in education and, indeed, every other sphere of life in Britain.' Schools 'perpetuate the status quo by consistently failing to meet the needs of West Indian children'. Gibson asserts that, for West Indian pupils, their peer groups provide some form of cultural protection but 'their identity problems remain unsolved'. They suffer from an identity crisis which has undermined their confidence. A major causal factor cited for under-achievement is stress - 'the stress of living in a society that devalues them because of their skin colour'. Stress finds expression in a lack of confidence, low self-esteem, poor sense of aspiration and the inability to cope with the challenges and demands presented in every day activities. Gibson also provides additional evidence that the language of the teacher is frequently unintelligible to West Indian pupils. His main contention is that:

West Indian youth stands alone and isolated. They are given no positive help in learning to respect themselves. They are given no encouragement in developing as a group, and such individualism as this generates is not likely to be characterised by autonomy and initiative. Individualism and organisation demands that the needs of the individual be submerged to those of the group.

That marginalisation is not confined to West Indian children is evident from research carried out by Verma and Ashworth (1986) which shows that Bangladeshi pupils are also under-achieving. A recent all-party Commons Committee found that 74% of 15 year-old Bangladeshi pupils cannot speak English fluently. They referred to the education of this group as 'an educational and social disaster' (HMSO 1986).

Despite the fact of differentiation, delineated in diversity of religion, custom, culture and ethnicity; not withstanding evidence of educational disaster which is the schooling experience of many children, a procrustean approach to education continues to prevail. Differentiated needs, being subsumed, are not met. A singular feature of government's educational responses is the assumption that 'we know best'. Closely associated is a determination to deal with minority concerns in no other ways than those which are prescribed as 'best' for these groups. That 'our educational system' unilaterally decides on the provision to be made for 'your children', no matter how inadequately is the unacceptable signal relayed daily to a differentiated society with differentiated drives, hopes, aspirations and ambitions.

Throughout its development an absence of consensus is characteristic of multicultural education. Goals and strategies are decided at the centre. With religious and cultural communities dialogue is at best fragmented and their presence mostly not yet admitted formally to educational structures. It follows that the term multi-cultural education does not attract any agreed definition. Banks (1986, p. 229) observes that multicultural education

> is searching for its soul and raison d'etre... Conservatives damn multi-cultural education because they fear it will revolutionise society. Radicals dismiss it as useless and harmful, as simply another rool of the ruling elite to contain black rage.

I have argued that an outmoded philosophy has sired what is at best a very imperfect expression of dialogue in differentiation. That philosophy carries with it a reluctance to respond structurally to the heterogenous needs of different sections of the school population. Significantly, it has failed to promote structural reform of educational institutions. The evidence of marginalisation, of educational and social disaster gives substance to demands that the processes and structures of educational institutions should be opened as a matter of urgency.

The reality of differentiation, evident on a local level as well as on a wider community level, demands an educational response on the structural level.

Religion, ethnicity and culture are all elements which are indicators of differentiation which characterise British society today. As we have seen it is only the Christian Churches and the Jewish community who in ordering their priorities today have differentiated access to maintained education. That it is possible for their schools to order their priorities in ways which differ from the mainstream County sector can be seen from an examination of pupil records. A response of schools to the local environment can also be gauged by comparing admissions policies and practices. To help identify variance in school priorities I will draw briefly upon comparative research recently carried out in sample of Church and County schools with specific reference to records of pupil composition (O'Keeffe 1986).

The differential powers accorded to governing bodies to exercise responsibility in the areas of pupil admissions, staff appointments and curriculum matters enable Church schools with a voluntary aided status to set, work through and order their priorities. The County school sector is subject to local education authority control in these areas.

Four indicators were used to collect information on the backgrounds of pupils - the percentage of pupils receiving free school meals, the percentage of pupils from single parent families and the parental occupations of pupils, which also provided statistics on unemployed parents. Details were also obtained on the academic ability of pupils. These statistics were collected for a sample of ten County and ten Church of England schools with a voluntary aided status within the Inner London Education Authority.

Making use of these measurements of disadvantage it became evident that in general County schools have - more pupils receiving free school meals; a higher percentage of pupils from single parent families (although the percentage differences are small); fewer pupils with parents in non-manual occupations and a higher incidence of parental unemployment than their matching Church secondary schools. In part reflecting a national unifying role the County school sector admits proportionately more disadvantaged children than does the Church school sector. It was seen that Church schools were more successful in filling their quota of Band 1 above average ability pupils and Band 2 average ability pupils than their matching County schools. The different starting points and priorities of County and Church schools can also be seen in the ways pupil admission policies are devised. In general, County schools set out to serve a given catchment area with defined geographical boundaries while endeavouring to place as many children as possible in schools of parental choice. First priority is given to children living in the neighbourhood of the school. Admissions policies for County schools are inclusive, in the sense that regardless of religion, race and ethnicity their doors are open to all pupils who apply for places, subject of course, to availability. Church schools, on the other hand, use a religious criterion in determining their pupil admissions policies. Out of a sample of thirty-eight Church of England secondary schools, thirty-three (87%) gave first preference to children from practising Anglican homes and second priority to children whose parents were practising members of other Christian traditions. Seventeen schools (45%) filled all their places with pupils who qualified on Church-related criteria. It is clear that for these schools their dominant role is the domestic one of providing a Christian education for Christian children and priority is given to fulfilling that obligation.

In areas where the demand for places in a Church school exceeds the supply of available places, the admissions criteria are used with precision. Where demand falls short of supply, admissions policies become flexible and open to a more varied pupil intake.

It was found that in pursuing their domestic role, many Church schools draw pupils from outside the immediate neighbourhood. Research findings show that 75% of head teachers questioned said that, because of their Church-related criteria, pupil intake in no way reflected the locality. On the other hand, 75% of head teachers in County schools confirmed that their pupil intake was a microcosm of their neighbourhood. It follows that a greater diversity of pupil population in terms of religious, cultural and racial backgrounds is to be found in County schools.

The presence of Asian families especially was not reflected in the local Church secondary school to the same extent as the local County school. Indeed, there is a total absence of Asian children in some popular over-subscribed Church schools. In a crucial sense Church related admissions policies impact on the local population by highlighting the non-availability of differentiated avenues to education for those who take their sense of belonging and identity from culturally, religiously and ethnically diverse sources.

Generally speaking, Church schools felt secure within their domestic role. It was within the area of their general role of service to the nation that tensions were more evident. A redefinition of the Church's approach which will take account of both the realities and the just demands of all sections of British society today remains a pressing need.

What has become of the comprehensive ideal which sought 'equality of opportunity', 'parity of prestige' between schools, ease of transfer and a pupil intake which would reflect a cross section of groups and social classes? At this point it is possible to assert that the strains which are evident spring from a tension drawing from priorities geared to a neutral order of neighbourhood in opposition to a religious sense of community.

The report of the Archbishop of Canterbury's Commission on urban priority areas tells us that the Church of England was traditionally middle class in character. It is no different today. That many Church schools mirror the membership of the Church does not come as a surprise. The report also notes that 'the Church of England's most enduring problem of the city has been its relationship with the urban working class' (1985 p. 16). Set alongside this concern must also be the changed face of the city today, displaying as it does the lively features of other historic faiths and cultural communities. Church schools will scrutinise their admissions record in the light of the Commission's observation: 'in a society where class divisions run so deeply any institution which attempts to identify itself simultaneously with both the privileged and the deprived 'faces a task so formidable that it will tend to side with one or the other' (p. 28). A concern to 'educate the poor' was a prime factor in the Church of England's pioneering role in education. Today that old simplicity is blurred. Meanwhile, pending a redefinition of a general national role those responsible for Church school education face widespread criticism of their endeavours. Much of the debate on the place of the Church schools in a multicultural and multifaith society revolves around the question of their divisive nature. Additionally, their admissions policies are increasingly seen as racist. These important issues are raised about social, educational and racial equality within a context where Church schools have chosen to serve in the main a relatively homogeneous social class intake. Such policies distance the Church of England from other groups particularly if these groups claim no allegiance to Christianity. We are thus presented with evidence of demands being made on Church schools to respond to the challenges of a multifaith, multicultural and multiracial society. How they respond to these challenges will depend upon whether they can redefine and reconcile their general and domestic roles. Seeking and finding goals and objectives which match our own time may recover for the Church's endeavour in education an earlier role of 'pioneer'. It seems to me that a major contribution to the reform of educational structures may be made by the Churches in a reinterpretation of educational goals which is calculated to promote and reflect human rights. It can be argued that the extent of marginalisation which so permeates mainstream school activity today constitutes a deprivation of human rights and a violation of the European Convention.

> No person shall be denied the right to education. In the exercise of any functions which it assumes in relation to education and to teaching, the State shall respect the right of parents to ensure such an education and teaching in conformity with their own religious and philosophical convictions. (First Protocol Article 2)

For those historic faith communities which are not permitted structural access to the maintained sector vital issues pertaining to school worship and the religious education of their children are inevitably sidetracked or down graded. The realities of contemporary British life have led to problems of a philosophical, theoretical and practical nature in the areas of school worship and religious education. Two factors are readily identifiable: first, the decline of institutional Christianity in society; second, the growing religious pluralism in Britain. The large numbers of Hindus, Muslims and other religious adherents in schools have turned an intellectual awareness of religious pluralism into a practical reality.

I have described in detail elsewhere how schools have responded to these changes (O'Keeffe 1986). However, I want to draw attention to evidence that formal religion has become marginalised in many County schools. For the most part an act of collective worship is seen as an inappropriate school activity and as coming into conflict with the dominant secular ethos. Indeed the presence of a wide range of religious beliefs has accelerated the movement in the direction of secular assemblies. In seeking to avoid ambiguity some County schools have developed patterns for assemblies centring around national, local and school themes which help to reinforce the school ethos and to develop a community spirit. For County school pupils in general, their religious beliefs and practices have become a private matter and, therefore are pushed to the margins of useful school activities. The approach adopted to religious pluralism is in character with an approach which the Schools Council describes as 'separatism'. They summarise its features as an 'avoidance of conflict where religion is a private matter for the individuals and minority cultures' (Wood 1985). In most Church schools, worship is seen as collective and Christian and a central feature in school life. In this way worship has a major role to play in contributing to school ethos in the primary as well as the secondary sector. However, some primary schools unlike their secondary counterparts are in the main neighbourhood schools. Within inner city areas they reflect a diverse school population. In these schools, some with large majorities of non-Christian pupils, school worship and school ethos continue to be strictly Christian in character and Christian in expression. In these schools what is religious observance for the Christian child becomes a matter of religious observation for children who adhere to other faiths. For these children their religion becomes invisible and it is confined to a private sphere located on the margins of school life.

The evidence presented points to the prevailing marginalisation endured by sections of County and Church school populations in the sphere of religion. I have argued that the extensive marginalisation of children in schools stems from structural and philosophical roots. But it must be said that teachers' attitudes are frequently cited as being contributory to the alienation process. Turning to an attitude survey of teachers in Church and County schools, it will be possible to look for indications of a general acceptance of differentiation both on a conceptual level and within pragmatic boundaries.

The data that I make use of is taken from postal questionnaires completed by 139 teachers in County schools and 178 teachers in Church of England schools. Questionnaires were given to head teachers to distribute to a random sample of 10% of staff in sixty-six secondary schools in London, the North West Region and the West Midlands. The questionnaire was in the first instance designed to ascertain the attitudes of teachers to the continuing partnership between the State and the Church of England in maintained education. Questions relating to accountability, autonomy and decision making were included.

I have already indicated that Church schools are not without their critics. To what extent do teachers share similar views? 50% of County school teachers compared with 80% of Church school teachers disagreed with the statement that Church schools perpetuate social discord to the extent that makes them indefensible. (Decimal points have been rounded up or down to the nearest whole numbers.) Significantly, 31% of County teachers (Church school teachers 10%) were not certain. The large measure of uncertainty reflects the continuing debate which takes as its focus the divisive nature of Church schools and whether they may be 'wittingly or unwittingly propping up racism and racial disadvantage' (Dummett & McNeal 1981, p. 17).

The Church's partnership in education was couched in terms of value systems by using the following statement - 'Education is so permeated with values that the Church has its own unique and distinctive contribution to make.' The majority of teachers (79%) agreed with this statement. In affirming the Church of England's distinctive contribution to education, these teachers are agreeing to give form to differentiation in State-maintained education. The protection and promotion of values is a prime stimulus for Muslim demands for a voice in education.

Is the greater parental choice afforded by the 1980 Education Act echoed in teachers' attitudes to parental choice of schools, with particular reference to Church schools? The majority of teachers (74%) believe that, as long as parents want a Church school education for their children, provision should be available. A minority (14%) did not believe parental choice to be an important factor for their retention; 11% were uncertain. Teachers' views on parental choice are linked to perceptions concerning the distinctive features of Church schools. For the majority of teachers in the sample the Church school was seen to provide Christian nurture. Christian nurture can no longer be guaranteed by most County schools. While the 1944 Education Act provided the basis for Christian nurture, in school today 'secular education has come of age'. It can no longer be assumed that it is the task of the County school to be involved in Christian nurture (BCC 1981). However, 77% of teachers agree with the statement - 'The Church school provides an opportunity for Christian nurture'. Teachers who were uncertain accounted for 14% of the sample while a minority (7%) disagreed.

One of the justifications advanced for the Church of England's continued partnership in education is that Church schools provide a distinctively Christian perspective on education. The majority of teachers who took part in the research endorsed this view. Church schools are seen as providing a religious base to education in which Christian values find expression through school worship, Christian nurture, religious education and the ethos of schools.

The general willingness to accept a sometimes little known and often much criticised partner suggests that County school teachers are in the main flexible and willing to accept a plurality of approaches to education.

Having identified some of the tensions manifest in comprehensive education today which have their origin in contrasting approaches to the admission of pupils and the place of religion within the school environment I now turn to look at a variety of proposals for structural change.

A call for reform of the dual system to cope better with the differentiated needs of a multicultural, multiethnic and multifaith school population springs from a variety of sources. Citing an over-riding need to support the principle of pluralism, the Bishop of Durham argues that Church schools should be phased out (Jenkins 1986). It is difficult to understand how it is possible to uphold a principle of pluralism in practice, while, at the same time, advocating the abolition of the very mechanism which has the potential to endow it with legitimacy and form. Professor Ayer (1986) and other members of the secular society also seek to abolish Church schools and end the dual system. Such a structural change is their response to the emerging Muslim claim to a voice in education and expresses their fears for the future needs of social cohesion.

A recent draft document for discussion compiled by the Socialist Education Association ('All Faiths in All Schools', 1986, p.27) states: 'No equitable policy for education of a multifaith society can proceed with the dual system operating as it has in the past.' The authors call for reform which will take positive advantage of our multifaith and multicultural society. They propose a new 'all faith' development. This would entail the establishment of a new unified system of maintained schools:

> in which voluntary schools, without sacrificing their ethos and individual approach, could gradually develop the capacity to educate a greater diversity of intake from their local communities, and where County schools, without sacrificing their unifying secular approach could gradually develop the capacity to meet more widely the religious and

cultural needs of their intakes. (p. 46)

They suggest that the development of a new 'all faiths' policy would require a new Education Act. New religious rights are proposed - the objective being not to decrease the religious rights of groups in education, but to extend them - to cover the right to request worship in their own faith, and classes specifically designed to study their own faith. They envisage that, by opening up the dual system in new ways, it would become possible to treat all faiths equally within the school. The authors of the SEA document advocate support, not segregation, and it is their answer to what they refer to as 'segregated schooling'.

The SEA reforms set out to relocate the religious dimension within society at a more visible location in the school environment. Their proposals are a means of restoring the balance of 'worldly' and 'other worldly' values within the comprehensive system.

In reviewing the inadequate educational responses of schools to the changing nature of society, the Swann Report calls for an approach which focuses on educating all children, whatever their background, to understand the 'shared values' of British society as a whole, and to enable them to appreciate 'the diversity of life styles and cultural and linguistic backgrounds' which are part of society (p. 316). The approach envisaged

> is one which both caters for the educational needs of all children with equal seriousness and sensitivity and which also prepares all children, both ethnic minority and majority, through a common educational experience, for life in today's society. (p. 317)

For the Swann Committee, the concept of 'Education for All' is the approach which will provide the way forward, to educate for diversity. For the Swann Committee, 'Education for All' is synonymous with a 'good' education. A 'good' education 'must reflect the diversity of British society and indeed of the contemporary world' (p. 318). This would involve replacing teaching resources which 'present an anachronistically Anglo-centric view of the world'; developing all areas of the curriculum in order to provide a multicultural perspective which permeates all aspects of the curriculum. A 'good' education must provide pupils with the knowledge, understanding and skills to function effectively as an individual and as a citizen of society. It has a major role to play in countering racism at all levels. As the Swann Report states:

> A crucial element in developing our aim of 'Education for All' is therefore to seek and identify and to remove those practices and procedures which work, directly or indirectly, and intentionally or unintentionally, against pupils from any ethnic minority group, and to promote, through the curriculum, an appreciation and commitment to the principles of equality and justice on the part of all pupils'. (p. 320)

An evaluation of the Swann Report presented by the Islamic Academy (Swann Committee Report, 1985), and expressing an Islamic educational viewpoint, highlights the inherent particularism central to its dominant philosophy. The Statement commences by commending the Swann Committee for aiming at an education system which allows the different communities to preserve their own identities and, at the same time, become part of 'pluralistic' democratic British society through commonly shared values. It then goes on to illustrate the gulf which exists between the views expressed in the Swann Report on education and the community's world view of education. The Muslim community rejects the purely secular basis of educational philosophy and the application of a secular approach adopted in schools to all areas of knowledge, because it undermines the concept of education which the Muslim community upholds.

The concept of 'integrational pluralism' which the Swann Report advocates in developing the notion of cultural pluralism is in direct conflict with the Muslim concept of 'dynamic pluralism'. For Muslims, shared values are those values which are 'actually shared in practice by various groups in the society including those values than can be 'justifiably presented as universally appropriate' (p. 4).

The Statement also rejects the view expressed that minorities may maintain their individual cultures only in so far as they do not come into conflict with rationally justifiable shared values of the wider pluralist society. A subordination of their values is regarded by Muslims as destructive to their own basic values - in other words, 'man-made criteria' as the basis for evaluating 'which values' are inappropriate.

The Swann Report in setting goals for religious education articulates a secular response to pluralism in society. This approach is rejected by the Muslim community for the following reasons:

> This sort of multi-culturalism claims to promote tolerance and understanding, it tacitly justifies cultural domination by the secularist anti-religious majority and, at the same time, systematically undermines the basic principles of Islam.
>
> The community wishes to preserve all elements of its culture and life-styles which are ultimately derived from the Qur'an and the Sunnah, and reinforced through the educational curricula that would acknowledge and allow those basic values of Islam to be preserved. (p. 6)

Furthermore, the 'national values' which the Swann Committee seeks to transmit are derived from 'pseudo-Christian and mainly secularist stances' with no recognition of the values upheld by Muslims, Hindus, Sikhs and other faith communities;

> Only when the basis of these 'national values' are sought in absolute principles which all these religions share in common...will the authorities, local and central, and the teachers and the all-white population become aware of the fact that age-old prejudices, the concept of white racial superiority, and negative stereotypes and myths about Muslims are false, and should not be regarded as part and parcel of 'national values'. (p.6)

The Swann Committee received evidence of the failure of schools to accord equal treatment to religious groups. Evidence was also given of an absence of provision of an acceptable form of religious education, stemming both from the approach adopted and by the low status accorded to that subject in many County schools. As a result, secularist humanistic values are seen to have become irreconcilable with religious values. Dissatisfaction and frustration are evident concerning the capacity of County schools to recognise and respond to 'other worldly' concerns.

The Muslim point of view asserts that Muslim voluntary schools would provide the opportunity for their children to learn and understand the religious traditions of their own faith community. Such schools would cater for the balanced growth of the child in all aspects.

The Swann Report received further evidence which showed that members of the Asian community are subject to extreme manifestations of racism. It was proposed that Muslim schools could provide a safe base thereby enabling children to become more secure in their religious and cultural roots having a sense of morality and responsibility. Not only would children be good citizens, but they 'would have a confident and balanced view of their place in society, free from a sense of alienation which is experienced by certain other ethnic minorities' (p. 502). Confronted with an abundance of evidence and considered proposals, the Swann Report decreeed that 'we do not believe that such 'separate' schools would be in the long term interest of the ethnic minority communities'. (p. 520)

Having further evaluated the concerns of the Muslims and other religious groups, the Swann Report concluded that:

> the best and perhaps the only way of ensuring that ethnic communities in this country are able both to retain their religious, cultural and linguistic heritages, as well as being accorded full equality alongside members of the majority community is within the broader pluralistic context for which we have argued in the report ... If the policies for 'Education for All' were adopted, the demands would be much diminished. (p. 509)

Dissenting members of the Swann Committee recognised that extending the dual system 'would not necessarily address the underlying concerns of ethnic minority communities and they might increase the very rejection and marginalisation which the communities seek to overcome'. They were of the view that to dismiss the requests of religious groups for their own schools is to deny a possible avenue in which progress towards 'Education for All' can become a reality. An extension of the dual system 'would provide invaluable experience and evidence in the long journey towards the goal 'Education for All', which all members of the Committee seek' (p. 515).

It is to be regretted that the majority Swann Report has

chosen to confront differentiation in society today. Showing a degree of inflexibility not evident in the views of teachers themselves the Report displays a singular unwillingness to accept structural change and diversity of approaches to education. The Swann Committee put forward 'Education for All' strictly on their own terms.

In this chapter I have from time to time suggested that the comprehensive ideal has been overly reliant on inadequate philosophical underpinnings and was and still is poorly served by multicultural initiatives. It seems to me that in order to preserve the virtues of comprehensive education it will be necessary to effect a rapprochement with the philosophical and structural factors which are inherent in our multicultural, multifaith and multiethnic society.

School provision which meets with justice the differentiated needs and rights of today's multicultural, multiethnic, multifaith school population is too important to be left to the vagaries of narrow exclusivist educational philosophies. To resist marginalisation, to counter alienation and to meet the demands of dignity for significant sections of society, it will instead be necessary to locate the dynamics of education for all within a wider framework. That such a framework exists I have no doubt, and can be seen to very properly rest within the wider domain of human rights. The role of education today both as a reflection on, and as a contributor to human rights needs urgent examination.

## REFERENCES

All Faiths in All Schools (1986) 2nd Report of the Socialist Education Association on Voluntary Schools and Religious Education.

Ashrif, S. (1985) 'An Anti-racist in Place of a Multicultural Education', Education Journal, January, p. 14.

Ayer, A. et al. (1986) 'The Educational Ghettos that Religions are Building', Guardian, 9 July.

Banks, J. (1986) 'Multicultural Education and Its Critics' in Modgil et al. (eds) Multicultural Education: the Interminable Debate, Lewes, Falmer Press, p. 229.

British Council of Churches (1981), Understanding Christian Nurture.

Council of Europe, Strasbourg (1983) The European Convention on Human Rights, p. 28.

Department of Education and Science (1986) Table 1DO1, January.

Dummett, A. and McNeal J. (1981) <u>Race in Schools</u>, The Runnymede Trust, p. 17.

'Education for All', <u>The Report of the Committee of Enquiry into the Education of Children from Ethnic Minority Groups</u> (The Swann Report), Cmnd 9453, HMSO.

Eggleston, J. <u>et al</u>. (1986) <u>The Educational and Vocational Experience of Ethnic Minority Groups</u>, Multicultural Studies, University of Warwick.

<u>Faith in the City</u> (1985) The Report of the Archbishop of Canterbury's Commission on Urban Priority Areas, London, Church House Publishing.

First Report of the Home Affairs Committee, Session 1986-1987, <u>Bangladeshis in Britain</u>, HMSO.

Gibson, A. (1986) <u>The Unequal Struggle</u>, London, Caribbean Centre for Educational Studies.

Hassan, L. and Beese B. (1985) 'Who's Educating Whom' in F. Dhondy (ed), <u>The Black Explosion in British Schools</u>, London, Race Today.

Hirst, P.H. (1972) 'Christian Education: A Contradiction in Terms?' in <u>Learning for Living</u>, 12, 4.

Jenkins, D. (1986) 'York Conference on Comprehensive Education', 27 July.

Mullard, C. (1982) 'Multicultural Education in Britain; from assimilation to cultural pluralism' in J. Tierney (ed.) <u>Race Migration and Schooling</u>, London, Holt, Rinehart and Winston.

National Society Annual Report (1812/1813).

Nixon, J. (1985) <u>A Teacher's Guide to Multicultural Education</u>, London, Basil Blackwell, reprinted 1986.

O'Keeffe, B. (1986) <u>Faith, Culture and the Dual System: A Comparative Study of Church and County Schools</u>, Lewes, Falmer Press.

<u>Religion in Schools</u> (1967) British Humanist Association.

<u>Signposts and Homecomings</u> (1981) A Report to the Bishops of England and Wales, London, St Paul Publications.

<u>Swann Committee Report: An Evaluation from the Muslim Point of View, An Agreed Statement</u> (1985) The Islamic Academy, Cambridge.

<u>Understanding Nurture</u> (1981) British Council of Churches.

Verma, G.K. and Ashworth B. (1986) <u>Ethnicity and Educational Achievement in British Schools</u>, London, Macmillan.

Wood, A. (1985) <u>Assessment in a Multicultural Society: Religious Studies at 16+</u>, Schools Council Programme 5, Improving the System.

# 13

# Progress and the Radical Educational Press

## Jenny Thewlis

In this chapter I want to chart the rise and fall of a phenomenon - the radical educational press of the 1970s - and to situate some examples of that phenomenon in relation to each other and to notions of progressive education.

The early 70s saw a plethora of publications on education ranging from cyclostyled pamphlets to relatively glossy editions. Some such as 'The Great Brain Robbery' (Paton 1971) were intended as one-off interventions, others saw themselves as contributing to a continuing debate. Most of them have disappeared. The virtual demise of what was a fertile arena for radical debate about the nature and purpose of education in late capitalist Britain is a reflection of the changes which have taken place in the field of state education and the social and economic matrix in which it is embedded.

This is not the place to discuss the background to the present situation in detail. Several studies, and in particular Unpopular Education (Baron et al. 1981) have concerned themselves with this and arrived at similar conclusions to that reached by Stuart Hall (1983): 'the awkward truth is that ... in education as elsewhere, the radical right has advanced by engaging the real weak points and exploiting the contradictions of the left.' Fifteen years ago some would have confidently expected that the radical left would be able to exploit the contradictions of capitalism! 

The radical educational press was one of the by-products of that period of optimism and the exploitation of contradictions within the education system was one of its aims. It represented a flowering of theoretical and practical initiatives mounted by socialist teachers working in the classroom, writing from a variety of ideological positions,

247

but sharing a critique of the status quo in education which had not been articulated to such a degree since the 1920s and the Teachers Labour League. Although there were already journals in existence which were clearly associated with progressive moves in education they were chiefly concerned with the 'more and better' philosophy which had formed the consensus of Labour Party thinking up to that point. The longest established, and still extant, journal was Forum for the Discussion of New Trends in Education, edited for many years by Brian Simon. Its founding editorial in 1958 detailed the new trends with which it proposed to concern itself:

> The new types of schools developing in different parts of the country; the steps taken by Secondary Modern schools to transcend their earlier limit- ations; re-appraisal of such features of internal school organisation as streaming; new approaches to the content of education.

In 1958 this represented the vanguard of progressive thought and was (and still is) important in offering comment on, and examples of, progressive teaching, whilst at the same time campaigning for the abolition of selective education.

Forum operated within the parameters of social democratic reform as did another long established educat- ional journal, Socialism and Education, the organ of the Socialist Education Association. But, whereas Forum stood at some remove from internal Labour Party politics, Socialism and Education was concerned to intervene in the educational policy making of the party and the debates surrounding it.

According to Clark and Davies (1981):

> educational policy within the social-democratic tradition aimed to increase access to educational institutions so that a more just and equal society could be achieved. This was to divorce the educational system almost entirely from the expectations and pressures of other societal systems and to give to education an ameliorative function it could never fulfil.

Nevertheless this sort of thinking had been at the core of Labour Party policy on education since the 20s. Rodney

Barker (1969) in reviewing the attitude towards education of the Labour Party and the TUC in the 20s and 30s states:

> the chief desire that emerged from the party's approach to education was not for the destruction of the old order nor for massive utilisation of unofficial voluntary agencies to counter the effects of teaching within that order, but for the broader dissemination of a tradition which by and large was accepted, admired, envied.

This attitude was formalised in the party's espousal of the ideology of equality of opportunity with its implicit acceptance of the bourgeois ethos of individualism. It reached its apotheosis in Harold Wilson's famous claim that comprehensive education would be grammar schools for all.

Education is seen from this perspective as a ladder by which the working class can achieve upward mobility, in which the question of educational provision is seen as one of social justice. Everyone (except the ruling class, who buy out of the state system) has an equal start. The existing educational and occupational hierarchies are taken for granted and it is only access which is a problem.

In the pamphlet Crisis in Education (1977) the Big Flame Collective state:

> the ideology of equality of opportunity has been a double-edged sword. Positively it has raised aspiration, challenged assumptions and provided an effective yardstick in judging how far educational reforms have affected the chances and performance of working class children. Negatively it has tended to individualise and de-politicise the educational process and its relation to the class structure ... this lessened their (the working classes') ability to view education as a class and push for collective solutions and changes.

There were, of course, many tangible improvements in education brought about by progressive measures such as de-streaming, collaborative learning and other classroom based reforms. Nevertheless, the ultimate failure of the social-democratic tradition to achieve justice and equality for the working class through the engine of state education, in spite of the move towards comprehensivisation, Educational

## Progress and the Radical Educational Press

Priority Areas and the expansion of higher education, was one of the main stimuli for the development of the radical educational press.

Another important factor was the historical conjuncture of the late 60s and early 70s which saw the confluence of changes in several areas, both within and without education and which influenced the thinking of many socialist teachers.

After decades of relative quiescence the teaching profession, through the teaching unions, had begun to engage in direct confrontation with employers and government. By the 1960s problems associated with over-large classes and high teacher turnover, as well as an erosion of living standards and status, had led to a state of dissatisfaction within the profession. The growth of militancy in other white collar sectors described by Terry Johnson (1972) had created a climate of opinion in which strike action could be undertaken, first over school meals supervision in 1967 and later in full scale stoppages over pay and conditions. These developments are fully charted by Vincent Burke (1971). To this must be added Mrs Thatcher's confrontational approach during her tenureship of the Ministry of Education. The chant much favoured by demonstrating teachers of 'Maggie Thatcher, milk snatcher!' summed up something of the antagonism felt towards her personally.

Although the militancy of the bulk of the teaching profession was short-lived and was not extended beyond the area of wage demands there were nevertheless some teachers who found a basis for further activity within the National Union of Teachers and within the school, where, partly because of massive teacher shortages, teachers had a greater leverage in school policy and control of their practice. This was often aided by the fact that many young teachers with progressive ideas rose rapidly to head of department status or the equivalent within schools and had the power to introduce new practices as a result. Some of them had been students during the period of student unrest in the late 60s. They had cut their radical teeth in confrontations with university and college bureaucracies. They were sometimes members of the newly emerging far left groupings, International Socialists or International Marxists, sometimes members of the Labour Party or the Communist Party. What set them apart from their predecessors, and many of their contemporaries, was that they brought their politics into classrooms and staffrooms and made explicit the political nature of their practice.

Within the National Union of Teachers the splinter group of Rank and File was a rallying point for many activists and radicals. But according to Nigel Wright (1976) it ultimately failed to mobilise the profession and alienated much sympathy through factional and dogmatic disputes. Nevertheless, the group produced several influential pamphlets (such as 'Education and Society' by C. Rosenberg) and a twice-termly journal, Rank and File, which reached a peak circulation of 9,000 in Spring 1972 - far higher than that attained by any other radical educational journal. It dealt mainly with Union issues, offering both critique and strategies for action. Among the issues it stood (and still stands) for were:

> Opposition to all cuts in educational expenditure ... a single salary scale for all teachers ... control of the NUT by rank and file membership ... free and compulsory comprehensive education ... the right of school students to form their own organisation. (Rank and File No. 1, 1976)

Not since the Teachers Labour League in the 1920s had such a militant critique of the education system been mounted from within. Rank and File's radical approach, coming at a time of growing dissatisfaction amongst teachers with many aspects of their occupation, contributed in no small measure to the climate in which other radical journals subsequently flourished.

Another factor which influenced and enabled their gestation was the new accessibility of cheap and attractive printing techniques. These were pioneered by the alternative and underground press of the 1960s and particularly by community publishers, such as Centreprise in Hackney, which produced a variety of writing by and for local residents. Parallels exist with the development of the radical 'unstamped' press in the 19th Century when developments in printing led to the publication of such journals as Poor Man's Guardian and Black Dwarf which disseminated radical political ideas to the working class. Reading societies were formed and the journals became instruments of education. Some of the radical journals under discussion here also organised readers' groups and conferences at which issues raised in the journals could be debated. In his analysis of the popular press Stanley Harrison

(1974) argues that the underground and alternative press reflected the credibility crisis with regard to the mass media, and stimulated the discontent, especially amongst students and young workers. Its weakness was that its links with organised labour were tenuous. He concludes:

> Underpinning the revolt against monopoly media, a number of journals emerged or increased their influence during the seventies particularly in the struggle to defend basic Trade Union rights. Ideas and moods generated amongst workers new to active class struggles, and among students looking for truthful answers and for exits from the social, economic and cultural chaos, offered a fertile ground for a wide range of left and lefter than left groups, each with its own journal.

Not only teachers, but other white collar occupations such as scientific and technical workers, health and social workers, were concerned with their economic situation. Alongside this was also developing a concern for the social purpose of their work, with democracy within their institutions and with their relationship to the rest of the labour movement. Scientists and technicians had begun to question what counted as science and the role of science in capitalist society in such journals as Undercurrents and Radical Science. Radical social workers produced the journal Case Con and organised conferences; psychologists produced Humpty Dumpty - 'for dissenting psychologists in public'.

The insights afforded by new developments in Sociology, Ethnomethodology and Marxist perspectives influenced these groups just as the new sociology of education had an influence amongst teachers. It marked a change of perspective on schooling as it focussed attention on the exploration of ways in which institutional practices, teacher expectations, the whole spectrum of the hidden curriculum and what counted as school knowledge helped to preserve inequality. This marked a distinct break with the explanations afforded by traditional empirical sociology and helped underline the fact that redistribution of resources alone would not alter the unequal practices in education. It led to an altered awareness on the part of those teachers who came into contact with it, leading them to question their own practice and leading to changes in pedagogy and approach. But lacking as it did an explicit structural analysis of the relationships of power and economic control which shape the education system, it gave rise to what Geoff Whitty (1977) has called 'romantic possibilitarianism' and was ultimately unthreatening to the status quo.

Many of the concerns of the new sociology were disseminated to a wider audience through the Open University 'School and Society' course, and particularly through the output of Penguin Education (now being reprinted by Bristol Classical Press), a short-lived but potent imprint, which brought the work of American educationalists such as John Holt, third world literacy workers such as Paolo Friere and new sociologists such as Nell Keddie to the notice of many teachers and students.

Schools themselves seemed to offer a site for change in the early 70s for a variety of reasons and the work already referred to seemed to suggest that change was possible. A large expansion of teacher training meant that there was a generation of new teachers many of whom were imbued with the ideas of progressive education. The move towards comprehensivisation, followed by the raising of the school leaving age in 1972 meant that new courses and approaches were admissible if for no other reason than to cater for the potentially disruptive and disaffected pupil. The new CSE examination, with its emphasis on course work and teacher assessment opened up a space which progressive teachers were not slow to occupy. The Plowden Report (Central Advisory Council for Education, 1967) had legitimised the development of progressive educational methods in primary schools whilst at secondary level the Schools Council had initiated a programme of curriculum reform which involved teachers in meeting to work on and monitor such undertakings as the Humanities Curriculum Project.

Change was occurring in both pedagogy and content. It was also occurring in the theoretical and ideological orientation of a sector of the teaching force. The radical educational journals were an outcome of these changes and the broader changes already discussed.

Radical Education, Teacher's Action, Socialist Teacher, Hard Cheese, Teaching London Kids, Rank and File, Libertarian Education occupied different positions on the radical/progressive continuum, but had many features in common. They were produced by, and directed towards, classroom teachers (although Hard Cheese was a product of students at Goldsmiths College in London); they were produced cheaply and strikingly in terms of format and layout: they were sold face to face in staff rooms and at meetings and demonstrations; they were mainly London based and concerned in particular with urban educational issues, particularly the problems of the inner city school. Their main audience was first and foremost educationalists. Although all the journals carried at times articles about students, parents and the wider community they were never really seen as a reachable readership. Their main thrust was within the profession in attempting to change teachers' consciousness and to re-inforce and resource radical and progressive practice.

The journals had different origins which were reflected in their theoretical orientations and which influenced the trajectory of their project. Libertarian Education (1972- ) was produced by a group of teachers and others active in the free school movement and based in Leicester; Teachers Action (1975-81) arose from the deliberations of a collective of teachers mostly working in the same London school and concerned with offering a materialist analysis of the education system. Teaching London Kids (1973- ) originated as a collection of papers from a conference organised by the London Association for the Teaching of English, whilst Radical Education (1974-79) was established by a group of teachers and lecturers who, disenchanted with the increasingly narrow sectarianism of Rank and File, were concerned with 'countering a certain fragmentation which characterises the radical movement in education' (Radical Education, no. 1, 1974).

None of these four journals were overtly connected with any political grouping on the left or with the NUT. I have deliberately not dealt here with the journals that were, although it could be argued that they constitute part of the radical educational press. The fact that they had in a sense a ready-made readership and a movement to support them set them apart from the journals I am considering. I would include here Education Today and Tomorrow, for many years the educational journal of the Communist Party, and Socialism and Education because of its strong connections with the Labour Party.

Although extremely influential amongst radical teachers I would not include Rank and File, located as it was entirely within the political struggles in the NUT or Socialist Teacher, produced by teachers within the Socialist Teachers Alliance (STA) and as such the mouth piece for that organisation. These three journals all had something to offer the radical teacher and much of what they had to say resonated with the concerns of the other journals. For example, Richard Hatcher, writing in Socialist Teacher 12 (1980) stated:

> The STA has always rejected the counter-position of, on the one hand, militant activity on the so-called 'trade-union' issues (salaries and conditions) and on the other hand, radical experiments as teachers in the classroom. However we are far from working out a developed analysis and programme for the class struggle in education along these lines. The Tory attacks, material and ideological, compel us to try and do so, because they raise the fundamental questions of the politics of education. Questions which we believe the dominant 'progressive' currents in British education - roughly speaking those centering on equality of opportunity ... and those centering on the freedom and growth of the individual child (ranging from Plowden to Neill) - cannot answer.

Such rhetoric could be encountered in the pages of all the radical educational press. Differences between the journals emerged in their approach to the politics of education and this varied according to where they were situated with respect to the nature of the child, the class location of teachers and pupils, the content and process of education and its relation to social and economic factors.

This determined their position in a continuum ranging from libertarian to radical marxist. At one end of this was Libertarian Education with its belief in the freedom of the individual child and teacher to grow and develop in their own way - a latter day apostle for the ideas of A.S. Neill and the practices of free-schools which his ideas informed. At the other end was the hard edge of the Teachers Action Collective, avowedly Marxist, their analysis of the education system rooted in class struggle.

Whatever their ideological stance each journal addressed itself, if only in opposition, to the question of progressivism, both as a theory and a practice. According to Raymond Williams (1976):

> In the 20th century progress has retained its primary sense of improvement, but has an

important (as well as an ironic) sense which takes
it simply as change.

The concepts of progressivism and progressive education
that derive from this, and from the philosophical position of
progressivism, have formed a powerful ideological and
practical intervention in the education system. Gerald
Grace (1978) sees this as tending to take a 'romantic' form
'in the sense that it looked substantially to education for
social regeneration and was naive about, or tended to
disregard, external power realities'. In practice it was
translated into child- and discovery-centred learning at
primary level, integration and curriculum development at
secondary levels, and reformist educational policies of the
'more and better' variety at local and national government
level.

The main critique of progressive education offered by
radicals and marxists is that it is soft, in that it lacks a
theory of the relationship of education to issues of power
and control within the State. According to Bowles and Gintis
(1976) 'changes in the structure of education are associated
historically with changes in the social organisation of
production. The fact that changes in the structure of
production have preceded parallel changes in schooling
establishes a strong <u>prima facie</u> case for causal importance
of economic structure as a major determinant of educational structure.'

Such an analysis could fruitfully be applied to the
current situation in Britain where some of the most far
reaching educational innovations of this century have been
set in motion by Kenneth Baker on behalf of a Tory
government which is presiding over one of the greatest
changes in the employment structure of the economy and
altering the whole infrastructure of work.

Nevertheless, the changes in education are couched in
what seem to be progressive terms. Indeed, the term
'progressive' has come to mean many things, depending on
who uses it.

Doug Holly (1974) comments that in a capitalist state
'Progressive developments in schools are to be encouraged,
especially when they chime in with the growth of new forms
of consumption, but progressives in education need to be
kept an eye on.'

Indeed, to the right wing press and to Tory back-
benchers, the term is treated as synonymous with socialist

or radical and exponents of progressive education have been regularly held up for vilification. The level of confusion and contradictions that surround progressive education were well illustrated in autumn 1986 when the head of a London primary school was suspended for refusing to introduce more progressive teaching methods while a Surrey head was suspended for abandoning 19th century traditional methods in favour of more informal teaching. At secondary level, the old Black Paperites of the seventies and their successors such as Roger Scruton could be mustered by the far right Social Affairs Unit to contribute to The Wayward Curriculum, edited by Dennis O Keeffe (1986) a vituperative and ill-informed attack on all levels of progressive curriculum innovation in secondary schools, from peace studies to anti-racist teaching. The tone is set by Geoffery Bantock, who confidently asserts, with no empirical evidence, that 'More teachers participate in the debased popular culture or in pseudo-Marxist attacks on "middle class values" than are concerned about the cultural effects of the school curriculum.'

The gains of progressivism - a more humane pedagogy, a more interesting curriculum, more democratic organisation, have been devalued by both right and left. It is not surprising that the radical educational journals occupied a complex and often contradictory stance towards those gains. Libertarian Education located itself at the outer limits of child-centred learning while Teachers Action 3 stated:

> We do not see that compulsory state education is in any way an expression of the benevolence of capitalism towards the working class. We do not see schools as being malfunctioning machines of enlightenment, institutions in which knowledge is magnanimously presented to the young masses for their intellectual betterment.

Radical Education and Teaching London Kids stood somewhere between these positions, the former opening up a theoretical debate around the concept of progressive education while the latter examined what passed for progressive pedagogy and curriculum content.

With these positions in mind I want to look more closely at what distinguished the journals I am dealing with from each other and locate their individual strengths and weaknesses.

Libertarian Education took the extreme child-centred view which represented the wilder shores of progressive ideology espoused by A.S. Neill and given material form at Summerhill and later in the brief burgeoning of free schools, organised on democratic, anti-hierarchical lines, of which White Lion Street in Islington was one of the first and most successful. Libertarian Education stood, and still stands, for individual freedom. Its anarchic overtones are well illustrated in the following statement from the summer '86 edition, the second edition to be published after a four year hiatus but still very much in the mode of the late '60s.

> This magazine is against authority. Schools and colleges use their authority to define, to grade and to discipline in order to transform the learners into the sort of 'products' the state demands. In contrast Libertarian Education sees education as liberation. The learner, young or old, is the best judge of what they should learn next. In our struggle to make sense out of life, the things we most need are the things we most want to learn. The liberated learner controls the process - no longer the victim.

Libertarian Education drew heavily on the work of A.S. Neill, John Holt, Ivan Illich and other apostles of the de-schooling movement. The bottom line of its belief was that children could only achieve their full potential away from the repressive, hierarchical institutions of state education. Such an assertion did little to help those teachers struggling to offer pupils some relevant and humane education within those institutions. What is missing from the journal is any analysis of the power structures it opposes. The romantic/anarchic stress on individual freedom excludes any perspective on the social and economic basis of the educational system and offers no coherent account of social class.

Teachers Action operated with a totally different model of the child. It saw pupils in state schools as members of the working class, 'wageless workers imprisoned by capital', rather than as individual spirits to be nurtured and enabled. Instead school students were seen as 'being a major force for change in school and society alike'. As such they were the natural allies of teachers, who are also seen as unambiguously members of the working class. In Teachers Action number 1 the collective spelt out its theoretical position:

> Teachers Action believes that the nature of the
> schooling system is directly attributable to the
> demands of monopoly capitalism. Just as machine
> tools are produced for industry, so is labour power
> produced for the same ends - capitalist production.
> We as teachers work on that assembly line and so
> put ourselves firmly, without pride or guilt, in the
> category of the productive worker. The conflicts in
> school, whether they are between headmaster and
> teacher, teacher and teacher, or teacher and pupil,
> arise from precisely the same forces that create
> conflict in industry between boss and worker and
> sometimes between worker and worker. They are
> not primarily conflicts of morality or of educa-
> tional philosophy; they are necessary by-products of
> the economic system, by-products that will tear it
> apart.

With their colours thus firmly nailed to the mast head the
Teachers Action Collective set forth to fight the system.

As a journal Teachers Action differed from the others
in that it articulated a clear theoretical position which was
traceable through most articles, which were usually written
by members of the collective, and reiterated its strong and
uncompromising editorial statements. Its position had been
developed through a series of pamphlets resulting from
collective discussion and which located its concerns firmly
in the class nature of the education system provided by the
state. It saw the way to change through class struggle within
the system, both teachers and pupils being members of the
working class. Teachers Action concentrated on the function
of education under capitalism rather than its content and as
such would reside at the radical end of the continuum.
However, a libertarian note was sometimes struck amongst
the revolutionary rhetoric.

> There are teachers, the large mass, who want a
> wage, want less work for it, want collective
> democracy in policy making, want not to be at odds
> with pupils, want to live in a world in which
> education has more to do with the mind and less to
> do with the survival of capitalism. This is a mass
> movement. It is in this mass movement that

> Teachers Action locates itself. We see this mass
> movement (and see our task in making it visible
> and viable) as the left movement in schools. We
> locate this movement in our theory and practice, in
> the general revolutionary movement of the working
> class. (Teachers Action, no. 7, 1977)

By concentrating on the school as factory and the teacher as
production line worker Teachers Action failed to acknowledge the spaces that did exist in areas such as curriculum
development and the pastoral system in schools which
radical and socialist teachers could occupy. It was this
overdetermined view of the education system that seemed
to imply that only a mass rising of the working classes, with
teachers in the vanguard, could bring about any meaningful
change. This was one of the main weaknesses of Teachers
Action's platform at a time when teachers were struggling
to hold on to the gains that had been fought for in many
areas of school life.

Teaching London Kids, on the other hand, constantly
pointed up those gains by foregrounding classroom practice
and the content of education. One reason for this lay in its
origin. It took its name from a conference organised by the
London Association for the Teaching of English and its focus
was the problems faced by progressive teachers of English in
London schools and the ways in which they could be overcome. Originally a series of conference papers, the response
to the first journal was such that it became a regular
publication and widened its frame of reference beyond the
concerns of English teaching, although this remained a key
area of interest, to those of all teachers in urban schools.

According to its mast head Teaching London Kids was
concerned with exploring among other things:

-   practice and dilemmas of progressive/socialist teachers
    in state schools, especially as experienced by young
    teachers;
-   notions of 'progressive' teaching methods and their
    impact on the education of working class children;
-   the concentration of educational problems in London
    schools;
-   the ways in which the power structure of society
    affects the organisation and curriculum of schools;
-   the potential role of the school in the community and
    vice versa;

- the critical importance of language in teaching and learning;

Above all Teaching London Kids is concerned with presenting positive strategies for action.

The positive strategies usually took the form of examples of good classroom practice from socialist teachers, but also considered organisational responses - to attacks on progressive methods, to the defence of gains within the examining and assessment machinery. This is not to say that Teaching London Kids failed to engage in debate about the broader issues of power and control within the system but it did so in relation to specific issues, such as the attempt by the Tory Government to abolish the ILEA in 1979.

What set Teaching London Kids apart from the other radical journals was its emphasis on what was achievable in terms of classroom practice. In an interview in Teaching London Kids No. 15 Gerald Grace refers to this as 'the transformation of the actual', and goes on to state that

a teacher should be very explicit about his or her role in the education system and present a radical thesis in strong and forceful terms.

This approach was best exemplified by the work of Chris Searle in the areas of working class and anti-imperialist education which were recorded by Teaching London Kids. In Teaching London Kids No. 7 Searle stated that

The only way I can really operate successfully is to take advantage of the contradictions within the classrooom and try thereby to persuade the children of the contradictions within society.

It was precisely these contradictions that the journal was urging teachers to exploit through the medium of new curriculum developments such as peace studies, anti-sexist and anti-racist teaching and media studies. However, this was seen as a weakness by its critics on the left. Ken Jones (1983) states:

In its efforts to present radical work in a positive, utilisable way, TLK avoids not only the snares of abstraction but also the necessary work of confronting the various premises of progressive education, and of beginning to elaborate an alternative to its methods inside and outside the classroom.

While it is true that Teaching London Kids did not offer a theoretical analysis of progressive education much of the work highlighted in the journal, and in particular the practice of Chris Searle, could not be incorporated into the system. Indeed it was seen as threatening the status quo, as witnessed by the furore in the media over the publication of his book Classrooms of Resistance (1975) which contained examples of work from working class pupils on subjects such as Chile and the closure of a local hospital.

The journal that came closest to mounting a theoretical critique of progressivism was Radical Education. Its founding editorial gave notice of its intention to try to develop a socialist theory of education to challenge the orthodox theories that had underpinned most educational thinking both at policy level and in universities and colleges up to that point. It stated:

A socialist theory of education will be developed not by academics in cloisters, but by the people at the coal face of education - the teachers and students.

The two key projects of the journal were to put 'education-as-radical' back on the agenda of the working class movement and to re-examine the process of education by subjecting it to radical critique. The former aim rested heavily on two articles by Richard Johnson (1976 & 1977) which examined forms of self-help working class education in the early years of the last century, in which workers sought to appropriate 'really useful knowledge' free from middle class control as an 'indispensable means of emancipation'. The relationship of the working class to education was an issue which concerned all the radical journals. Radical Education attempted to locate it historically and to examine the antecedents which influence that relationship today and in particular the alliance between progressivism and labourism which gave rise to the post-war settlement.

The way that the processes of education have served ruling class interests was a second strand in Radical

Education's attempt to formulate a socialist theory of education. Doug Holly (1974) got to the heart of the matter by looking at 'the politics of the learning process itself'. In an article which was a spirited defence of the best of progressive teaching methods, as opposed to the philosophical position of 'progressivism' which he characterised as the mysticism of method, he elaborated on the dilemma facing radical teachers, and in particular the editorial board of Radical Education, namely the relationship between reformism and radicalism. He argued that 'a dialectical view of history does not so easily characterise reform in general as anti-proletarian or any particular reform as "bourgeois". To so characterise most of what reactionaries now call "progressive methods" would be especially myopic.' He went on to attempt a definition of a socialist view of learning which 'must start by defining quite clearly the basis of curriculum and methodology because each is seen not as an end in itself but as a means. Systematic learning in schools and colleges is what education is all about: socially organised learning, the planned development of consciousness.'

An emphasis on the dialectic, the examples of history and a concern for the process of education formed the planks of Radical Education's embryonic socialist theory of education. The demise of the journal in 1979 meant that the theory never reached full term, though a lengthy editorial in the ninth edition (Summer 1977) spelt out in some detail the sort of analysis and action necessary to move towards such a theory, and its concomitant radical practice. Taking as its starting point the 'Great Debate' initiated by Callaghan's 1976 Ruskin College speech, the editorial charted the history of education in the 20th century and looked at the ways in which the post-war consensus over education was coming under attack from central government. While urging teachers to resist the attack, Radical Education criticised the analyses and strategies on offer from the left at the time.

> We think that the limitations of all the positions that we have described are a result of a historical separation of the questions of educational provision and of educational ideology ... There is a failure to understand that in order to raise again questions that relate to the class nature of education inside the working class movement, it is necessary to

relate them to the movement <u>that is already going</u> <u>on</u>, dominated though it is by reformist ideology.

<u>Radical Education</u> could not have anticipated that the attack signalled in 1976 could have gathered the force that it has. Although editorials and articles in all the radical journals had highlighted the attacks and argued for a common resistance on the part of radical and progressive teachers, this never materialised.

At the time of writing (1987) <u>Teaching London Kids</u> and <u>Libertarian Education</u> still survive, if tenuously, <u>Radical Education</u> and <u>Teachers Action</u> ceased production in 1979 and 1981 respectively, and for a variety of reasons. These were both personal, in terms of the energies and commitments of the members of the editorial collectives and political, in terms of the prevailing social and economic climate. Certainly, their self-appointed tasks were far from complete when they disappeared - the hoped for mass movement of teachers and pupils united with fellow workers espoused by <u>Teachers Action</u> had failed to materialise, while <u>Radical Education's</u> socialist theory of education remained untested. It was not a problem of available ideologies nor was it that there was no further need for those journals. Rather it was a failure of the Left to unite around a common cause, to seize the initiative by offering a determined resistance to the attacks on schooling, and a cohesive and popular programme for educational reform.

Since Callaghan's Ruskin speech it had become clear that radical teachers could hope for nothing more from a Labour government than a diluted version of the educational policies zealously being pursued by the Right.

But as Brian Simon (1985) perceptively comments

> it is not only Labour which may be criticised; the Left as a whole, fragmented (particularly in education), failed to develop agreed alternative policies uniting the struggle for educational change with relevant and realisable political perspectives. This is undoubtedly partly due to the failure of the Left to tackle theoretical or ideological issues affecting both the content and process of education itself, and its relation to social and political change.

He goes on to criticise radical and socialist groupings of

teachers, characterised by the journals they produced, as being equally guilty of this failure. Although the journals paid lip service to the notion of a united front, and indeed made several attempts both informally, through meetings of the editorial collectives, and more formally under the aegis of the Socialist Teachers Alliance, none of them were ultimately prepared to submerge their particular ideological line in the common cause. They continued to struggle in isolation from each other and from any mass movement which could have supported them.

But it was not only ideological disunity which affected them. By the end of the decade the atmosphere of retrenchment in schools beset by cuts and closures was very different from the expansionist era, particularly for inner city schools, of the early seventies. The right wing press launched witch hunts against radical and socialist teachers - nothing new, as the persecution of the William Tyndale staff described by Terry Ellis (1977) and Chris Searle (Teaching London Kids no.7) had shown, but in the climate of the times, harder to resist. The shrinkage of teacher training with the concomitant closure and amalgamation of many colleges, the movement to the right of the student body also helped contribute to a situation inimical to the survival of radical educational journals.

There were other more pressing, if more mundane, considerations. By 1980 Libertarian Education ran a page headed Crisis! which enumerated the problems, common to all the journals, of rising printing costs, falling markets, problems of sales and distribution and lack of feedback. These continued to be real problems for the surviving journals, especially those lacking an organisational base for support. (Teaching London Kids, which in the early seventies had a print run of anything from four to six thousand now produces fifteen hundred copies.)

The 'vigorous development of radical teachers' journals' described by Baron et al. (1981) is a thing of the past, yet this is at a time when the need for resistance is greater than ever. The attacks on the content and process of progressive and radical education have never been better orchestrated, or more singularly pursued, than by the present Tory administration.

The movement towards a centralised curriculum, the increasing influence of the Manpower Services Commission, the removal of teachers' negotiating rights all signal the government's intentions to remove control of education from the teaching profession to the Department of State for Education. The thrust to remove educational policy making from the hands of Local Authorities, coupled with the removal of <u>their</u> negotiating role in teachers' pay settlements prefigures the breakdown of the traditional educational partnership between central government, the LEAs and the teaching unions which has existed since the 1944 Education Act. All this, coupled with the stated intention of the government to allow market forces to determine the success or failure of schools points to a radical reshaping of the education system by the Right.

Education has always been an important issue for Socialists and has always occupied a key position in Labour Party policies. The fact that the Left seems powerless to resist the current onslaught is a function of several things: that the attack from the Right is not just on education but on every aspect of the welfare state; that the teacher unions, so long engaged in a battle of attrition over pay and conditions, have failed to engage the sympathies of parents and so paved the way for the Tories to claim a populist appeal for their policies; the decline in the power of the trades unions.

Not all is gloom. The eighties have seen positive developments in policy making by many metropolitan education authorities, particularly in the areas of race and gender. Ironically, the introduction of the GCSE examination gives teachers more control over what they teach and how they assess it at a time when the government is moving to impose a centralised curriculum on all schools. And faced with a common threat, the NUT and the NAS/UWT are at last discussing common action.

In spite of this, the situation is such that it is becoming increasingly difficult for radical teachers 'to turn the few weapons they can find in the history and learning to "teach" against the ideology, the system and the practices in which they are trapped' (L. Althusser, 1972).

This is what the radical educational journals of the seventies attempted to do. It is more important than ever to hang on to the gains made by progressivism and to celebrate and publicise them; to provide theoretical and ideological support to radical and progressive teachers; to furnish ammunition in the form of examples of good practice.

The question is, who is going to do so?

266

# REFERENCES

Althusser L. (1972) 'Ideology and Ideological State Apparatuses' in Education: Structure and Society ed Cosin B., Penguin Books in association with the Open University, Harmondsworth.

Barker, R. (1969) 'The Labour Party and Education for Socialism', International Review of Labour History, 14.

Baron S. et al. (1981) Unpopular Education, Hutchinson and Co.

Bowles, S. and Gintis H. (1976) Schooling in Capitalist America, Routledge & Kegan Paul, London.

Burke, V. (1971) Teachers in Turmoil, Penguin Education, Harmondsworth.

Central Advisory Council for Education (1967) Children and their Primary Schools, HMSO.

Clark, M. and Davies, D. (1981) 'Radical Education: the Pedagogic Subtext' in Rethinking Curriculum Studies ed Lawn M. and Barton L., Croom Helm, London.

Ellis, T. et al. (1977) William Tyndale: the Teachers' Story, Writers and Readers Coop.

Grace, G. (1978) Teachers, Ideology and Control, Routledge & Kegan Paul, London.

Hall, S. (1983) 'Education in Crisis' in Is There Anyone Here From Education? ed Wolpe A.M. and Donald J., Pluto Press.

Harrison, S. (1974) Poor Mens' Guardians, Lawrence and Wishart.

Holly, D. (1974) 'The Invisible Ruling Class' in Education or Domination? ed Holly D., Arrow Books.

Johnson, R. (1976/7) 'Really Useful Knowledge' in Radical Education No. 7 and No. 8.

Johnson, T. (1972) Professions and Power, Macmillan, London.

Jones, K. (1983) Beyond Progressive Education, Macmillan, London.

O'Keeffe, D. (ed.) (1986) The Wayward Curriculum, Social Affairs Unit.

Paton, K. (1971) The Great Brain Robbery, Moss Side Press.

Searle, C. (1975) Classrooms of Resistance, Writers and Readers Coop.

Simon, B. (1985) Does Education Matter? Lawrence and Wishart.

Whitty, G. (1977) 'Sociology and the Problem of Radical Educational Change' in Society, State and Schooling ed

Young M. and Whitty G., Falmer Press, Lewes.
Williams, R. (1976) Keywords, Fontana.
Wright, N. (1976) 'Teacher Politics and Educational Change'
    in Explorations in the Politics of School Knowledge, ed
    Whitty G. and Young M., Nafferton Books.

# Index